FAMOUS ENGLISH
SERMONS

FAMOUS ENGLISH SERMONS

Edited, with an introduction, by
ASHLEY SAMPSON

THE RELIGIOUS BOOK CLUB
121 CHARING CROSS ROAD
LONDON, W.C. 2

This edition, 1942

CONTENTS

CONTENTS

INTRODUCTION

THE SERMON has never been given its rightful place in our heritage of English literature; and, when we remember Donne, Jeremy Taylor, Joseph Butler, and Newman, we may well ask why. For it is as though the literature of religion were disqualified as such. Most of the literature of the Middle Ages is regarded as literature before it is considered as religious apologetics, while the *Utopia* of Thomas More (though originally in Latin), the *Religio Medici*, the devotional poetry of the seventeenth century, and even the Homilies of Bede, are treasured as literature before anything else. Perhaps it is because of our English shyness that the sermon has not shared this honour—a feeling that the sermon, like one's neighbour's morals, is a fugitive problem—something far too intimate and private for the prying eye of the professional critic. The Bible is different. That is public property—the fruit of a national mind; but sermons are too mixed up with particular circumstances and individual reactions to admit of general criticism.

That, I suppose, is a fair summary of the layman's attitude; and yet, once committed to print (or even to ink) the sermon is literature. This does not mean that a good sermon is a good work of prose; but it does mean that the sermon is a work of prose—a thing to be read as well as heard—subject to all the possibilities and potentialities of prose, and consequently vulnerable to literary criticism. I think it may be said of the sermon what Burnet once said of Charles the Second—that he 'had little or no literature, but true and sound sense, and a right notion of style.' It would certainly surprise some readers to know how radically that cynical monarch transformed the English sermon of his day by changing the shambling and interminable harangues of the puritan preachers into a bold and effective pulpit oratory.

Nevertheless it is a common failing to suppose that preaching as an art was never understood in England before the Reformation. Not much has come down to us of pulpit literature in the Middle Ages, and most of what has survived is in Latin; but much of it was preached in a direct, racy style; and the preacher in ' Merrie England ' possessed this advantage over the preachers of our modern England— that he had all his Black Sheep under his eye. Where a preacher of the twentieth century has to cast his net wide in the vague hope of catching some renegade, his early predecessor could score some direct hits without raising his voice very high ! It was a temptation that could not, even if it should, be resisted ; and no anthology of English sermons which claims to be thoroughly representative can afford entirely to ignore the Middle Ages.

The sermon of Richard Wimbledon here included— preached at Paul's Cross in 1388—is one of the few which have survived in the original English. Latin examples of this piece of oratory exist in abundance ; but this edition, preserved in Foxe's *Acts and Monuments* as a relic of the Middle Ages, is regarded by Professor Owst as a good translation from the Middle English. Owing to the inordinate length of the sermon, only the first part is reproduced here, and the spelling has been modernised.

At the Reformation the English sermon naturally assumed a more controversial aspect, much of which was dross ; but there is pure gold at the core of it— like the jewel in the brain of the toad, and a deep-seated sense of human needs that had never been granted to the mass of Christians. The sermon I have given from Latimer, though less well known than his sermon on the plough, is less well worn and also less controversial than most of what he preached. It possesses something that created an epoch in pulpit oratory—the translation of the Bible into English. The oratory of the Authorized Version is a thing much older than 1611. It is the ripened and gathered fruit of a harvest which had been growing steadily, from translation to translation ; but always the same green growth—the same golden grain. When Tyndale was garroted and burnt outside the city of Brussels in 1537 he had done much more than sow the seed. It is his Bible that the ploughboy learnt and the parson preached from his own day until ours. Even Donne, of all stylists perhaps the most original, cannot escape that influence. In the famous passage from the *Death's Duel* sermon on birth into the world he rivals Job when he declaims :

' This issue, this deliverance from that death, the death of the womb, is an entrance, a delivery over to another death, the manifold deaths of this world. We have a winding sheet in our mother's womb, which grows with us from our conception, and we come into the world wound up in that winding sheet, for we come to seek a grave. And as prisoners discharged of action may lie for fees, so when the womb hath discharged us, yet are we bound to it by cords of flesh by such a string, as that we cannot go thence, nor stay there ; we celebrate our own funerals with cries, even at our birth ; as though our three score and ten years life were spent in our mother's labour, and our circle made up in the first point thereof.'

This is an echo of the Bible. The darker moods of Job or the great rhetorical passages of St Paul's epistles are in it ; and its rhythm is surely that of the Authorized Version. Sir Thomas More had his Cicero and Seneca, and Chaucer his Greek poets ; but Latimer, Foxe, Baxter, and Bunyan, whether they were Protestant or Catholic, poet or peasant, knew their Bible. It is true, of course, that the Bible was the crowning pinnacle of England's golden age of literature. It did not burst upon it unawares ; but it stayed while mortal men perished ; reading, both in public and private, gave it a place in the moulding of our language that no other piece of literature has even dimly rivalled. Despite much individual genius, both inside and outside the pulpit, it has seldom been escaped.

The sermon in the present volume whose style most resembles the language of Holy Writ is that which Richard Baxter preached before Charles II. at his restoration—although it remains guilty of that hot verbosity which had been the curse of the English pulpit under the recent Commonwealth. For this reason, and even more because its abundance of quotations becomes a burden, the original text has been abridged—nearly all the Biblical quotations have been removed—with such parts of the sermon as would have made them inevitable ; but the address as a whole has been left *en bloc*—its vital message for that day and ours in no sense mitigated by this abridgment. Swift, on the other hand, wrote in a style independent of most influences—though touched with, rather than adorned by, his study of the Classics. His prose was astonishingly free from mannerisms for an era of polished adornments ; but the fact that he is here represented by an address to the public which cannot be regarded as a sermon in the stricter sense, brings out the rough parts of his secular style to better advantage. Swift's sermons were not great literature.

There are indeed some lovely gems of English prose for an anthology of English sermons ; and one sees again and again how the fire of moral indignation or the cool shade of some happy and tender thought will drop a sudden thunderbolt or shoot a sudden greenness into the preacher's style. James Martineau, who was no famous stylist, could be moved in the pulpit to say of Christian love, joy, and peace : 'They have a higher origin than a physical frame happily moulded, or even a will dutifully disposed. There is something in them of more heavenly fire, lighting up our human nature, but not entirely kindled there ; leaving us with the blessing, but rendering back to God the praise.' Of a different hue was Latimer's outburst against 'umpreaching prelates,' who 'are so troubled with lordly living, they be so placed in palaces, couched in courts, ruffling in their rents, dancing in their dominions, burdened with ambassage, pampering of their paunches, like a monk that maketh his jubilee ; munching in their mangers, and mocking in their gay manors and mansions and so troubled with loitering in their lordships, that they cannot attend to it.' Not Wyclif in all his zeal against the pride of princes or the idleness of prelates ever burst into quite such alliterative venom !

It was indeed against invective of this kind—abuse which soon lost its moral immediacy in a wild torrent of words like a storm in a wilderness—that the Church reacted in the reign of Charles the Second. For there was as little style in those colourless ramblings of the Puritan preachers as there was in the 'hell fire' sermons of Jonathan Edwards and his school. It is in the burning indignation of a Tertullian or a Savonarola—or, to bring it within the covers of this present book, of a Dean Colet, a Donne, or a Swift—that such invective becomes a blazing fire

of living language. Those 'shambling harangues' of
the Puritan, as Bishop Henson not unjustly calls them,
are tawdry by comparison.

The sermon, however, is less concerned with
language than with life—less with the power of
dramatic or poetic interpretation than with the great
or little problems which it seeks to interpret. In this
the sermon differs from all other forms of literature—
that it deliberately propagates ideas. It is of course
true that the plays of Æschylus, the novels of Dickens,
the masterpiece of Cervantes, and the *Divine Comedy*
of Dante were written with a purpose in mind ; but
that purpose can never be separated from those
elements that make each one of them a great work
of art. Theme, story, style, and purpose are all
blended into a single effect ; but with the sermon
it is different. For here it is possible to separate the
message from the medium, and even to summarise it
in words that the preacher never uses. Its moral
purpose is its outstanding quality ; and all other
elements are subordinated to it—all arts which the
preacher uses being legitimate only in so far as they
intensify this. That is why an anthology of sermons
can never be regarded simply as a literary product.

Nevertheless each era of preaching is redolent of
the age that produces it, and an anthology of English
sermons that missed any one of the phases through
which English Christianity has passed would do so
at its peril. That green and mellow age of English
literature—the age of Addison and Steele—had its

moments of fire and intensity ; and the earthquake which John Wesley and his Methodists created in the midst of it reverberated for at least a century beyond. So the Evangelical Revival is followed by the Oxford Movement ; but an age which saw Newman at Oxford, Robertson at Brighton, Dale in Birmingham, and Magee in Ireland, defies analysis in the last resort. It can only be said that, where ties of blood and tradition separate men in literature and life, the pulpit can unite them.

This book, however, would not be justified unless the greatest preacher used all the arts of literature to round off the rough edges of his rhetoric and sought to shape his thought into the most beautiful and satisfying form that words will allow. Sometimes the very spontaneity of his utterance gives dynamite to his thought and fire to his speech ; and sometimes a richly human nature will light them with a glow as brilliant and tender as the sunset. I have often wished, for this latter reason, that the sermons which St. Francis preached to the birds and beasts had been preserved. They were probably as fresh and fragrant as the morning dew ; but the preacher's task has generally been to sharpen our blunted sensibilities and tell us in language which the human mind can understand of realities that are beyond its understanding. Perhaps none excelled John Henry Newman in his genius for getting the maximum of heaven out of the minimum of earth. In his sermon on the Invisible World he speaks of the animals :

' They have apparently passion, habits, and a certain
accountableness, but all is mystery about them. We
do not know whether they can sin or not, whether
they are under punishment, whether they are to live
after this life. We inflict very great suffering on a
portion of them, and they in turn every now and
then seem to retaliate upon us, as if by a wonderful
law. We depend upon them in various ways ; we
use their labour, we eat their flesh. This however
relates to such of them as come near us : cast your
thoughts abroad on the whole realm of them, large
and small, in vast forests, or in the water, or in the
air, and then say whether the presence of such multitudes, so various in their nature, so strange and wild
in their shapes, living on the earth without ascertainable object, is not as mysterious as anything which
Scripture says about angels ? '

That is an instance from a preacher who was also
a poet—a man who was at home in two worlds ; and
the sermons of Donne, Joseph Butler, and Jeremy
Taylor, here republished, declaim the same two-edged
sword. For the preacher wields a weapon that may
or may not be effective in two forms. There are
voices which in these days come to us effectively
over the air whose message is never quite the same
when it is reborn into the cold light of print ; but
there are others who reach the heart and the mind as
well through the eye as through the ear. It is my
own conviction that those whom I have chosen shall
be represented in this volume can stand the test of

both. Some are voices that have come to us by the written word through many ages—testifying to the deathlessness of their message ; and the others are, I truly believe, in the same tradition of prophecy.

This note of prophecy applies in a special sense to the last sermon in the book. For Europe would seem to have entered upon a new phase of her history—in which there is little else but darkness to be seen as yet. Nevertheless it is a part of the prophet's function to detect whatever gleam of light there may be ahead, and Mr. C. S. Lewis, in his sermon preached before the University of Oxford early in the Lent Term, 1939, has put out a feeler for that light which is all that we can see as yet of the world that is ahead of us—the hope of Christian culture. Mr. Lewis is a Fellow of Magdalen College and a young novelist of some distinction ; and the inclusion of his sermon in this varied anthology, preached at a dramatic moment in the world's history, would seem to form a fitting climax to a book of Famous Sermons.

ASHLEY SAMPSON

Note.—The Editor is under a debt of deep gratitude to Professor Owst for his tireless efforts and inexhaustible knowledge on the subject of the English Sermon. His assistance has been of the greatest value in tracking down rare specimens and unearthing editions that are hard to come by at the present time.—A. S.

Sermon from the Latin

THE VENERABLE BEDE

✠

SERMON FROM THE LATIN

THE VENERABLE BEDE

THE HOLY GOSPEL which has been read to you, my brethren, is worthy of your utmost attention, and should be kept in constant remembrance. For it commends to us perfect faith, and shows the strength of such perfect faith against all temptations. If you would know how one ought to believe in Christ, what can be more clear than this which Peter says to Him, ' Thou art the Christ, the Son of the living God ' ? If you would hear of what avail is this belief, what can be more plain than this which the Lord says of the Church to be builded upon Him, ' The gates of hell shall not prevail against it ' ? These points will be more fully considered hereafter, each in its own place. I will now proceed to the explanation of the whole passage, taking the sentences in their natural order.

And first, of the place in which the Lord's words were spoken. ' *Jesus came into the coasts of Cæsarea Philippi.*' Philip, as Luke informs us, was tetrarch of Iturea and of the region of Trachonitis. He built a city in the district where the Jordan rises, at the foot of Mount Lebanon, a district which bounds Judea towards the north, and he named it Cæsarea Philippi, after his own name, and at the same time in honour of Tiberius Cæsar, under whom he governed the country.

'*Jesus asked His disciples, saying, Whom do men say that I, the Son of Man, am ?*' He does not ask as though He knew not what His disciples and others thought of Him. He questions the disciples as to their opinion, in order that He may worthily reward their confession of a true faith. For as, when all were questioned, Peter alone answered for all, so what the Lord answered to Peter, in Peter He answered to all. And He asks what others think of Him, in order that the erroneous opinions of others might be exposed, and so it would be shown that the disciples received the truth of their confession not from the common belief, but from the very secrets of revelation from the Lord. ' Whom do men say that I, the Son of Man, am ? ' He asks. Right well does He call them ' men ' who spoke of Him only as Son of Man, because they knew not the secrets of His Divinity. For they who can receive the mysteries of His Divinity are deservedly said to be more than men. The Apostle [meaning of course St. Paul, known in the mediæval times as ' The Apostle '] himself beareth witness, ' Eye hath not seen, nor ear heard, nor have entered into the heart of man, the things which God hath prepared for them that love Him.' And having premised this of men, that is, of those whose knowledge is from the human heart, the human ear, the human eye, the Apostle presently adds, of himself and of those like him who surpassed the ordinary knowledge of the human race, ' but God hath revealed them unto us by His Spirit.' In the same way here, when the Lord had questioned the disciples as to whom men held Him to be, and they had stated the different views of different persons, He says to them :

' *But whom do ye say that I am ?* ' as though setting them apart from ordinary men, and implying that they were made gods and sons of God by adoption, according to that saying of the Psalmist, ' I have said, Ye are gods, and ye are all the children of the Most Highest.'

' *Simon Peter answered and said, Thou art the Christ, the Son of the living God.*' He calls Him the ' living ' God by way of distinction from the false gods which heathendom in its various delusions made to itself to worship, either of dead men, or—greater folly still— of insensate matter. Of which false gods it is sung in the Psalm, ' their idols are silver and gold, the work of men's hands.' And mark well, my beloved, for it is worthy of all admiration, how, when the true view of both the natures of the same Lord our Saviour is to be expressed, it is the Lord who sets forth the humility of the manhood He had taken upon Him, the disciple who shows the excellency of the divine eternity. The Lord says of Himself that which is the less, the disciple says of the Lord that which is the greater. So, too, in the Gospel, the Lord was accustomed to speak of Himself much more often as Son of Man than as Son of God, that He might admonish us of the dispensation which He undertook for us. And we ought the more humbly to reverence the high things of His divinity, the more we remember that for our exaltation He descended to the low estate of manhood. For if among the mysteries of the Incarnation, by which we have been redeemed, we cherish always in pious memory the power of the divinity by which we have been created, we too with Peter are rewarded with blessing from on high. For when Peter confesses Him to be the Christ, the Son of the living God, see what follows : ' *Jesus answered and said, Blessed art thou, Simon Bar-Jona.*' It is certain, then, that after true confession of Christ there remain the true rewards of blessedness.

Let us now consider attentively what and how great is that name with which He glorifies the perfect confessor of His name, that by a true confession we may deserve to be partakers of this also. ' Blessed art thou, Simon Bar-Jona.' Bar-Jona in Syriac signifies ' son of a dove.' And rightly is the Apostle Peter called son of a dove, for the dove is without guile, and Peter followed his Lord in prudent and pious guilelessness, mindful of that precept of guile-lessness and truth which he and his fellow-disciples received from the same Master—' Be ye wise as serpents, and harmless as doves.' And surely, since the Holy Spirit descended upon the Lord in the form

of a dove, he is rightly called ' Son of a Dove ' who is
shown to have been filled with the grace of the Spirit.
And justly does the Lord reward him who loved Him
and confessed Him, by declaring that he, who asserted
Him to be Son of the living God, is son of the Holy
Spirit. Of course no faithful man doubts that these
two sonships are very different. For the Lord Christ
is Son of God by nature : Peter, as also the other
elect, son of the Holy Spirit by grace. Christ is
Son of the living God, because He is born of Him :
Peter is son of the Holy Spirit, because he is born
again of Him. Christ is Son of God before all time,
for He is that virtue of God and wisdom of God
which saith, ' The Lord possessed Me in the beginning
of His way, before His works of old.' Peter is son
of the Holy Spirit from the time when, illumined by
Him, he received the grace of divine knowledge.
And because the will of the Holy Trinity is one, and
the operation one, when the Lord had said, ' Blessed
art thou, Simon Bar-Jona,' that is, son of the grace of
the Spirit, He rightly proceeded to say :

' *For flesh and blood hath not revealed it unto thee ; but
my Father which is in Heaven.*' It was indeed the
Father who revealed it : for the grace of the Father
and of the Holy Spirit is one, as also that of the
Son, which may be proved very easily from sacred
Scripture. For the Apostle says of the Father, ' God
hath sent forth the Spirit of His Son into your
hearts.' The Son Himself says of the Holy Spirit,
' But when the Comforter is come, whom I will send

unto you from the Father.' The Apostle says of the Holy Spirit, ' But all these worketh that one and the selfsame Spirit, dividing to every man severally as He will.' The Father therefore sends the Spirit, the Son sends the Spirit : the Spirit Himself breatheth where He listeth, because, as we have said, the will and the operation of the Father, the Son, and the Holy Spirit is one. And hence it is fittingly said, that the Father which is in heaven revealed to the son of the dove that mystery of faith which flesh and blood could not reveal. Now flesh and blood we rightly understand to mean men puffed up with the wisdom of the flesh, ignorant of the guilelessness of the dove, and thus as far as possible removed from the wisdom of the Spirit. Of whom it has been said above, that in their ignorance of Christ some said that He was John the Baptist ; some Elias ; and others Jeremias, or one of the prophets. Of such men the Apostle saith : ' But the natural man receiveth not the things of the Spirit of God.'

To proceed. ' *And I say unto thee, That thou art Peter, and upon this rock I will build my Church.*' Peter, who was before named Simon, received from the Lord the name of Peter on account of the strength of his faith and the constancy of his confession ; for his mind clung firmly to That of which it is written, ' that rock was Christ.' ' And upon this rock,' that is, upon the Lord and Saviour who gave to him that knew Him, loved Him, confessed Him, a share in His own name, so that from the Rock he should be called Peter ; on which Rock the Church is builded, because only by believing and loving Christ, by receiving the Sacraments of Christ, by observing the commandments of Christ, can man arrive at the lot of the elect, at eternal life. To this the Apostle [again of course St. Paul] beareth witness when he saith, ' For other foundation can no man lay than that is laid, which is Jesus Christ.'

' *And the gates of Hell shall not prevail against it.*' The gates of Hell are wicked doctrines, which seduce men and bring them to Hell. The gates of Hell, further, are the tortures and the blandishments of persecutors, who by terrifying and enticing unstable souls, open unto them an entrance into eternal death. Further, the gates of Hell are the evil deeds and the unseemly words of believers, inasmuch as they show the way of perdition to those who allow them or follow their example. For even faith, if it have not works, is dead in itself, and evil communications corrupt good manners. Many, then, are the gates of Hell ; but not one of them prevails against the Church which is builded on the Rock : for one who has received the faith of Christ with the inmost love of his heart, easily puts down every temptation from without. But a believer who has depraved and betrayed his belief, either by wrongdoing or by denial, is to be taken as having built the house of his confession, not on a rock with the Lord as his helper, but on sand with no foundation : that is, he must be held to have made pretence of being a Christian, with no simple and true determination to follow Christ, but with some frail earthly purpose.

' *And I will give unto thee the keys of the kingdom of Heaven.*' He who confessed the King of Heaven with a devotion beyond that of others, had worthily conferred upon him beyond others the keys of the kingdom of Heaven ; that all might know, how that without such confession and faith none may enter into the kingdom of Heaven. And He describes, as ' the keys of the kingdom of Heaven,' that knowledge and power of discerning by which the worthy would be received into the kingdom, the unworthy rejected. It is evidently on this account that He added :

'*And whatsoever thou shalt bind on earth shall be bound in Heaven : and whatsoever thou shalt loose on earth shall be loosed in Heaven.*' This power of binding and of loosing seems to be given by the Lord to Peter alone ; but without the slightest doubt it is given to the other Apostles also. Christ Himself bears witness to this, for after the triumph of His Passion and Resurrection He appeared to them, and breathing on them said, ' Receive ye the Holy Ghost : whosoever sins ye remit, they are remitted unto them ; and whosoever sins ye retain, they are retained.' Nay, the same function is committed now, in the person of the bishops and priests, to the whole Church, so that after knowledge of the case of sinners it may take pity on those whom it sees to be humble and truly penitent, and absolve them from the fear of eternal death ; while it marks as bound under everlasting punishments those whom it finds to be persistent in their sins. Whence in another place the Lord says of one who is once and again taken in a fault and yet repenteth not, ' But if he neglect to hear the Church, let him be unto thee as an heathen man and a publican.' And lest any should deem it a light thing to be condemned by the judgment of the Church, He adds presently these terrible words, ' Verily I say unto you, whatsoever ye shall bind on earth shall be bound in Heaven ; and whatsoever ye shall loose on earth shall be loosed in Heaven.' To the whole Church, then, of the elect is there given authority to bind and loose according to the measure of sins and of repentance. But the blessed Peter, who confessed Christ with a true faith, and followed Him with a true love, received in a special manner the keys of the kingdom of Heaven and the first place of the power of judgment ; in order that all believers throughout the world may understand that no man who in any way separates himself from the unity of faith and fellowship can be absolved from the chains of sin or enter the gate of the kingdom of Heaven. So that, my dearest brethren, we must of necessity learn with the utmost care the sacraments of the faith which he taught, and show forth works meet for faith. We must with all vigilance beware of the manifold and subtle snares of the gates of Hell, that so we may be worthy to enter into the gates of the daughter of Sion, that is, into the joys of the city which is on high. And let us not suppose that it suffices for salvation that we be like unto the crowds of careless and ignorant persons in faith or in deeds, for there is in the sacred writings one only rule laid down for faith and life. But as often as the examples of those who err are brought before us, let us turn away the eyes of our mind lest they behold vanity, and carefully investigate what truth itself teaches. Let us follow the example of the blessed Peter, who rejected the errors of others, and made with the mouth an unwavering profession of the hidden things of the true faith which he had learned, and kept them in his heart with invincible care. For in this place we learn of the faithfulness of confession ; while of the virtue of single love for Christ He beareth witness Himself in another place, when some of His disciples went back, and He said unto the twelve, ' Will ye also go away ? ' ' Peter answered Him, Lord, to whom shall we go ? Thou hast the words of eternal life. And we believe and are sure that Thou art that Christ, the son of the living God.' If we set ourselves to follow his example, my brethren, according to our ability, we too shall be able with him to be called blessed and to be blessed ; to us, too, the name of Simon will be meet, that is, of one that obeys Christ ; we too, on account of the guilelessness of our faith that is not feigned, and the grace we receive from the Lord, shall be called sons of the virtue of the dove ; and He Himself, rejoicing with us in the spiritual progress of our soul, shall say, ' Behold thou art fair, my love ; behold, thou art fair ; thou hast dove's eyes.' And so it cometh to pass that if we build on the rock of faith, gold, silver, precious stones, that is, the perfect works of virtues, the fires of tribulation shall bring no harm, the storms of temptation shall not prevail. Nay, rather, proved by adversity, we shall receive the crown of life, promised before the ages by Him who liveth and reigneth God, with the Father, in the unity of the Holy Spirit, for ever and ever. Amen.

A Sermon no less Godly
than Learned

RICHARD WIMBLEDON

✠

' Redde rationem villicationis tuae '—
LUCAE xvi. 2.

A SERMON NO LESS GODLY
THAN LEARNED

RICHARD WIMBLEDON

MY DEAR FRIENDS, ye shall understand that Christ, author and doctor of truth, in His book of the gospel (likening the kingdom of heaven to an householder) saith on this manner : ' Like is the kingdom of heaven to an holding man, that went out first on the morrow to hire workmen into his vine : also, about the third, sixth, ninth, and eleventh hours he went out, and found men standing idle, and said to them, Go ye into my vineyard, and that right is I will get you. When the day was gone, he cleped [1] his steward and high [2] to give each man a penny.'

The spiritual understanding of this householder is our Lord Jesus Christ, that is head of the household of Holy Church, and thus clepeth men in divers hours of the day, that is in divers ages of the world ; as in time of law of kind [3] He cleped, by inspiring Abel, Enoch, Noah, and Abraham ; in time of the old law, Moses, Daniel, Isaiah, and Jeremiah ; and

---

[1] ' Cleped ' : called.   [2] ' High ' : ordered.
[3] ' Law of kind ' : nature.

30

in time of grace, apostles, martyrs, and confessors and virgins. Also He cleped men in divers ages : some in childhood, as John Baptist ; some in state of waxing, as John the Evangelist ; some in state of manhood, as Peter and Andrew ; and some in old age, as Gamaliel, and Joseph of Arimathea ; and all these He clepeth to travail in His vine, that is the Church, and that in divers manners. For, right as ye see, that in tilling of the material vine there be divers labours, for some cut away the void branches, some make forks and rails to bear up the vine, and some dig away the old earth from the root, and lay there fatter ; and all these offices be so necessary to the vine, that if any of them fail it shall harm greatly, or destroy the vine ; for but-if [1] the vine be cut, she shall wax wild, but-if she be railed, she shall be overcome with nettles and weeds, and but-if the root be fatted with dung, she for feebleness should wax barren. Right so in the Church be needful these three offices, priesthood, knighthood and labourers. To priesthood it falleth to cut away the void branches of sins with the sword of their tongue. To knighthood it falleth to let [2] wrongs, and hests [3] to be done, and to maintain God's law, and them that be teachers thereof, and also to keep the land from enemies of other lands. And to labourers it falleth to travail bodily, and with their sore sweat to get out of the earth bodily livelihood for them and other

[1] 'But-if' : unless.   [2] 'Let' : prevent.
[3] 'Hests' : commands.

31

parties.[1] And these states be also needful to the
Church, that none may well be without other : for
if priesthood lacked, the people, for default of
knowing God's law, would wax wild in vices, and
die ghostly [2] ; and if the knighthood lacked, and
men to rule the people by law and hardiness,[3] thieves
and enemies would so increase, that no man would
live in peace : and if there were no labourers, both
knights and priests must become acre men [4] and
shepherds ; and else they would, for default of bodily
sustenance, die.   And therefore, saith the clerk [5]
Avicenna, that every unreasonable beast, if he hath
that, that kind [6] hath ordained for him, as kind hath
ordained it, he has sufficient to live by himself without
any help of others of the same kind.   And if there
were but one horse, or one sheep in the world, yet,
if he had grass and corn, as kind hath ordained for
such beasts, he would live well enough.   But if there
were but one man in the world, though he had all
that good that is therein, yet, for default, he would
die, or his life would be worse than if he were naught :
and the cause is this, for that thing that kind ordaineth
for man's sustenance, without other arraying than it
hath of kind, accordeth not [7] to him.   As though a
man have corn as it cometh from the earth, yet it is
no meat according to him, until it be, by man's craft,
changed into bread ; and though he have flesh or

---

[1] ' Parties ' : persons.   [2] ' Ghostly ' : spiritually.
[3] ' Hardiness ' : boldness.   [4] ' Acre men ' : small-holders.
[5] ' Clerk ' : scholar.   [6] ' Kind ' : nature.
[7] ' Accordeth not ' : is not suitable.

fish, yet, while it is raw as kind ordained it, till it be by man's travail sodden, roasted, or baked, it accords not to man's livelihood. And right so wool, that the sheep beareth, must, by man's divers crafts and travails, be changed ere it be able to clothe any man ; and certes one man, by himself, should never do all these labours. And therefore, saith this clerk, it is need that some be acre men, some bakers, some makers of cloth ; and some merchants, to fetch that, that one land fetcheth from another, as there it is plentiful.

And certes this should be a cause why every state should love others ; and men of one craft should not despise or hate man of none other craft, since they be so needful every to other ; and oft the very crafts that be most unhonest,[1] might worst be forborn.[2] And one thing I dare well say, that he that is neither travailing in this world on studying, on prayers, on preaching for help of the people (as it falleth to priests), nor ruling the people, maintaining or defending from enemies (as it falleth to knights), nor travailing on earth in divers crafts (as it falleth to labourers), when the day of reckoning cometh, that is, the end of this life, right as he lived here without travail, so he shall there lack the reward of the ' penny,' that is, the endless joy of heaven ; and, as he was here living after no state nor order, so he shall be put then in that place that no order is in, but everlasting horror and sorrow, that is, in hell.

[1] ' Unhonest ' : dishonourable.   [2] ' Forborn ' : dispensed with.

Therefore, every man see to what state God hath cleped him, and dwell he therein by travail, according to his degree. Thou that art a labourer or a crafty man,[1] do this truly. If thou art a servant or a bondman, be subject and low, in dread of displeasing thy lord. If thou art a merchant, deceive not thy brother in chaffering.[2] If thou art a knight or a lord, defend the poor man and needy from hands that will harm them. If thou art a justice or a judge, go not on the right hand by favour, neither on the left hand, to punish any man for hate. If thou art a priest, undernime,[3] praise, and reprove, in all manner of patience and doctrine. Undernime those that be negligent, praise those that be obedient, reprove those that be disobedient to God, so every man travail in his degree : for when the evening is come, that is, the end of this world, then every man shall take reward, good or evil, after that he hath travailed here.

The words that I have taken to make of my sermon, be thus much to say : ' Yield reckoning of thy baily.[4] ' Christ, author of pity, the lover of the salvation of His people, in the process of this gospel informeth every man what is his baily, by manner of a parable of a baily that He speaketh of, to array him to answer of the goods that God hath taken [5] him, when the day of strait reckoning shall be come,

---

[1] ' Crafty man ' : craftsman.   [2] ' Chaffering ' : bargaining.
[3] ' Undernime ' : instruct.   [4] ' Baily ' : stewardship.
[5] ' Taken ' : entrusted to.

that is, the day of doom.[1] And so I, at this time,
through the help of God, following Him that is so
great a master of authority, because that I know
nothing that should more draw away man's unreasonable love from the passing joy of this world, than the
mind [2] of the dreadful reckoning. As much as
suffice, I shall show you how ye shall dispose you to
avoid the vengeance of God, when there shall be time
of so strait doom, that we shall give reckoning of
every idle word that we have spoken. For then it
shall be said to us, and we shall not flee it : ' Yield
reckoning of thy baily.'

But, for the further process of the first part of this
sermon, ye shall wit [3] that there shall be three bailiffs
that shall be cleped to this strait reckoning : twain,
to answer for themselves and for others. That be,
priests, that have cure of men's souls, and temporal
men, that have governance of people. And the third
bailiff shall account only for himself, and that is,
every Christian man, of that he hath received of God.
And each of these shall answer to three questions :
to the first question, How hast thou entered ? the
second, How hast thou ruled ? and to the third,
How hast thou lived ? And if thou canst well
assoil [4] these three questions, was there never none
earthly lord that ever so well rewarded his servant
without comparison, as thy Lord God shall reward
thee : that is, with bliss, and joy, and life that ever

---

[1] ' Doom ' : judgment.   [2] ' Mind ' : memory.
[3] ' Wit ' : know.   [4] ' Assoil ' : answer.

shall last. But on that other side, if thou wilt now be reckless of thine own welfare, and take no heed of this reckoning : if that day take thee suddenly, so that thou pass hence in deadly sin (as thou wittest never what shall befall thee), all the tongues that ever were, or ever shall be, may not tell the sorrow and woe that thou shalt ever be in and suffer. Therefore for the desire of so great joy, and the dread of so great pain, though love nor dread of God were not in thine heart, yet should thou make thee afraid to sin, for to think that thou shalt give reckoning of thy baily.

Therefore, as I say to thee, the first question that shall be proposed to the first bailiff (that is a prelate, or a curate of men's souls) is this : How hast thou entered ? (Matt. xxii.). ' Friend, how enteredst thou hither ? ' Who brought thee into this office ? truth or simony ? God or the devil ? grace or money ? the flesh or the spirit ? Give thou thy reckoning if thou canst. If thou canst not, I rede [1] that thou tarry for to learn ; for up-hap [2] ere night thou shalt be cleped. And if thou stand dumb for uncunning,[3] or else for confusion of thy conscience, thou fall into the sentence that anon followeth : ' Bind his hands and his feet, and cast him into the outermost of darkness ; there shall be weeping and grinding of teeth.' Therefore I rede thee, thou advise thee how thou shalt answer to the question : How hast thou

[1] ' Rede ' : advise.   [2] ' Up-hap ' : perhaps
[3] ' Uncunning ' : ignorance.

entered ? whether by cleping, or by thine own procuring : for that thou wouldst travail in God's gospel, or for thou wouldst be richly arrayed ? Answer now to thine own conscience, as thou shalt answer to God, thou that hast taken now the order of priest (whether thou be curate or none). Who stirred thee to take upon thee so high an estate ? whether for thou wouldst live as a priest ought to do, studying of God's law to preach, and most heartily to pray for the people ; or for to live upon other men's travail, and thyself travail not ?

Why, also, set men their sons or their cousins to school ? whereto ? but for to get them great advancements, or to make them the better to know how they should serve God. This, men may see openly, by the sciences that they set them to. Why, I pray you, put men their sons to the law civil, or to the king's court to write letters and writs, rather than to philosophy or divinity, but for the hope that these occupations should be ever means to make them great in the world. I hope that there will no man say, that they should not better learn the rule of good living in the book of God's law, than in any books of man's worldly wisdom ? But certes now it is truth that John Chrysostom saith : ' Mothers be loving to the bodies of their children, but the soul they despise ; they desire them to welfare in this world, but they take no heed what they shall suffer in the other. Some ordain fees [1] for their children, but none ordain

---

[1] ' Fees ' : property.

37

them to God. The loss of their bodies they will sore bewail, but the health of their souls they reckon naught of. If they see them sore or sick, they sorrow and sigh ; but though they see them sin, they sorrow not. And in this they shew that they brought forth the bodies, but not the souls.'

And, if we take heed truly what abominations be scattered and spread abroad in Holy Church nowadays among priests, we shall well wit that they come not all to the fold of Christ, by Christ's cleping, for to profit, but by other ways, to get them worldly wealth : and this is the cause of losing of souls that Christ bought so dear, and of many errors among the people. And, therefore, it is writ in the book of Mourning, where the prophet speaketh thus to God (Lam. i. 10) : ' The enemy hath put his hand to all things desirable to him ; for he hath let lawless folk enter into the sanctuary, of the which thou hadst commanded that they should not enter into the church.' This enemy is Satan, as his name soundeth,[1] that hath put his hand to all that he liketh. What sin, I pray you, will the fiend have sown among men, that is not now used ? In what plenty is now pride, envy, wrath, and covetousness ? When were they so great as they be now ? and so of all other sins. And why, trowest thou ? But for there be a lawless people entered into thy sanctuary, that neither keep in themselves the law of God, nor can teach others. And to every such saith God by the prophet (Hosea iv.) : ' For that

[1] ' As his name soundeth ' : the Hebrew name ' Satan ' means ' Enemy.'

thou hast put away cunning,[1] I shall put thee away, that thou shalt use no priesthood to me.' Lo that God expressly here in Holy Writ forbiddeth men to take the state of priesthood on them, but-if they have cunning that they need. Thou, then, that canst neither rule thyself nor others after the law of God, beware how thou wilt answer to God, at His dreadful doom, when He shall say to thee, that which I took to my theme : 'Yield the reckoning of thy baily, how thou hast entered.'

The second question, that every curate and prelate of holy church shall answer to, is this : How hast thou ruled? that is to say, the souls of thy subjects, and the goods of poor men : give now thine account. First, how thou hast governed God's folk that were taken thee to keep? Whether thou art an herd, or an hired man, that dost all for bodily hire ; as a father, or as a wolf that eateth his sheep and keepeth them not? Say, whom hast thou turned from his cursed living, by thy devout preaching? Whom hast thou taught the love of God, that was once un-cunning? There shall be heard a grievous accusing of fatherless children, and a hard alleging that priests have lived by their wages, and not done away their sins. Yield also reckoning how thou hast ruled, and spent the goods of poor men. Hark what Saint Bernard saith : 'Dread [2] clerks, dread the ministers of the church, the which be in the place of saints, that they do so wickedly ; not holding themselves

---

[1] 'Cunning' : knowledge.   [2] 'Dread' : beware of.

paid with such wages that were sufficient to them.'
That overplus that needy men would be sustained by,
they be not ashamed to waste in the house of their
pride and lechery, and withhold to themselves
wickedly and cursedly that which should be the
livelihood of poor men. With double wickedness
truly they sin : first, for they receive other men's
goods, and secondly, they misuse holy things in their
vanities and in their filthiness. Every such bailiff
therefore beware, for anon to the last farthing he
shall reckon with Christ. Trowest thou not then,
that thou shalt not be disallowed of God, of that
thou hast mis-spended in feeding of fat palfreys, of
hounds, of hawks, and if it so be, that is worst of
all, on lecherous women ? Hear what is said of
such : ' They have led their days in wealth ; and, in
a point, they be gone down into hell.' Think,
therefore, I rede thee, that thou shalt yield reckoning
of thy baily.

The third question that this bailiff shall answer to
is this : How hast thou lived ? what light of holiness
hast thou showed, in thy living, to the people, or
what mirror hast thou been of holiness to them ?
Give now thy reckoning, how thou hast lived, as a
priest or as a lewd [1] man, as a man or as a beast ?
That is to wonder truly, how the life of priests is
changed ! They be clothed as knights ; they speak
as unhonestly as carls,[2] or of winning [3] as merchants ;

[1] ' Lewd ' : unlearned.   [2] ' Carls ' : labourers.
[3] ' Winning ' : profit-making.

they ride as princes : and all that is thus spent, is of the goods of poor men, and of Christ's heritage. Therefore, saith an holy doctor, ' The clay of Egypt was tough and sticky, and meddled [1] with blood. The slates were hard to be undone, for they were baked with the fire of covetousness, and with a layer of lust. In this travail rich men, in this they wake, awaiting poor men.[2] In these travail prelates, that be too much blinded with too much shining of riches, that make them houses like churches in greatness, that with divers paintings colour their chambers, that with divers clothings of colours make images gay : but the poor man, for default of clothes, beggeth, and with an empty womb crieth at the door. And if I shall the truth say,' saith this doctor, ' oft time poor men be robbed for to clothe the trees and stones.' Of such speaketh the prophet : ' How art thou here, or as who art thou ? ' Here thou art occupying the place of Peter and Paul, or of Thomas or of Martin. But how ? As Judas among the apostles, as Simon Magus among the disciples ; as a candle now quenched, that stinketh all the house, instead of a light lantern ; as a smoke that blindeth men's eyes, in place of clean fire. If thou contrary thus the form of living that Christ and His disciples left to priests, Lo, what saith the prophet Jeremiah : ' They have entered, and they have had, and not been obedient.'

[1] ' Meddled ' : mixed.
[2] ' They wake, awaiting poor men ' : they keep watch, lying in wait for poor men.

41

They, with false title, or with their corrupt and false intention, had poor men's goods to their misusing; and they have not been obedient to the law of God in their own living. Therefore it is written, that the hardest doom shall fall on such. An hard doom, for they have mis-entered; and harder doom, for they have misruled; and the hardest doom for they have so cursedly lived. Think, therefore, I rede, how thou wilt give reckoning of thy baily!

The second bailiff that accounteth at this doom for himself, and also for others, is he that keeping hath of any community, as kings, princes, mayors, and sheriffs, and justices: and these shall also answer to the same three questions. The first question: How hast thou entered (that is to say, into thine office)? for the help of the people, to destroy falsehood and further truth, or for desire of winning, or worldly worship? If thou take such an office more for thine own worldly profit than for the help of the community, thou art a tyrant, as the philosopher saith. For it is to be feared lest there be too many that desire such states, that they may rather oppress those that they hate, and take gifts to spare to punish those that have trespassed, and so make them partners of their sins; and for bribes they work all things. And many such, when they be so high, they reckon not that they be poor men's brethren; but they ween to pass them in kind,[1] as they pass in worldly

---

[1] 'They ween to pass them in kind': they think that they are superior to them by nature.

worship, that is but wind : of which God saith by the prophet, 'They have reigned, but not of me ; they have been princes, but I know not.' So we read of Rehoboam, that was the son of King Solomon ; what time he was first king the people of Israel came to him and said, 'Thy father, in his last days, put on us great charge. We pray thee somewhat make it lighter, and we will serve thee.' And the king took counsel of the old wise men, and they counselled to answer them fairly, and that should be for the best. But he left these old wise men's counsel, and did after the counsel of children that were his playmates, and said to the people when they came again, 'My left finger is greater than my father's backbone. My father grieved you somewhat, but I will add more thereto.' And the people heard this, and rebelled to him, and took them another king ; and since, the kingdom never came whole again. And therefore it is good that every ruler of communities, that they be not led by follies, nor by none other ear-rowner,[1] so that he have not an eye of love to the community that he hath to rule. For wit ye well, be he never so high, that he shall come before his higher, to yield reckoning of his baily.

The second question is, How hast thou ruled the people and the office that thou hadst to govern ? thou that has been a judge in causes of poor men, how hast thou kept this hest of God ? 'Thou shalt not take heed to the person of a poor man, to be to him

---

[1] 'Ear-rowner' : whisperer.

the harder for his poverty, and thou shalt not behold a rich man's semblance, to spare or to favour him in his wrong for his riches ? ' O Lord ! what abuse there is among officers of both laws nowadays. If a great man pleadeth with a poor man, to have aught that he holdeth, every officer shall be ready to hasten all that he may, that the rich man might have such an end as he desired. But if a poor man plead with a rich man, then there shall be so many delays, that though the poor man's right be open to all the country, for pure fault of spending he shall be glad to cease. Sheriffs and bailiffs will return poor men's writs, with ' tarde venit,' but-if they feel meed [1] in their hands : and yet I hear say (men that have seen both laws) that the court that is cleped Christ's court is much more cursed. Therefore it is written : ' Gifts they take out of men's bosoms, to overturn the right way of doom ' ; but it is to dread, the word of Christ : ' In what doom ye deem,[2] ye shall be deemed, when ye come to yield a reckoning of your baily.'

The third question is, How hast thou lived, that thou deemest and punishest other men for their trespass ? A great doctor saith : ' Thee behoveth to flee the wickedness of other men, that thou chastisest them for their trespass. For if thyself do unlawfully, in deeming other men thou condemnest thyself, since thou doest that thou condemnest.' And Paul saith : ' Why teachest thou not thyself, that thou teachest

---

[1] ' Meed ' : reward.   [2] ' Deem ' : judge.

others ? why stealest thou, that teacheth not other men to steal ? ' Saint Gregory saith : ' He shall not take governance of others, that cannot go before them in good living. And when any man stand before him in doom, he must take heed to before what Judge he shall stand himself, to take his doom after his deeds.' But it is to dread, that many fare as two false priests, that would have condemned to death holy Susannah, for she would not assent to their lechery ; of the which it is written : ' They turned away their eyes, for they would not see heaven, nor have mind of rightful dooms.' So it happeneth often, they that were more worthy to be hanged condemn them that be less worthy ; as a clerk telleth of Socrates the philosopher. Saith he, ' Upon a day a man asked of him, why he laughed. And he said, For I see great thieves leading a little thief to hanging.' I pray thee, whether is he a greater thief that benimeth [1] a man his house and his land from him and from his heirs for evermore, or he that, for making of great need, stealeth a sheep or a calf ? Or trow we not that it happeneth such extortioners to be otherwhile judges, and deem men thus : but I rede thee, that thus deemest others, think on that doom that thou shalt come to, to yield the reckoning of thy baily.

The third bailiff that shall be cleped to this dreadful account shall be every Christian man, that shall give reckoning to his Lord God for goods that he hath had of his own. And here I will speak but of the

---

[1] ' Benimeth ' : depriveth.

first question, that is this : How enterest thou ?
And here, by the way, ye that have got any wordly
goods, or taken by extortion, by ruin, by usury, or
by deceit, ' Woe shall be to him at this dreadful
day,' as Saint Augustine saith. If he be cast into the
fire, that hath not given of his own goods, where,
trowest thou, shall he be cast that hath reved [1] other
men's from them ? And if he shall burn with the
fiend, that hath not clothed the naked, where, trowest
thou, shall he burn that hath made him naked that
was once clothed ? But, as Saint Gregory saith,
' Two things make men to live thus by ruin of other
neighbours ; that they desire heyness,[2] and dread
poverty.'

And what vengeance falleth of this sin of covetousness, I may see by figure in Holy Writ, when the
angel saith to the prophet Zacharias : ' Rear up thine
eyes, and see what is, that goeth out. And the
prophet said, What is it ? Then the angel said,
This is the pot going out ; this is the eize [3] of them
on all the earth. And there was a weight of lead I
bore, and there was a woman sitting in the middle
of this pot. And the angel said : This is impiety.
And he took her, and cast her into the middle of this
pot ; and he took the gobbet of lead, and cast it
into the pot's mouth. And the prophet lifted up his
eyes, and he saw two women coming out, and spirits
in their wings, like two kites or gledes [4] ; and they

---

[1] ' Reved ' : stolen. [2] ' Heyness ' : high position
[3] ' Eize ' : resemblance. [4] ' Gledes ' : hawks.

46

carried up this pot between heaven and the earth.
And then the prophet spake to the angel, Whither
will these bear this pot? And he said, Into the land
of Sennar.' This pot is covetousness; for right as a
pot hath a wide open mouth, so covetousness gapeth
after worldly goods. And right as the liquor in the
pot profiteth not to the pot, but to men that draw
and drink thereof; so worldly goods, often, profit
not to churls,[1] but to others that come after; as it
is written, ' He that hath money, shall have no fruit
of it.' And this covetousness is the eye of covetous
men, for they be blind to see how they should see to
go to heaven, but to winning of worldly things they
see many ways, like to owls and nightcrows, that see
better by night than by day. The gobbet of lead, is
the sin of obstinacy. The woman that sat in the
pot, is unpity,[2] as the angel said, that followeth
unrighteousness and avarice. For through avarice, a
man loseth the pity that he should have of the
mischief of his soul. For, oft time, men lose the life
of their soul, by pity that they should have of their
body, putting themselves to many great bodily
travails and perils both by sea and land; and
covetousness maketh all. This pot is stopped with
the gobbet of lead, when unpity is thus, by sin of
obstinacy, closed in covetousness, that he may go not
out of the chinche's [3] heart by penance. For, as Job
saith : ' When he is fulfilled, he shall be stopped.'

[1] ' Churls ' : men.   [2] ' Unpity ' : lack of feeling.
[3] ' Chinche ' : keeper.

47

The two women that bear up this pot, are pride, and lust of the flesh, that he cleped, in Holy Writ, ' the two daughters of the water-leech, crying, bring, bring.' And they had wings : the first wing is grace spiritual, as cunning, wisdom, and counsel, with such others many ; for which gifts many men wax proud. The second wing is bodily grace, as strength, fairness, gentleness, and many other such, whereof men wax proud. The wings of the second woman, that is fleshly desire, be gluttony and sloth. Of gluttony, speaketh Saint Gregory : ' When the womb is fulfilled, the pricks of lechery be moved.' And of sloth Saint Augustine saith : ' Lot, the while he dwelled in business among shrews [1] in Sodom, he was a good man : but, when he was on the hill, slow,[2] for sikkerness,[3] in his drunkenness lay by his daughters.' And these women had wings like kites, that with a crying voice seek their meat, as Saint Bartholomew saith. And thus fareth covetousness of men, witnessing Saint Augustine, what is the greediness of fleshly desire : ' Inasmuch as the ravenous fishes have sometimes measure, yet when they hunger they rapine,[4] and when they fulfil they spare ; but only covetousness of men may not be fulfilled. For ever he taketh, and never hath enough ; neither he dreadeth God, nor shame of men : he spareth not his father, he knoweth not his mother, he accordeth not with his brethren, neither keepeth truth with his

---

[1] ' Shrews ' : wicked people.   [2] ' Slow ' : idle.
[3] ' Sikkerness ' : security.   [4] ' Rapine ' : plunder.

friend : he oppresseth widows and fatherless children. Freemen he maketh bond, and bringeth forth false witness, and occupieth dead men things, as if he should never die.' 'What madness is this,' saith this doctor, ' thus to lose life and grace, and get death of soul ? win gold, and lose heaven ? ' And therefore saith the prophet : ' Have travail in the midst, and leave unrighteousness.' Also Innocent, speaking of the harms that come of covetousness, saith thus : ' O how many men hath covetousness deceived and spilt ? ' When covetous Balaam would, for gifts that the king proffered him, have cursed God's people, his own ass reproved him, and hurt his foot against a wall : and yet was overcome and led away with covetousness, which enforced him what he might. Achor was stoned to death, for covetousness made him steal gold and clothes, against the commandment of God. Gehazi was smitten with mesilrie,[1] for he sold Naaman's healing, that came of God's grace. Judas, for covetousness, sold Christ, and afterwards hanged himself. Ananias, and Sapphira his wife, were dead suddenly, for they forsook to give Peter their money that they had.

And covetousness maketh also that rich men eat the poor, as beasts do their losous, holding them low.[2] This may we see all day indeed, I dread : For if a rich man have a field, and a poor man have in the midst, or in the side thereof, one acre ; and a

---

[1] ' Mesilrie ' : leprosy.
[2] ' Their losous, holding them low ' : their pasture, keeping it down.

rich man have all a street, save one house that some
poor brother of his owneth ; he ceaseth never till he
get it out of the poor man's hand, either by prayer,
or by buying, or by pursuing of deceit. Thus fared
it by King Ahab, that, through his false queen's gin,[1]
slew the poor man Naboth, for that he would not
sell him his vineyard that was nigh to the king's
palace. Upon which process, thus saith Saint
Ambrose : ' How far will ye rich men stretch your
covetousness ? will ye dwell alone upon the earth
and have no poor man with you ? ' Why put ye out
your fellow by kind, and challenge [2] to yourself the
possession coming by kind ? In common to all rich
and poor, the earth was made. Why will ye rich
challenge proper right herein ? Kind knoweth no
riches, and bringeth forth all men poor ; for he
bringeth them to this world, needy of meat, and of
drink, and clothing. Naked the earth taketh us, as
naked she brought us hither. She cannot close with
us our possession in the sepulchre ; for kind maketh
no difference between poor and rich in coming hither,
nor in going hence. All in one manner he bringeth
forth ; all in one manner he closeth in grave.
Whosoever will make difference of poor and rich,
abide till they have a little while lain in the grave.
Then open, and look among dead bones, who was
rich, and who was poor ; but if it be thus : that
more clothes rot with the rich than with the poor,
and that harms them that be alive, and profits not

[1] ' Gin ' : snare.   [2] ' Challenge ' : claim.

them that be dead. Thus saith the doctor, of such extortion, as it is written : ' Other men's fields they reap, and from the vine of him that harm oppressed, they pluck away the grapes.' They leave men naked, and take away their clothes that have naught where-with to helle [1] them in cold, and lift up this pot between heaven and earth. For covetous men neither have charity to their brethren upon earth, not to God in heaven ; and they bear this pot into the land of Sennar, that is to say, into the land of stench, that is, hell ; ' for there shall be stench, instead of sweet smelling,' as Isaiah saith.

Beware, I rede, that ye naught have to do with this pot, nor with the woman therein ; and, on all manner, that ye be not wedded to her, for then ye must be both one. This is that foul lecherous woman the kings and merchants of the earth have done lechery with, and of her virtue they have been made rich ; whose damnation is written in the Book of Privities [2] in these words : ' In one day shall come all these vengeances of her death : weeping, and hunger ; and fire shall burn her ; for strong is God that shall avenge Himself on her. And then shall weep and howl upon her the kings of the earth, that have done lechery with her, and have lived in delights, when they shall see the smoke of her burning, standing afar off, weeping and wailing, and saying, Alas ! alas ! that great city that was clothed with bis,[3] and

[1] ' Helle ' : cover.   [2] ' Privities ' : the Apocalypse.
[3] ' Bis ' : fine linen.

purple, and brasile,[1] and overgilt with gold, and
precious stones, and pearl ; for in one hour all these
great riches shall be destroyed.   Then shall they say,
that shall be damned with her, We have erred from
the way of truth and righteousness, light has not
shined to us, and the sun of understanding has not
risen to us : we have been made weary in every way
of wickedness and of lust, and have gone hard ways ;
but the ways of God we knew not.   What hath pride
profited us, or the boast of riches what hath it brought
to us ?   All this is a shadow of death, and we may now
show no token of holiness ; in our wickedness we
be wasted away.'   Think, therefore, I rede, that thou
shalt yield reckoning of thy baily.

[1] ' Brasile ' : red colour.

A Sermon before the
Convocation at St. Paul's

JOHN COLET

✛

A SERMON BEFORE THE
CONVOCATION AT ST. PAUL'S

JOHN COLET

YE are come together to-day, fathers and right
wise men, to enter council ; in the which, what
ye will do, and what matters ye will handle, yet we
understand not. But we wish that once, remembering
your name and profession, ye would mind the
reformation of the Churches' matter. For it was
never more need, and the state of the Church did
never desire more your endeavours. For the spouse
of Christ, the Church, whom ye would should be
without spot or wrinkle, is made foul and evil favoured,
as saith Isaias : *The faithful city is made an harlot.*
And as saith Jeremiah : *She hath done lechery with many
lovers, whereby she hath conceived many seeds of wickedness,
and daily bringeth forth very foul fruit.*

Wherefore I came hither to-day, fathers, to warn
you that in this your council, with all your mind,
ye think upon the reformation of the Church. But
forsooth I came not willingly, for I knew mine
unworthiness. I saw beside how hard it was to please
the precise judgment of so many men. For I judged

it utterly unworthy and unmeet, yea and almost to malapert, that I, a servant, should counsel my lords ; that I, a son, should teach you, my fathers. Truly it had been meeter for some one of the fathers ; that is to say, you prelates might have done it with more grave authority and greater wisdom. But the commandment was to be obeyed of the most reverent father and lord the Archbishop, President of this council, which laid upon me this burden, truly too heavy for me. We read that the prophet Samuel said : *Obedience is better than sacrifice.* Wherefore, fathers and right worthy men, I pray you and beseech you that this day ye would sustain my weakness with your goodness and patience ; furthermore, to help me at the beginning with your good prayers.

And before all things let us pray unto God the Father Almighty ; first remembering our most holy Father the Pope, and all the spiritual pastors, with all Christian people ; furthermore the most reverent Father and Lord the Archbishop, President of this council, and all bishops, and all the clergy, and all the people of England ; remembering finally this your congregation, desiring God to inspire your minds so accordingly to agree, to such profit and fruit of the Church, that ye seem not, after the council finished, to have been gathered together in vain and without cause. Let us all say *Pater noster.*

To exhort you, reverent fathers, to the endeavour of reformation of the Church's estate (because that nothing hath so disfigured the face of the Church as hath the fashion of secular and worldly living in clerks and priests), I know not where more conveniently to take beginning of my tale than of the Apostle Paul, in whose temple ye are gathered together. For he, writing unto the Romans, and under their name unto you, saith : *Be you not conformed to this world, but be you reformed in the newness of your understanding, that ye may prove what is the good will of God, well pleasing and perfect.* This did the Apostle write to all Christian men, but most chiefly unto priests and bishops. Priests and bishops are the light of the world. For unto them said our Saviour : *You are the light of the world.* And He said also : *If the light that is in thee be darkness, how dark shall the darkness be ?* That is to say, if priests and bishops, that should be as lights, run in the dark way of the world, how dark then shall the secular people be ? Wherefore Saint Paul said chiefly unto priests and bishops : *Be you not conformable to this world, but be ye reformed.*

In the which words the Apostle doth two things. First, he doth forbid that we be not conformable to the world and be made carnal. Furthermore, he doth command that we be reformed in the Spirit of God, whereby we are spiritual.

I intending to follow this order, I will speak first of confirmation, then after of reformation.

Be you not (saith he) *conformable to this world.*

The Apostle calleth the *world* the ways and manner of secular living, the which chiefly doth rest in four

evils of this world : that is to say, in devilish pride,
in carnal concupiscence, in worldly covetousness, in
secular business. These are in the world, as Saint
John the apostle witnesseth in his epistle canonical.
For he saith : *All thing that is in the world* is either
the *concupiscence of the flesh*, or the *concupiscence of the*
eyes, or *pride of life*. The same are now and reign in
the Church, and in men of the Church ; that we
may seem truly to say, all thing that is in the church
is either concupiscence of flesh, or eyes, or pride of
life.

And first for to speak of pride of life : how much
greediness and appetite of honour and dignity is
nowadays in men of the Church ? How run they,
yea almost out of breath, from one benefice to another ;
from the less to the more, from the lower to the
higher ? Who seeth not this ? Who seeing this
sorroweth not ? Moreover these that are in the same
dignities, the most part of them doth go with so
stately a countenance and with so high looks, that
they seem not to be put in the humble bishopric of
Christ, but rather in the high lordship and power of
the world, not knowing nor advertising what Christ
the master of all meekness said unto His disciples,
whom He called to be bishops and priests : *The*
princes of people (saith He) *have lordship of them, and those*
that be in authority have power ; but do ye not so ; but he
that is greater among you, let him be minister ; he that is
highest in dignity, be he the servant of all men. The Son
of man came not to be ministered unto, but to minister. By

which words our Saviour doth plainly teach that the
ministry in the Church is none other thing than a
ministration, and the high dignity in a man of the
Church to be none other thing than a meek service.

The second secular evil is carnal concupiscence.
Hath not this vice so grown and waxed in the
Church as a flood of their lust, so that there is
nothing looked for more diligently in this most busy
time of the most part of priests than that that doth
delight and please the senses ? They give themselves
to feasts and banqueting ; they spend themselves in
vain babbling ; they give themselves to sports and
plays ; they apply themselves to hunting and hawking ;
they drown themselves in the delights of this world.
Procurers and finders of lusts they set by. Against
the which kind of men Judas the apostle crieth out
in his epistle, saying : *Woe unto them which have gone
the way of Cain. They are foul and beastly, feasting in
their meats, without fear feeding themselves ; floods of the
wild sea, foaming out their confusions ; unto whom the
storm of darkness is reserved for everlasting.*

Covetousness is the third secular evil, the which
Saint John the apostle calleth concupiscence of the
eyes. Saint Paul calleth it idolatry. This abominable pestilence hath so entered in the mind almost of
all priests, and so hath blinded the eyes of the mind,
that we are blind to all things but only unto those
which seem to bring unto us some gains. For what
other thing seek we nowadays in the Church than fat
benefices and high promotions ? Yea, and in the

same promotions, of what other thing do we pass upon than our tithes and rents? that we care not how many, how chargeful, how great benefices we take, so that they be of great value. O covetousness! Saint Paul justly called thee the root of all evil. Of thee cometh this heaping of benefices upon benefices. Of thee, so great pensions assigned of many benefices resigned. Of thee, all the suing for tithes, for offerings, for mortuaries, for dilapidations, by the right and title of the Church. For the which thing we strive no less than for our own life. O covetousness! of thee cometh these chargeful visitations of bishops. Of thee cometh the corruptions of courts, and these daily new inventions wherewith the silly people are sore vexed. Of thee cometh the besyte and wantonness of officials. O covetousness! mother of all iniquity, of thee cometh this fervent study of ordinaries to dilate their jurisdictions. Of thee cometh this woode and raging contention in ordinaries; of thee, insinuation of testaments; of thee cometh the undue sequestration of fruits; of thee cometh the superstitious observing of all those laws that sounde to any lucre, setting aside and despising those that concern the amendment of manners. What, should I rehearse the rest? To be short, and to conclude at one word: all corruptness, all the decay of the Church, all the offences of the world, come of the covetousness of priests; according to that of Saint Paul, that here I repeat again and beat into your ears: *covetousness is the root of all evil.*

The fourth secular evil that spotteth and maketh ill favoured the face of the Church is the continual secular occupation, wherein priests and bishops nowadays doth busy themselves, the servants rather of men than of God ; the warriors rather of this world than of Christ. For the Apostle Paul writeth unto Timothy : *No man, being God's soldier, turmoil himself with secular business.* The warring of them is not carnal but spiritual. For our warring is to pray, to read and study scriptures, to preach the word of God, to minister the sacraments of health, to do sacrifice for the people, and to offer hosts for their sins. For we are mediators and means unto God for men. The which Saint Paul witnesseth, writing to the Hebrews : *Every bishop* (saith he) *taken of men, is ordained for men in those things that be unto God, that he may offer gifts and sacrifices for sins.* Wherefore those Apostles, that were the first priests and bishops, did so much abhor from all manner of meddling of secular things, that they would not minister the meat that was necessary to poor people, although that were a great work of virtue ; but they said : *it is not meet that we should leave the word of God and serve tables ; we will be continually in prayer, and preaching the word of God.* And Saint Paul crieth unto the Corinthians : *If you have any secular business, ordain them to be judges that be most in contempt in the Church.* Without doubt, of this secularity, and that clerks and priests, leaving all spiritualness, do turmoil themselves with earthly occupations, many evils do follow.

First, the dignity of priesthood is dishonoured ; the which is greater than other the kings and emperors : it is equal with the dignity of angels. But the brightness of this great dignity is sore shadowed, when priests are occupied in earthly things, whose conversation ought to be in heaven.

Secondarily, priesthood is despised, when there is no difference betwixt such priests and lay people, but, according to the prophecy of Hosea : *as the people be, so are the priests.*

Thirdly, the beautiful order and holy dignity in the Church is confused, when the highest in the Church do meddle with vile and earthly things, and in their stead vile and abject persons do exercise high and heavenly things.

Fourthly, the lay people have great occasion of evils, and cause to fall, when those men whose duty is to draw men from the affection of this world, by their continual conversation in this world teach men to love this world, and of the love of the world cast them down headlong into hell.

Moreover in such priests that are so busied there must needs follow hypocrisy. For when they be so mixed and confused with the lay people, under the garment and habit of a priest they live plainly after the lay fashion. Also by spiritual weakness and bondage fear, when they are made weak with the waters of this world, they dare neither do nor say but such things as they know to be pleasant and thankful to their princes.

At last, ignorance and blindness : when they are blinded with the darkness of this world, they see nothing but earthly things. Wherefore our Saviour Christ, not without cause, did warn the prelates of His Church : *Take heed*, said He, *lest your hearts be filled with gluttony and drunkenness and with the cares of this world. With the cares*, saith He, *of this world*, wherewith the hearts of priests being sore charged they cannot hold and lift up their minds to high and heavenly things.

Many other evils there be beside those, that follow of the secularity of priests, which were long here to rehearse. But I make an end.

These be the four evils that I have spoken of, O Fathers, O priests, by the which we are conformable to this world, by the which the face of the Church is made evil favoured, by the which the state of it is destroyed truly much more than it was in the beginning by the persecution of tyrants, or afterwards by the invasion that followed of heretics. For, in the persecution of tyrants, the Church being vexed was made stronger and brighter. In the invasion of heretics, the Church being shaken was made wiser and more cunning in Holy Writ. But since this secularity was brought in, after that the secular manner of living crept in in the men of the Church, the root of all spiritual life—that is to say, charity—was extinct. The which taken away there can neither wise nor strong Church be in God.

In this time also we perceive contradiction of the

lay people. But they are not so much contrary unto
us, as we are ourselves ; nor their contrariness hurteth
not us so much as the contrariness of our evil life,
the which is contrary both to God and Christ. For
he said : *Who that is not with Me, is against Me.*

We are also nowadays grieved of heretics, men mad
with marvellous foolishness. But the heresies of them
are not so pestilent and pernicious unto us and the
people, as the evil and wicked life of priests ; the
which, if we believe Saint Bernard, is a certain kind
of heresy, and chief of all and most perilous. For
that same holy Father, in a certain convocation,
preaching unto the priests of his time, in a certain
sermon so he said by these words : ' There be many
Catholic and faithful men in speaking and preaching,
the which same men are heretics in working. For
that that heretics do by evil teaching, that same do
they through evil example : they lead the people out
of the right way, and bring them into error of life.
And so much they are worse than heretics, how much
their works prevail their words.' This that holy
Father Saint Bernard, with a great and fervent spirit,
said against the sect of evil priests in his time. By
which words he sheweth plainly to be two manner
of heresies ; the one to be of perverse teaching, and
the other of naughty life : of which this later is
worse and more perilous. The which reigneth now
in the Church in priests not living priestly but
secularly, to the utter and miserable destruction of
the Church.

Wherefore, you Fathers, you priests, and all you of the clergy, at the last look up and awake from this your sleep in this forgetful world ; and at the last being well awaked hear Paul crying unto you : *Be you not conformable unto this world.*

And this for the first part. Now let us come to the second.

THE SECOND PART, OF REFORMATION

But be you reformed in the newness of your understanding.
The second thing that Saint Paul commandeth, is that we be reformed into a new understanding ; that we smell those things that be of God. Be we reformed unto those things that are contrary to those I spake of even now : that is to say, to meekness, to soberness, to charity, to spiritual occupation ; that, as the said Paul writeth unto Titus, *renouncing all wickedness and worldly desires, we live in this world, soberly, truly, and virtuously.*

This reformation and restoring of the Church's estate must needs begin of you our Fathers, and so follow in us your priests and in all the clergy. You are our heads, you are an example of living unto us. Unto you we look as unto marks of our direction. In you and in your life we desire to read, as in lively books, how and after what fashion we may live. Wherefore, if you will ponder and look upon our motives, first take away the blocks out of your eyes.

It is an old proverb : *Physician, heal thyself*. You spiritual physicians, first taste you this medicine of purgation of manners, and then after offer us the same to taste.

The way whereby the Church may be reformed into better fashion is not for to make new laws. For there be laws many enough and out of number, as Solomon saith : *nothing is new under the sun*. For the evils that are now in the Church were before in time past ; and there is no fault but that Fathers have provided very good remedies for it. There are no trespasses but that there be laws against them in the body of the Canon law. Therefore it is no need that new laws and constitutions be made, but that those that are made already be kept. Wherefore in this your assembly let those laws that are made be called before you and rehearsed ; those laws, I say, that restrain vice, and those that further virtue.

First, let those laws be rehearsed, that do warn you Fathers that ye put not over soon your hands on every man, or admit unto holy orders. For there is the well of evils, that, the broad gate of holy orders opened, every man that offereth himself is everywhere admitted without pulling back. Thereof springeth and cometh out of the people that are in the Church both of unlearned and evil priests. It is not enough for a priest, after my judgment, to construe a collect, to put forth a question, or to answer a sophism ; but much more a good, a pure, and a holy life, approved manners, meetly learning of Holy Scriptures, some knowledge of the sacraments ; chiefly and above all things, the fear of God, and love of the heavenly life.

Let the laws be rehearsed, that command that benefices of the Church be given to those that are worthy ; and that promotions be made in the Church by the right balance of virtue, not by carnal affection, not by the acception of persons ; whereby it happeneth nowadays that boys for old men, fools for wise men, evil for good, do reign and rule.

Let the laws be rehearsed, that warreth against the spot of Symony. The which corruption, the which infection, the which cruel and odious pestilence, so creepeth now abroad, as the canker evil in the minds of priests, that many of them are not afraid nowadays both by prayer and service, rewards and promises, to get them great dignities.

Let the laws be rehearsed, that command personal residence of curates in their churches. For of this many evils grow, because all things nowadays are done by vicars and parish priests ; yea, and those foolish also and unmeet, and oftentimes wicked ; that seek none other thing in the people than foul lucre, whereof cometh occasion of evil heresies and ill Christendom in the people.

Let be rehearsed the laws and holy rules given of Fathers, of the life and honesty of clerks ; that forbid that a clerk be no merchant, that he be no usurer, that he be no hunter, that he be no common player, that he bear no weapon ; the laws that forbid clerks to haunt taverns, that forbid them to have suspect familiarity with women ; the laws that command soberness, and a measureableness in apparel, and temperance in adorning of the body.

Let be rehearsed also to my Lords these monks, canons, and religious men, the laws that command them to go the straight way that leadeth unto heaven, leaving the broad way of the world ; that commandeth them not to turmoil themselves in business, neither secular nor other ; that command that they sue not in princes' courts for earthly things. For it is in the council of Chalcedon that monks ought only to give themselves to prayer and fasting, and to the chastizing of their flesh, and observing of their rules.

Above all things, let the laws be rehearsed, that pertain and concern you my reverent Fathers and Lords Bishops, laws of your just and canonical election, in the chapters of your churches, with the calling of the Holy Ghost. For because that is not done nowadays, and because prelates are chosen oftentimes more by favour of men than by the grace of God ; therefore truly have we not a few times bishops full little spiritual men, rather worldly than heavenly, savouring more the spirit of this world than the Spirit of Christ.

Let the laws be rehearsed of the residence of bishops in their dioceses ; that command, that they look diligently, and take heed to the health of souls ; that they sow the word of God ; that they show themselves in their churches at the least on great holydays ; that they do sacrifice for their people ; that they hear the causes and matters of poor men ; that they sustain fatherless children and widows ; that they exercise themselves in works of virtue.

Let the laws be rehearsed of the good bestowing of the patrimony of Christ : the laws that command that the goods of the Church be spent, not in costly building, not in sumptuous apparel and pomps, not in feasting and banqueting, not in excess and wantonness, not in enriching of kinsfolk, not in keeping of dogs, but in things profitable and necessary to the Church. For when Saint Augustine, sometime Bishop of England, did ask the Pope Gregory how that the bishops and prelates of England should spend their goods, that were the offerings of faithful people, the said Pope answered (and his answer is put in the Decrees, in the xii chap. and second question), that the goods of bishops ought to be divided into iiii parts ; whereof one part ought to be to the bishop and his household, another to his clerks, the third to repair and uphold his tenements, the fourth to the poor people.

Let the laws be rehearsed, yea, and that oftentimes, that take away the filths and uncleanliness of courts ; that take away those daily new-found crafts for lucre ; that busy them to pull away this foul covetousness, the which is the spring and cause of all evils, the which is the well of all iniquity.

At the last let be renewed those laws and constitutions of Fathers of the celebration of councils, that command provincial councils to be oftener used for the reformation of the Church. For there never happeneth nothing more hurtful to the Church of Christ, than the lack of both council general and provincial.

When these laws and such other are rehearsed, that be for us, and that concern the correction of manners, there lacketh nothing but that the same be put in execution with all authority and power ; that once, seeing we have a law, we live after the law. For the which things, with all due reverence, I call chiefly upon you Fathers. For this execution of the laws and observing of the constitutions must needs begin of you, that ye may teach us priests to follow you by lively examples ; or else truly it will be said of you : *They lay grievous burdens upon other men's backs, and they themselves will not as much touch it with their little finger.*

Forsooth if you keep the laws, and if you reform first your life to the rules of the Canon laws, then shall ye give us light, in the which we may see what is to be done of our part,—that is to say, the light of your good example. And we, seeing our Fathers so keeping the laws, will gladly follow the steps of our Fathers.

The clergies and spiritual part once reformed in the Church, then may we with a just order proceed to the reformation of the lay part ; the which truly will be very easy to do, if we first be reformed. For the body followeth the soul ; and, such rulers as are in the city, like dwellers be in it. Wherefore if priests that have the charge of souls be good, straight the people will be good. Our goodness shall teach them more clearly to be good than all other teachings and preachings. Our goodness shall compel them into the right way truly more effectually than all your suspendings and cursings.

Wherefore, if ye will have the lay people to live after your wish and will, first live you yourself after the will of God ; and so, trust me, ye shall get in them whatsoever ye will.

Ye will be obeyed of them : and right it is. For in the epistle to the Hebrews these are the words of Saint Paul to the lay people : *Obey*, saith he, *to your rulers, and be you under them.* But if ye will have this obedience, first perform in you the reason and cause of obedience ; the which the said Paul doth teach, and it followeth in the text : that is, *Take you heed also diligently, as though ye should give a reckoning for their souls :* and they will obey you.

You will be honoured of the people. It is reason. For Saint Paul writeth unto Timothy : *Priests that rule well are worthy double honours, chiefly those that labour in word and teaching.* Therefore, if ye desire to be honoured, first look that ye rule well, and that ye labour in word and teaching ; and then shall the people have you in all honour.

You will reap their carnal things, and gather tithes and offerings without any striving. Right it is. For Saint Paul, writing unto the Romans saith : *They are debtors, and ought to minister unto you in carnal things.*

First sow you your spiritual things, and then ye shall reap plentifully their carnal things. For truly that man is very hard and unjust, that will *reap where he never did sow, and that will gather where he never scattered.*

Ye will have the Church's liberty, and not to be drawn before secular judges : and that also is right. For it is in the Psalms : *Touch ye not mine anointed.* But if ye desire this liberty, first unloose yourself from the worldly bondage, and from the services of men ; and lift up yourself into the true liberty, the spiritual liberty of Christ, into grace from sins ; and serve you God, and reign in Him. And then, believe me, the people will not touch the anointed of their Lord God.

Ye would be out of business in rest and peace : and that is convenient. But if ye will have peace, come again to the God of peace and love. Come again to Christ, in whom is the very true peace of the Ghost, the which passeth all wit. Come again to yourself, and to your priestly living. And, to make an end, as Saint Paul saith : *Be you reformed in the newness of your understanding, that you savour those things that are of God ; and the peace of God shall be with you.*

These are they, reverent Fathers, and right famous men, that I thought to be said for the reformation of the Church's estate. I trust ye will take them of your gentleness to the best. And if peradventure it be thought that I have past my bounds in this sermon, or have said anything out of temper, forgive it me ; and ye shall forgive a man speaking of very zeal, [to]

71

a man sorrowing the decay of the Church. And consider the thing itself, not regarding any foolishness. Consider the miserable form and state of the Church, and endeavour yourselves with all your minds to reform it. Suffer not, Fathers, this your so great a gathering to depart in vain. Suffer not this your congregation to slip for naught. Truly ye are gathered oftentimes together ; but, by your favour to speak the truth, yet I see not what fruit cometh of your assembling, namely to the Church.

Go ye now in the Spirit that ye have called on, that, by the help of It, ye may in this your council find out, discern, and ordain those things that may be profitable to the Church, praise unto you, and honour unto God. *Unto whom be all honour and glory for evermore. Amen.*

First Sermon on the Lord's Prayer

HUGH LATIMER

✠

Our Father, which art in heaven—MATT. vi. 9.

FIRST SERMON ON THE
LORD'S PRAYER

HUGH LATIMER

I HAVE entered of late in the way of preaching, and spoken many things of prayer, and rather of prayer than of any other thing : for I think there is nothing more necessary to be spoken of, nor more abused than prayer was by the craft and subtilty of the devil ; for many things were taken for prayer when they were nothing less. Therefore at this same time also I have thought it good to entreat of prayer, to the intent that it might be known how precious a thing right prayer is. I told you,

First, What prayer is.

Secondarily, To whom we ought to pray.

Thirdly, Where, and in what place we ought to pray. And,

Fourthly, I told you the diversity of prayer, namely, of the common prayer, and the private.

These and such like things I have dilated and expounded unto you in the open pulpit.

Now at this present time I intend as by the way of a lecture, at the request of my most gracious lady, to expound unto you, her household servants, and other that be willing to hear, the right understanding and meaning of this most perfect prayer which our Saviour himself taught us, at the request of his disciples, which prayer we call the *Paternoster*. This prayer of our Lord may be called a prayer above all prayers ; the principal and most perfect prayer ; which prayer ought to be regarded above all others, considering that our Saviour himself is the author of it ; he was the maker of this prayer, being very God and very man. He taught us this prayer, which is a most perfect schoolmaster, and commanded us to say it : which prayer containeth great and wonderful things, if a learned man had the handling of it. But as for me, such things as I have conceived by the reading of learned men's books, so far forth as God will give me his grace and Spirit, I will shew unto you touching the very meaning of it, and what is to be understood by every word contained in this prayer ; for there is no word idle or spoken in vain. For it must needs be perfect, good, and of great importance, being our Saviour's teaching, which is the wisdom of God itself. There be many other psalms and prayers in scripture very good and godly ; and it is good to know them : but it is with this prayer, the Lord's Prayer, I say, like as with the law of love. All the laws of Moses, as concerning what is to be done to please God, how to walk before him uprightly and godly, all such laws are contained in this law of love, *Diliges Dominum Deum tuum ex toto*

75

corde tuo, et in tota anima tuo, et in tota mente tua ; et proximum sicut teipsum : 'Thou shalt love the Lord thy God with all thy heart, with all thy soul, and with all thy mind ; and thy neighbour as thyself.' Even so is it with this prayer. For like as the law of love is the sum and abridgment of the other laws, so this prayer is the sum and abridgment of all other prayers : all the other prayers are contained in this prayer ; yea, whatsoever mankind hath need of to soul and body, that same is contained in this prayer.

This prayer hath two parts : it hath a preface, which some call a salutation or a loving entrance ; secondarily, the prayer itself. The entrance is this : *Cum oratis, dicite, Pater noster, qui es in cœlis ;* 'When ye pray, say, Our Father, which art in heaven.' As who should say, ' You christian people, you that bear the name of Christians, must pray so.'

Before I go any further, I must put you in remembrance to consider how much we be bound to our Saviour Christ, that he would vouchsafe to teach us to pray, and in this prayer to signify unto us the good-will which our heavenly Father beareth towards us. Now to the matter.

' Our Father.' These words pertain not to the petitions : they be but an entering, a seeking favour at God's hand : yet if we well weigh and consider them, they admonish us of many things and strengthen our faith wondrous well. For this word, ' Father,' signifieth that we be Christ's brothers, and that God is our Father. He is the eldest Son : he is the

76

Son of God by nature, we be his sons by adoption through his goodness ; therefore he biddeth us to call him our Father ; which is to be had in fresh memory and great reputation. For here we are admonished how that we be reconciled unto God ; we, which before-times were his enemies, are made now the children of God, and inheritors of everlasting life. This we be admonished by this word, 'Father.' So that it is a word of much importance and great reputation : for it confirmeth our faith, when we call him Father. Therefore our Saviour, when he teacheth us to call God 'Father,' teacheth us to understand the fatherly affection which God beareth towards us ; which thing maketh us bold and hearty to call upon him, knowing that he beareth a good-will towards us, and that he will surely hear our prayers. When we be in trouble, we doubt of a stranger, whether he will help us or not : but our Saviour commanding us to call God, 'Father,' teacheth us to be assured of the love and good-will of God toward us. So by this word 'Father,' we learn to stablish and to comfort our faith, knowing most assuredly that he will be good unto us. For Christ was a perfect schoolmaster : he lacked no wisdom : he knew his Father's will and pleasure : he teacheth us, yea, and most certainly assureth us, that God will be no cruel judge, but a loving Father. Here we see what commodities we have in this word, 'Father.'

Seeing now that we find such commodities by this one word, we ought to consider the whole prayer with great diligence and earnest mind. For there is no word nor letter contained in this prayer, but it is of great importance and weight; and therefore it is necessary for us to know and understand it thoroughly, and then to speak it considerately with great devotion : else it is to no purpose to speak the words without understanding ; it is but lip-labour and vain babbling, and so unworthy to be called prayer ; as it was in times past used in England. Therefore when you say this prayer, you must well consider what you say : for it is better once said deliberately with understanding, than a thousand times without understanding : which is in very deed but vain babbling, and so more a displeasure than pleasure unto God. For the matter lieth not in much saying, but in well saying. So, if it be said to the honour of God, then it hath his effect, and we shall have our petitions. For God is true in his promises : and our Saviour, knowing him to be well affected towards us, commandeth us therefore to call him Father.

Here you must understand, that like as our Saviour was most earnest and fervent in teaching us how to pray, and call upon God for aid and help, and for things necessary both to our souls and bodies ; so the devil, that old serpent, with no less diligence endeavoureth himself to let and stop our prayers, so that we shall not call upon God. And amongst other his lets, he hath one especially wherewith he thinketh to keep us from prayer, which is, the remembrance of our sins. When he perceiveth us to be disposed to pray, he cometh with his craft and subtile conveyances, saying, ' What, wilt thou pray unto God for aid and help ? Knowest thou not that thou art a wicked sinner, and a transgressor of the law of God ? Look rather to be damned, and judged for thy ill doings, than to receive any benefit at his hands. Wilt thou call him ' Father,' which is so holy a God, and thou art so wicked and miserable a sinner ? ' This the devil will say, and trouble our minds, to stop and let us from our prayer ; and so to give us occasion not to pray unto God. In this temptation we must seek for some remedy and comfort : for the devil doth put us in remembrance of our sins to that end, to keep us from prayer and invocation of God. The remedy for this temptation is to call our Saviour to remembrance, who hath taught us to say this prayer. He knew his Father's pleasure ; he knew what he did. When he commanded us to call God our Father, he knew we should find fatherly affections in God towards us. Call this, I say, to remembrance, and again remember that our Saviour hath cleansed through his passion all our sins, and taken away all our wickedness ; so that as many as believe in him shall be the children of God. In such wise let us strive and fight against the temptations of the devil ; which would not have us to call upon God, because we be sinners. Catch thou hold of our Saviour, believe in him, be assured in thy heart that he with his suffering took away all thy sins. Consider again, that our Saviour calleth us to prayer, and commandeth us to pray. Our sins let

us, and withdraw us from prayer ; but our Saviour
maketh them nothing : when we believe in him, it
is like as if we had no sins. For he changeth with us :
he taketh our sins and wickedness from us, and
giveth unto us his holiness, righteousness, justice,
fulfilling of the law, and so, consequently, everlasting
life : so that we be like as if we had done no sin at
all ; for his righteousness standeth us in so good
stead, as though we of our own selves had fulfilled
the law to the uttermost. Therefore our sins cannot
let us, nor withdraw us from prayer : for they be
gone ; they are no sins ; they cannot be hurtful unto
us. Christ dying for us, as all the scripture, both of
the new and old Testament, witnesseth, *Dolores nostros
ipse portavit,* ' He hath taken away our sorrows.' Like
as when I owe unto a man an hundred pound : the
day is expired, he will have his money ; I have it
not, and for lack of it I am laid in prison. In such
distress cometh a good friend, and saith, ' Sir, be of
good cheer, I will pay thy debts ' ; and forthwith
payeth the whole sum, and setteth me at liberty.
Such a friend is our Saviour. He hath paid our debts,
and set us at liberty ; else we should have been
damned world without end in everlasting prison and
darkness. Therefore, though our sins condemn us,
yet when we allege Christ and believe in him, our
sins shall not hurt us. For St. John saith, *Si quis
peccaverit, advocatum habemus apud Patrem, Jesum Christum
justum,* ' We have an advocate with God the Father,
Jesus Christ the righteous.' Mark that he saith,

Advocatum, non advocatos. He speaketh singularly, not plurally. We have one advocate, not many ; neither saints, nor any body else, but only him, and none other, neither by the way of mediation, nor by the way of redemption. He only is sufficient, for he only is all the doer. Let him have all the whole praise ! Let us not withdraw from him his majesty, and give it to creatures : for he only satisfieth for the sins of the whole world ; so that all that believe in Christ be clean from all the filthiness of their sins. For St. John Baptist saith, *Ecce Agnus Dei qui tollit peccata mundi,* 'Behold the Lamb of God which taketh away the sins of the world.' Doth the devil call thee from prayer ? Christ calleth thee unto it again : for so it is written, *In hoc apparuit Filius Dei, ut destruat opera diaboli ;* 'To that end the Son of God appeared, to destroy the works of the devil.'

But mark here : scripture speaketh not of impenitent sinners ; Christ suffered not for them : his death remedieth not their sins. For they be the bondmen of the devil, and his slaves ; and therefore Christ's benefits pertain not unto them. It is a wonderful saying that St. John hath, 'Behold the Lamb of God, that taketh away the sins of the world.' The devil saith unto me, 'Thou art a sinner.' 'No,' saith St. John, 'the Lamb of God hath taken away thy sins.' Item, *Habentes igitur Pontificem magnum qui penetravit cœlos, Jesum Filium Dei, accedamus cum fiducia ad thronum gratiæ, ut consequamur misericordiam ;* 'We therefore having a great high Priest, which hath passed through the heavens, even Jesus the Son of God, let us with boldness go unto the seat of his grace, that we may obtain mercy.' O, it is a comfortable thing that we have an access unto God! Esay saith, *In livore ejus sanati sumus ;* 'The pain of our punishment was laid upon him, and with his stripes are we healed.' Further, in the new Testament we read, *Huic omnes prophetæ testimonium perhibent, remissionem peccatorum accipere per nomen ejus omnes qui credunt in eum ;* 'Unto the same bear all prophets witness, that all they do receive forgiveness of sins by his name, which believe on him.'

Now you see how ye be remedied from your sins ; you hear how you shall withstand the devil, when he will withdraw you from prayer. Let us therefore not give over prayer, but stick unto it. Let us rather believe Christ our Saviour than the devil, which was a liar from the beginning. You know now how you may prevent him, how you may put him off and avoid his temptations.

There is one other addition afore we come to the petitions, which doth much confirm our faith and increase the same : *Qui es in cœlis,* 'which art in heaven.' These words put a diversity between the heavenly Father, and our temporal fathers. There be some temporal fathers which would fain help their children, but they cannot ; they be not able to help them. Again, there be some fathers which are rich, and might help their children, but they be so unnatural, they will not help them. But our heavenly

Father, in that we call him, ' Father,' we learn that he will help, that he beareth a fatherly love towards us.

' In heaven.' Here we learn that he is able to help us, to give us all good things necessary to soul and body ; and is mighty to defend us from all ill and peril. So it appeareth that he is a Father which will help ; and that he being celestial, he is able to help us. Therefore we may have a boldness and confidence, that he may help us : and that he will help us, where and whensoever we call, he saith, *Cælum et terram impleo*, ' I fill heaven and earth.' And again, *Cælum mihi sedes est, et terra scabellum pedum meorum ;* ' Heaven is my seat, and the earth is my footstool.' Where we see, that he is a mighty God ; that he is in heaven and earth, with his power and might. In heaven he is apparently, where face to face he sheweth himself unto his angels and saints. In earth he is not so apparently, but darkly, and obscurely he exhibiteth himself unto us ; for our corrupt and feeble flesh could not bear his majesty. Yet he filleth the earth ; that is to say, he ruleth and governeth the same, ordering all things according unto his will and pleasure. Therefore we must learn to persuade ourselves, and undoubtedly believe, that he is able to help ; and that he beareth a good and fatherly will towards us ; that he will not forget us. Therefore the king and prophet David saith, *Dominus de cælo prospexit*, ' The Lord hath seen down from heaven.' As far as the earth is from the heaven yet God looketh

down, he seeth all things, he is in every corner. He
saith, The Lord hath looked down, not the saints.
No, he saith not so ; for the saints have not so sharp
eyes to see down from heaven : they be pur-blind,
and sand-blind, they cannot see so far ; nor have
not so long ears to hear. And therefore our petition
and prayer should be unto him, which will hear and
can hear. For it is the Lord that looketh down.
He is here in earth, as I told you, very darkly ; but
he is in heaven most manifestly ; where he sheweth
himself unto his angels and saints face to face. We
read in scripture, that Abel's blood did cry unto
God. Where it appeareth that he can hear, yea, not
only hear, but also see, and feel : for he seeth over
all things, so that the least thought of our hearts is
not hid from him. Therefore ponder and consider
these words well, for they fortify our faith. We call
him ' Father,' to put ourselves in remembrance of
his good-will towards us. ' Heavenly ' we call him,
signifying his might and power, that he may help
and do all things according to his will and pleasure.
So it appeareth most manifestly, that there lacketh
neither good-will nor power in him. There was once
a prophet, which, when he was ill entreated of King
Joash, said, *Dominus videat et requirat ;* ' The Lord look
upon it, and requite it.' There be many men in
England, and other where else, which care not for
God, yea, they be clean without God ; which say in
their hearts, *Nubes latibulum ejus, nec nostra considerat,
et circa cardines cœli ambulat :* ' Tush, the clouds cover

him that he may not see, and he dwelleth above in heaven.' But, as I told you before, Abel's blood may certify of his present knowledge. Let us therefore take heed that we do nothing that might displease his majesty, neither openly nor secretly : for he is every where, and nothing can be hid from him. *Videt et requiret*, ' He seeth, and will punish it.'

Further, this word ' Father ' is not only apt and convenient for us to strengthen our faith withal, as I told you ; but also it moveth God the sooner to hear us, when we call him by that name, ' Father.' For he, perceiving our confidence in him, cannot choose but shew him like a Father. So that this word, ' Father,' is most meet to move God to pity and to grant our requests. Certain it is, and proved by holy scripture, that God hath a fatherly and loving affection towards us, far passing the love of bodily parents to their children. Yea, as far as heaven and earth is asunder, so far his love towards mankind exceedeth the love of natural parents to their children : which love is set out by the mouth of his holy prophet Esay, where he saith, *Num oblivioni tradet mulier infantem suum, quo minus misereatur filii uteri sui ? Et si obliviscatur illa, ego tamen tui non obliviscar :* ' Can a wife forget the child of her womb, and the son whom she hath borne ? And though she do forget him, yet will I not forget thee.' Here are shewed the affections and unspeakable love which God beareth towards us. He saith, *Nunquid potest mulier*, ' May a woman ? ' He speaketh of the woman, meaning the man too ;

but because women most commonly are more affected towards their children than men be, therefore he nameth the woman. And it is a very unnatural woman, that hateth her child, or neglecteth the same. But, O Lord, what crafts and conveyances useth the devil abroad, that he can bring his matters so to pass, that some women set aside not only all motherly affections, but also all natural humanity, insomuch that they kill their own children, their own blood and flesh ! I was a late credibly informed of a priest, which had taken in hand to be a midwife. O what an abominable thing is this ! But what followed ? He ordered the matter so, that the poor innocent was lost in the mean season. Such things the devil can bring to pass ; but what then ? God saith, ' Though a woman do forget her children, though they kill them, yet will I not forget thee, saith the Lord God Almighty.' Truth it is, there be some women very unnatural and unkind, which shall receive their punishments of God for it ; but for all that, we ought to beware and not to believe every tale told unto us, and so rashly judge. I know what I mean. There hath been a late such tales spread abroad, and most untruly. Such false tale-tellers shall have a grievous punishment of the Lord, when he shall come to reward every one according unto his deserts.

Here I have occasion to tell you a story which happened at Cambridge. Master Bilney, or rather Saint Bilney, that suffered death for God's word sake ; the same Bilney was the instrument whereby

God called me to knowledge ; for I may thank him, next to God, for that knowledge that I have in the word of God. For I was as obstinate a papist as any was in England, insomuch that when I should be made bachelor of divinity, my whole oration went against Philip Melancthon and against his opinions. Bilney heard me at that time, and perceived that I was zealous without knowledge : and he came to me afterward in my study, and desired me, for God's sake, to hear his confession. I did so ; and, to say the truth, by his confession I learned more than before in many years. So from that time forward I began to smell the word of God, and forsook the school-doctors and such fooleries. Now, after I had been acquainted with him, I went with him to visit the prisoners in the tower at Cambridge ; for he was ever visiting prisoners and sick folk. So we went together, and exhorted them as well as we were able to do ; moving them to patience, and to acknowledge their faults. Among other prisoners, there was a woman which was accused that she had killed her own child, which act she plainly and stedfastly denied, and could not be brought to confess the act ; which denying gave us occasion to search for the matter, and so we did. And at the length we found that her husband loved her not ; and therefore he sought means to make her out of the way. The matter was thus : a child of hers had been sick by the space of a year, and so decayed as it were in a consumption. At the length it died in harvest-time. She went to her neighbours and other friends to desire their help, to prepare the child to the burial ; but there was nobody at home : every man was in the field. The woman, in an heaviness and trouble of spirit, went, and being herself alone, prepared the child to the burial. Her husband coming home, not having great love towards her, accused her of the murder ; and so she was taken and brought to Cambridge. But as far forth as I could learn through earnest inquisition, I thought in my conscience the woman was not guilty, all the circumstances well considered. Immediately after this I was called to preach before the king, which was my first sermon that I made before his majesty, and it was done at Windsor ; where his majesty, after the sermon was done, did most familiarly talk with me in a gallery. Now, when I saw my time, I kneeled down before his majesty, opening the whole matter ; and afterwards most humbly desired his majesty to pardon that woman. For I thought in my conscience she was not guilty ; else I would not for all the world sue for a murderer. The king most graciously heard my humble request, insomuch that I had a pardon ready for her at my return homeward. In the mean season that same woman was delivered of a child in the tower at Cambridge, whose godfather I was, and Mistress Cheke was godmother. But all that time I hid my pardon, and told her nothing of it, only exhorting her to confess the truth. At the length the time came when she looked to suffer : I came, as I was wont to do, to instruct her ; she made great moan to me, and most earnestly required me that I would find the means that she might be purified before her suffering ; for she thought she should have been damned, if she should suffer without purification. Where Master Bilney and I told her, that that law was made unto the Jews, and not unto us ; and that women lying in child-bed be not unclean before God ; neither is purification used to that end, that it should cleanse from sin ; but rather a civil and politic law, made for natural honesty sake ; signifying, that a woman before the time of her purification, that is to say, as long as she is a green woman, is not meet to do such acts as other women, nor to have company with her husband : for it is against natural honesty, and against the commonwealth. To that end purification is kept and used, not to make a superstition or holiness of it, as some do ; which think that they may not fetch neither fire nor any thing in that house where there is a green woman ; which opinion is erroneous and wicked. For women, as I said afore, be as well in the favour of God before they be purified as after. So we travailed with this woman till we brought her to a good trade ; and at the length shewed her the king's pardon, and let her go.

This tale I told you by this occasion, that though some women be very unnatural, and forget their children, yet when we hear any body so report, we should not be too hasty in believing the tale, but rather suspend our judgments till we know the truth.

And again, we shall mark hereby the great love and loving-kindness of God our loving Father, who sheweth himself so loving unto us, that notwithstanding women forget sometimes their own natural children, yet he will not forget us; he will hear us when we call upon him; as he saith by the evangelist Matthew: 'Ask, and it shall be given unto you; seek, and ye shall find; knock, and it shall be opened unto you,' etc. Then he cometh and bringeth in a pretty similitude, saying: 'Is there any man amongst you, which, if his son ask bread, will offer him a stone? If ye then,' *cum sitis mali*, 'being evil, can give your children good gifts,' etc. In these words, where he saith, *cum sitis mali*, 'which be evil,' he giveth us our own proper name; he painteth us out, he pincheth us; he cutteth off our combs; he plucketh down our stomachs. And here we learn to acknowledge ourselves to be wicked, and to know him to be the well-spring and fountain of all goodness, and that all good things come of him. Therefore let every man think lowly of himself, humble himself and call upon God, which is ready to give us not only bread and drink, or other necessaries, but the Holy Ghost. To whom will he give the Holy Ghost? To lords and ladies, to gentlemen or gentlewomen? No, not so. He is not ruled by affections: he hath not respect unto personages. *Poscentibus*, saith he, 'unto those which call upon him,' being rich or poor, lords or knights, beggars or rich; he is ready to give unto them when they come to him. And this is a

great comfort unto those which be poor and miserable
in this world ; for they may be assured of the help of
God, yea, and as boldly go unto him, and desire his
help, as the greatest king in earth. But we must
ask, we must inquire for it ; he would have us to be
importunate, to be earnest and diligent in desiring ;
then we shall receive when we come with a good faith
and confidence. To whom shall we call ? Not unto
the saints. *Poscentibus illum*, saith he. Those that
call upon him shall be heard. Therefore we ought
to come to him only, and not unto his saints.

But one word is left, which we must needs consider ; *Noster*, ' our.' He saith not ' my,' but ' our.'
Wherefore saith he ' our ? ' This word ' our '
teacheth us to consider that the Father of heaven is a
common Father ; as well my neighbour's Father as
mine ; as well the poor man's Father as the rich : so
that he is not a peculiar Father, but a Father to the
whole church and congregation, to all the faithful.
Be they never so poor, so vile, so foul and despised,
yet he is their Father as well as mine : and therefore
I should not despise them, but consider that God is
their Father as well as mine. Here may we perceive
what communion is between us ; so that when I
pray, I pray not for myself alone, but for all the rest :
again, when they pray, they pray not for themselves
only, but for me : for Christ hath so framed this
prayer, that I must needs include my neighbour in
it. Therefore all those which pray this prayer, they
pray as well for me as for themselves ; which is a

great comfort to every faithful heart, when he con-
sidereth that all the church prayeth for him. For
amongst such a great number there be some which be
good, and whose prayer God will hear : as it appeared
by Abraham's prayer, which prayer was so effectuous,
that God would have pardoned Sodome and Gomorre,
if he might have found but ten good persons therein.
Likewise St. Paul in shipwreck preserved his company
by his prayer. So that it is a great comfort unto
us to know that all good and faithful persons pray
for us.

There be some learned men which gather out of
scripture, that the prayer of St. Stephen was the
occasion of the conversion of St. Paul. St. Chrysostom
saith, that that prayer that I make for myself is the
best, and is of more efficacy than that which is made
in common. Which saying I like not very well. For
our Saviour was better learned than St. Chrysostom.
He taught us to pray in common for all ; therefore
we ought to follow him, and to be glad to pray one
for another : for we have a common saying among
us, ' Whosoever loveth me, loveth my hound.' So,
whosoever loveth God, will love his neighbour, which
is made after the image of God.

And here is to be noted, that prayer hath one
property before all other good works : for with my
alms I help but one or two at once, but with my
faithful prayer I help all. I desire God to comfort
all men living, but specially *domesticos fidei*, ' those
which be of the household of faith.' Yet we ought

to pray with all our hearts for the other, which believe not, that God will turn their hearts and renew them with his Spirit ; yea, our prayers reach so far, that our very capital enemy ought not to be omitted. Here you see what an excellent thing prayer is, when it proceedeth from a faithful heart ; it doth far pass all the good works that men can do.

Now to make an end ; we are monished here of charity, and taught that God is not only a private Father, but a common Father unto the whole world, unto all faithful ; be they never so poor and miserable in this world, yet he is their Father. Where we may learn humility and lowliness : specially great and rich men shall learn here not to be lofty or to despise the poor. For when ye despise the poor miserable man, whom despise ye ? Ye despise him which calleth God his Father as well as you ; and peradventure more acceptable and more regarded in his sight than you be. Those proud persons may learn here to leave their stubbornness and loftiness. But there be a great many which little regard this : they think themselves better than other men be, and so despise and contemn the poor ; insomuch that they will not hear poor men's causes, nor defend them from wrong and oppression of the rich and mighty. Such proud men despise the Lord's prayer : they should be as careful for their brethren as for themselves. And such humility, such love and carefulness towards our neighbours, we learn by this word ' Our.' Therefore I desire you on God's behalf, let us cast away all disdainfulness, all proudness, yea, and all bibble-babble. Let us pray this prayer with understanding and great deliberation ; not following the trade of monkery, which was without all devotion and under-standing. There be but few which can say from the bottom of their hearts, ' Our Father ' ; a little number. Neither the Turks, neither the Jews, not yet the impenitent sinners, can call God their Father. Therefore it is but vain babbling, whatsoever they pray : God heareth them not, he will not receive their prayers. The promise of hearing is made unto them only which be faithful and believe in God ; which endeavour themselves to live according unto his commandments. For scripture saith, *Oculi Domini super justos ;* ' The eyes of the Lord are over the righteous, and his ears open unto their prayers.' But who are those righteous ? Every penitent sinner, that is sorry from the bottom of his heart for his wickedness, and believeth that God will forgive him his sins for his Son our Saviour Jesus Christ's sake. This is called in scripture ' a just man,' that endeavoureth himself to leave all wickedness. In such sort Peter and Paul were just, because they did repent, and believe in Christ, and so endeavoured themselves to live according unto God's laws. Therefore like as they were made just before God, so may we too ; for we have even the self-same promise. Let us therefore follow their ensample. Let us forsake all sins and wickedness ; then God will hear our prayers. For scripture saith, *Dominus facit quicquid volunt timentes eum, et clamorem eorum exaudit ac servat eos :* ' The Lord fulfilleth the desire of them that fear him ; he also will hear their cry, and help them.' In another place he saith, *Si manseritis in sermone meo, et verba mea custodiveritis, quicquid volueritis petentes accipietis :* ' If ye abide in me, and my words abide in you, ask what ye will, and it shall be done for you.' So we see that the promises pertain only to the faithful ; to those which endeavour themselves to live according to God's will and pleasure ; which can be content to leave their wickedness, and follow godliness : those God will hear at all times, whensoever they shall call upon him.

Remember now what I have said : remember what is meant by this word ' our ' ; namely, that it admonisheth us of love and charity ; it teacheth us to beware of stubbornness and proudness ; considering that God loveth as well the beggar as the rich man, for he regardeth no persons. Again, what is to be understood by this word ' Father ' ; namely, that he beareth a good will towards us, that he is ready and willing to help us. ' Heavenly,' that admonisheth us of his potency and ability, that he is ruler over all things. This, I say, remember, and follow it : then we shall receive all things necessary for this life ; and finally everlasting joy and felicity. Amen. Let us pray, ' Our Father.'

Death's Duel

JOHN DONNE

✝

And unto God the Lord belong the issues of death (i.e. from death).—PSALM lxviii. 20.

DEATH'S DUEL

JOHN DONNE

BUILDINGS stand by the benefit of their foundations that sustain and support them, and of
their buttresses that comprehend and embrace them,
and of their contignations that knit and unite
them : The foundations suffer them not to sink, the
buttresses suffer them not to swerve, and the contignation and knitting suffers them not to cleave.
The body of our building is in the former part of
this verse. It is this : he that is our God is the God
of salvation ; *ad salutes*, of salvations in the plural
(so it is in the original) ; the God that gives us
spiritual and temporal salvation too. But of this
building, the foundation, the buttresses, the contignations are in this part of the verse, which constitutes
our text, and in the three divers acceptations of the
words amongst our expositors. Unto God the Lord
belong the issues from death. For first the foundation
of this building (that our God is the God of all
salvations) is laid in this : that unto this God the
Lord belong the issues of death ; that is, it is in
his power to give us an issue and deliverance, even

then when we are brought to the jaws and teeth of
death, and to the lips of that whirlpool, the grave.
And so in this acceptation, this *exitus mortis*, this
'issue of death' is *liberatio a morte*, 'a deliverance
from death,' and this is the most obvious and most
ordinary acceptation of these words, and that upon
which our translation lays hold, 'The issues from
death.' And then secondly the buttresses that
comprehend and settle this building: That he that
is our God, is the God of all salvations, are thus
raised; 'Unto God the Lord belong the issues of
death,' that is, the disposition and manner of our
death: what kind of issue and transmigration we
shall have out of this world, whether prepared or
sudden, whether violent or natural, whether in our
perfect senses or shaken and disordered by sickness;
there is no condemnation to be argued out of that,
no judgement to be made upon that, for howsoever
they die, 'previous in his sight is the death of his
saints,' and with him are the issues of death; the
ways of our departing out of this life are in his hands.
And so in this sense of the words, this *exitus mortis*,
the issue of death, is *liberatio in morte*, a deliverance
in death. Not that God will deliver us from dying,
but that he will have a care of us in the hour of death,
of what kind soever our passage be. And in this
sense and acceptation of the words, the natural frame
and contexture doth well and pregnantly administer
unto us. And then lastly the contignation and
knitting of this building, that he that is our God is

the God of all salvations, consists in this, ' Unto this God the Lord belong the issues of death,' that is, that this God the Lord having united and knit both natures in one, and being God, having also come into this world, in our flesh, he could have no other means to save us, he could have no other issue out of this world, not return to his former glory, but by death. And so in this sense, this *exitus mortis*, this issue of death, is *liberatio per mortem*, a deliverance by death, by the death of this God our Lord Christ Jesus. And this is Saint Augustine's acceptation of the words, and those many and great persons that have adhered to him. In all these three lines then, we shall look upon these words. First, as the God of power, the Almighty Father rescues his servants from the jaws of death. And then, as the God of mercy, the glorious Son rescued us, by taking upon himself this issue of death. And then between these two, as the God of comfort, the Holy Ghost rescues us from all discomfort by his blessed impressions beforehand, that what manner of death soever be ordained for us, yet this *exitus mortis* shall be *introitus in vitam*, our issue in death shall be an entrance into everlasting life. And these three considerations, our deliverance *a morte, in morte, per mortem*, from death, in death, and by death, will abundantly do all the offices of the foundations, of the buttresses, of the contignation of this our building : That he that is our God, is the God of all salvations, because unto this God the Lord belong the issues of death.

First, then, we consider this *exitus mortis*, to be *liberatio a morte*, that with God the Lord are the issues of death, and therefore in all our deaths, and deadly calamities of this life, we may justly hope of a good issue from him. And all our periods and transitions in this life, are so many passages from death to death ; our very birth and entrance into this life, is *exitus a morte*, an issue from death, for in our mother's womb we are dead, so as that we do not know we live, not so much as we do in our sleep, neither is there any grave so close, or so putrid a prison, as the womb would be unto us, if we stayed in it beyond our time, or died there before our time. In the grave the worms do not kill us, we breed and feed, and then kill those worms which we ourselves produced. In the womb the dead child kills the mother that conceived it, and is a murderer, nay a parricide, even after it is dead. And if we be not dead so in the womb, so as that being dead we kill her that gave us our first life, our life of vegetation, yet we are dead so, as David's idols are dead. In the womb we have eyes and see not, ears and hear not. There in the womb we are fitted for works of darkness, all the while deprived of light. And there in the womb we are taught cruelty, by being fed with blood, and may be damned, though we be never born. Of our very making in the womb, David says, ' I am wonderfully and fearfully made,' and, ' Such knowledge is too excellent for me,' for even that ' is the Lord's doing,' and it ' is wonderful in our eyes.' *Ipse fecit nos*, ' it is he that hath made us, and not we ourselves ' nor our parents neither. ' Thy hands have made me and fashioned me round about,' saith Job, and (as the original word is) ' thou hast taken pains about me,' and yet, says he, ' thou dost destroy me.' Though I be the masterpiece of the greatest Master (man is so), yet if thou do no more for me, if thou leave me where thou madest me, destruction will follow. The womb which should be the house of life, becomes death itself, if God leave us there. That which God threatens so often, the shutting of the womb, is not so heavy, not so discomfortable a curse in the first, as in the latter shutting, nor in the shutting of barrenness, as in the shutting of weakness, when ' children are come to the birth,' and ' there is not strength to bring forth.'

It is the exaltation of misery, to fall from a near hope of happiness. And in that vehement impre-cation, the Prophet expresses the highest of God's anger, ' give them, O Lord,' what wilt thou give them ? give them ' a miscarrying womb.' Therefore as soon as we are men (that is, inanimated, quickened in the womb), though we cannot ourselves, our parents have reason to say in our behalf, ' wretched man that he is, who shall deliver him from this body of death ? ' for even the womb is a body of death, if there be no deliverer. It must be he that said to Jeremy, ' Before I formed thee I knew thee, and before thou camest out of the womb I sanctified thee.' We are not sure that there was no kind of ship nor boat to fish in, nor to pass by, till God prescribed Noah that absolute form of the Ark. That word which the Holy Ghost by Moses useth for the Ark, is common to all kind of boats, 'Thebah,' and is the same word that Moses useth for the boat that he was exposed in, that ' his mother laid him in an ark of bulrushes.' But we are sure that Eve had no midwife when she was delivered of Cain, therefore she might well say, *possedi virum a Domino*, ' I have gotten a man from the Lord,' wholly, entirely from the Lord ; It is the Lord that enabled me to conceive, the Lord that infused a quickening soul into that conception, the Lord that brought into the world that which himself had quickened, without all this might Eve say, My body had been but the house of death, and *Domini Domini sunt exitus mortis*, ' to God the Lord belong the issues of death.'

But then this *exitus a morte*, is but *introitus in mortem*, this issue, this deliverance from that death, the death of the womb, is an entrance, a delivering over to another death, the manifold deaths of this world. We have a winding-sheet in our mother's womb, which grows with us from our conception, and we come into the world, wound up in that winding-sheet, for we come to seek a grave. And as prisoners discharged of actions may lie for fees, so when the womb hath discharged us, yet we are bound to it by cords of flesh by such a string, as that we cannot go thence, nor stay there ; we celebrate our own funerals with cries, even at our birth ; as

though our threescore and ten years life were spent in
our mother's labour, and our circle made up in the
first point thereof, we beg our Baptism, with another
Sacrament, with tears, and we come into a world that
lasts many ages, but we last not ; *in domo Patris*, says
our Saviour, speaking of heaven, *multae mansiones*,
there are many mansions, divers and durable, so that
if a man cannot possess a martyr's house (he hath
shed no blood for Christ) yet he may have a confessor's,
he hath been ready to glorify God in the shedding of
his blood. And if a woman cannot possess a virgin's
house (she hath embraced the holy state of marriage)
yet she may have a matron's house, she hath brought
forth and brought up children in the fear of God.
In domo Patris, ' in my Father's house,' in heaven
' there are many mansions ' ; but here upon earth
' the son of man hath not where to lay his head,'
says he himself. *Nonne terram dedit filiis hominum?*
how then hath God given this earth to the sons of
men ? he hath given them earth for their materials
to be made of earth, and he hath given them earth
for their grave and sepulture, to return and resolve
to earth, but not for their possession : ' Here we
have no continuing city,' nay no cottage that continues,
nay no persons, no bodies that continue. Whatsoever
moved Saint Jerome to call the journeys of the
Israelites, in the wilderness, mansions, the word (the
word is *nasang*) signifies but a journey, but a peregrina-
tion. Even the Israel of God hath no mansions ; but
journeys, pilgrimages in this life. By that measure

did Jacob measure his life to Pharaoh; 'the days of the years of my pilgrimage.' And though the Apostle would not say *morimur*, that, whilst we are in the body we are dead, yet he says, *peregrinamur*, whilst we are in the body, we are but in a pilgrimage, and we are absent from the Lord; he might have said dead, for this whole world is but a universal churchyard, but one common grave, and the life and motion that the greatest persons have in it, is but as the shaking of buried bodies in the grave, by an earthquake. That which we call life, is but *hebdomada mortium*, a week of deaths, seven days, seven periods of our life spent in dying, a dying seven times over; and there is an end. Our birth dies in infancy, and our infancy dies in youth, and youth and the rest die in age, and age also dies, and determines all. Nor do all these, youth out of infancy, or age out of youth arise so, as a phoenix out of the ashes of another phoenix formerly dead, but as a wasp or a serpent out of a carrion, or as a snake out of dung. Our youth is worse than our infancy, and our age worse than our youth. Our youth is hungry and thirsty, after those sins which our infancy knew not. And our age is sorry and angry, that it cannot pursue those sins which our youth did; and besides, all the way, so many deaths, that is, so many deadly calamities accompany every condition, and every period of this life, as that death itself would be an ease to them that suffer them. Upon this sense doth Job wish that God had not given him as issue from the first

death, from the womb, ' Wherefore hast thou brought
me forth out of the womb ? O that I had given up
the ghost, and no eye seen me ! I should have been
as though I had not been.' And not only the impatient Israelites in their murmuring (' would to God
we had died by the hand of the Lord in the land of
Egypt '), but Elijah himself, when he fled from
Jezebel, and went for his life, as that text says, under
the juniper tree, requested that he might die, and
said, ' it is enough now, O Lord, take away my life.'
So Jonah justifies his impatience, nay his anger towards
God himself. ' Now, O Lord, take, I beseech thee,
my life from me, for it is better to die than to live.'
And when God asked him, ' dost thou well to be
angry for this ? ' he replies, ' I do well to be angry,
even unto death.' How much worse a death than
death, is this life, which so good men would so often
change for death ! But if my case be as Saint Paul's
case, *quotidie morior*, that ' I die daily,' that something
heavier than death falls upon me every day ; if my
case be David's case, *tota die mortificamur* ; ' all the
day long we are killed,' that not only every day, but
every hour of the day some thing heavier than death
falls upon me, though that be true of me, *Conceptus
in peccatis*, ' I was shapen in iniquity, and in sin did
my mother conceive me ' (there I died one death),
though that be true of me (*Natus filius irae*) I was born
not only the child of sin, but the child of wrath, of
the wrath of God for sin, which is a heavier death ;
Yet, *Domini Domini sunt exitus mortis*, ' with God the

Lord are the issues of death,' and after a Job, and a Joseph, and a Jeremy, and a Daniel, I cannot doubt of a deliverance. And if no other deliverance conduce more to his glory and my good, yet he hath the keys of death, and he can let me out at that door, that is, deliver me from the manifold deaths of this world, the *omni die* and the *tota die*, the every day's death and every hour's death, by that one death, the final dissolution of body and soul, the end of all. But then is that the end of all? Is that dissolution of body and soul, the last death that the body shall suffer? (for of spiritual death we speak not now). It is not. Though this be *exitus a morte*, it is *introitus in mortem*; though it be an issue from the manifold deaths of this world, yet it is an entrance into the death of corruption and putrefaction and vermiculation and incineration, and dispersion in and from the grave, in which every dead man dies over again. It was a prerogative peculiar to Christ, not to die this death, not to see corruption. What gave him this privilege? Not Joseph's great proportion of gums and spices, that might have preserved his body from corruption and incineration longer than he needed it, longer than three days, but would not have done it for ever. What preserved him then? Did his exemption and freedom from original sin preserve him from this corruption and incineration? 'Tis true that original sin hath induced this corruption and incineration upon us. If we had not sinned in Adam, mortality had not ' put on immortality ' (as the Apostle speaks),

nor corruption had not ' put on incorruption,' but we
had had our transmigration from this to the other
world, without any mortality, any corruption at all.
But yet since Christ took sin upon him, so far as
made him mortal, he had it so far too, as might have
made him see this corruption and incineration, though
he had no original sin in himself. What preserved
him then ? Did the hypostatical union of both
natures, God and Man, preserve him from this
corruption and incineration ? 'Tis true that this was
a most powerful embalming, to be embalmed with
the divine nature itself, to be embalmed with eternity,
was able to preserve him from corruption and incineration for ever. And he was embalmed so, embalmed
with the divine nature itself, even in his body as
well as in his soul ; for the Godhead, the divine
nature did not depart, but remained still united to
his dead body in the grave. But yet for all this
powerful embalming, this hypostatical union of both
natures, we see Christ did die ; and for all this union
which made him God and Man, he became no man
(for the union of the body and soul makes the man,
and he whose soul and body are separated by death
as long as that state lasts is properly no man). And
therefore as in him the dissolution of body and soul
was no dissolution of the hypostatical union ; so is
there nothing that constrains us to say, that though
the flesh of Christ had seen corruption and incineration in the grave, this had been any dissolution of
the hypostatical union, for the divine nature, the

Godhead, might have remained with all the elements and principles of Christ's body, as well as it did with the two constitutive parts of his person, his body and his soul. This incorruption then was not in Joseph's gums and spices, nor was it in Christ's innocency, and exemption from original sin, nor was it (that is, it is not necessary to say it was) in the hypostatical union. But this incorruptibleness of his flesh is most conveniently placed in that, *Non dabis*, ' thou wilt not suffer thy holy one to see corruption ' : we look no further for causes or reasons in the mysteries of religion, but to the will and pleasure of God : Christ himself limited his inquisition in that *ita est*, ' even so, Father, for so it seemeth good in thy sight.' Christ's body did not see corruption, therefore, because God had decreed it should not. The humble soul (and only the humble soul is the religious soul) rests himself upon God's purposes and the decrees of God, which he hath declared and manifested, not such as are conceived and imagined in ourselves, though upon some probability, some verisimilitude. So in our present case Peter proceeds in his Sermon at Jerusalem, and so Paul in his at Antioch. They preached Christ to have been risen without seeing corruption not only because God had decreed it, but because he had manifested that decree in his Prophet. Therefore doth St. Paul cite by special number the second Psalm for that decree. And therefore both St. Peter and St. Paul cite for it that place in the sixteenth Psalm, for when God declares his decree

and purpose in the express words of his Prophet, or
when he declares it in the real execution of the decree,
then he makes it ours, then he manifests it to us.
And therefore as the Mysteries of our Religion are
not the objects of our reason, but by faith we rest on
God's decree and purpose (it is so, O God, because it
is thy will it should be so), so God's decrees are ever
to be considered in the manifestation thereof. All
manifestation is either in the word of God, or in
the execution of the decree. And when these two
concur and meet, it is the strongest demonstration
that can be : when therefore I find those marks of
adoption and spiritual filiation, which are delivered
in the word of God to be upon me, when I find
that real execution of his good purpose upon me, as
that actually I do live under the obedience, and under
the conditions which are evidences of adoption and
spiritual filiation—then so long as I see these marks
and live so, I may safely comfort myself in a holy
certitude and a modest infallibility of my adoption.
Christ determines himself in that, the purpose of
God was manifest to him : St. Peter and St. Paul
determine themselves in those two ways of knowing
the purpose of God, the word of God before, the
execution of the decree in the fullness of time. It
was prophesied before, say they, and it is performed
now, Christ is risen without seeing corruption. Now
this which is so singularly peculiar to him, that ' his
flesh should not see corruption,' at his second coming,
his coming to judgement, shall extend to all that are

then alive, their flesh shall not see corruption, because as the Apostle says, and says as a secret, as a mystery : ' Behold I show you a mystery, we shall not all sleep ' (that is, not continue in the state of the dead in the grave) ' but we shall all be changed in an instant,' we shall have a dissolution, and in the same instant a redintegration, a recompacting of body and soul, and that shall be truly a death and truly a resurrection, but no sleeping in corruption. But for us that die now and sleep in the state of the dead, we must all pass this posthume death, this death after death, nay this death after burial, this dissolution after dissolution, this death of corruption and putrefaction, of vermiculation and incineration, of dissolution and dispersion in and from the grave, when these bodies that have been the children of royal parents, and the parents of royal children, must say with Job, ' Corruption, thou art my father,' and to the worm, ' thou art my mother and my sister.' Miserable riddle, when the same worm must be my mother, and my sister, and myself ! Miserable incest, when I must be married to my mother and my sister, and be both father and mother to my own mother and sister, beget and bear that worm which is all that miserable penury ; when my mouth shall be filled with dust, and the worm shall feed, and feed sweetly upon me, when the ambitious man shall have no satisfaction, if the poorest alive tread upon him, nor the poorest receive any contentment in being made equal to princes, for they shall be equal but in dust.

One dieth at his full strength, being wholly at ease and in quiet, and another dies in the bitterness of his soul, and never eats with pleasure, but they lie down alike in the dust, and the worm covers them. In Job and in Isaiah, it covers them and is spread under them, ' the worm is spread under thee, and the worm covers thee.' There's the mats and the carpets that lie under, and there's the state and the canopy that hang over the greatest of the sons of men. Even those bodies that were the temples of the Holy Ghost, come to this dilapidation, to ruin, to rubbish, to dust, even the Israel of the Lord, and Jacob himself hath no other specification, no other denomination, but that *vermis Jacob*, ' thou worm of Jacob.' Truly the consideration of this posthume death, this death after burial, that after God (with whom are the issues of death) hath delivered me from the death of the womb, by bringing me into the world, and from the manifold deaths of the world, by laying me in the grave, I must die again in an incineration of this flesh, and in a dispersion of that dust. That that monarch, who spread over many nations alive, must in his dust lie in a corner of that sheet of lead, and there, but so long as that lead will last, and that private and retired man, that thought himself his own for ever, and never came forth, must in his dust of the grave be published, and (such are the revolutions of the graves) be mingled with the dust of every highway, and of every dunghill, and swallowed in every puddle and pond : this is the most inglorious and contemptible

vilification, the most deadly and peremptory nullifica-
tion of man, that we can consider. God seems to
have carried the declaration of his power to a great
height, when he sets the prophet Ezekiel in the valley
of dry bones, and says, ' Son of man, can these bones
live ? ' as though it had been impossible, and yet
they did. The Lord laid sinews upon them, and flesh,
and breathed into them, and they did live. But in
that case there were bones to be seen, something
visible, of which it might be said, can this thing
live ? But in this death of incineration, and dispersion
of dust, we see nothing that we call that man's. If
we say, ' Can this dust live ? ' perchance it cannot, it
may be the mere dust of the earth, which never did
live, never shall. It may be the dust of that man's
worm, which did live, but shall no more. It may be
the dust of another man, that concerns not him of
whom it is asked. This death of incineration and
dispersion is, to natural reason, the most irrecover-
able death of all, and yet *Domini Domini sunt exitus
mortis*, ' unto God the Lord belong the issues of
death,' and by recompacting this dust into the same
body, and reinanimating the same body with the
same soul, he shall in a blessed and glorious resurrection give me such an issue from this death, as
shall never pass into any other death, but establish
me into a life that shall last as long as the Lord of
life himself.

And so have you that that belongs to the first
acceptation of these words (' unto God the Lord

belong the issues of death ') that though from the
womb to the grave and in the grave itself we pass
from death to death, yet, as Daniel speaks, ' the
Lord our God is able to deliver us, and he will
deliver us.'

And so we pass unto our second accommodation
of these words (' unto God the Lord belong the issues
of death ') that it belongs to God, and not to man to
pass a judgement upon us at our death, or to conclude
a dereliction on God's part upon the manner thereof.

Those indications which the physicians receive, and
those presagitions which they give for death or
recovery in the patient, they receive and they give
out of the grounds and the rules of their art ; but
we have no such rule or art to give a presagition of
spiritual death and damnation upon any such
indication as we see in any dying man ; we see often
enough to be sorry, but not to despair ; we may be
deceived both ways ; we use to comfort ourself in
the death of a friend, if it be testified that he went
away like a lamb, that is, without any reluctation.
But, God knows, that [he] may be accompanied with
a dangerous damp and stupefaction, and insensibility
of his present state. Our blessed Saviour suffered
colluctations with death, and a sadness even in his
soul to death, and an agony even to a bloody sweat
in his body, and expostulations with God, and
exclamations upon the cross. He was a devout man,
who said upon his deathbed, or dead-turf (for he was
an hermit) *septuaginta annis Domino servivisti, et mori*

times ? ' hast thou served a good Master threescore
and ten years, and now art thou loath to go into his
presence ? ' yet Hilarion was loath ; Barlaam was a
devout man (an hermit too) that said that day he
died : *Cogita te hodie cœpisse servire Domino, et hodie
finiturum,* ' Consider this to be the first day's service
that ever thou didst thy Master,' to glorify him in a
Christianly and a constant death, and if thy first day
be thy last day too, how soon dost thou come to
receive thy wages ? yet Barlaam could have been
content to have stayed longer for it. Make no ill
conclusions upon any man's lothness to die, for the
mercies of God work momentarily in minutes, and
many times insensibly to bystanders or any other
than the party departing. And then upon violent
deaths inflicted, as upon malefactors, Christ himself
hath forbidden us by his own death to make any ill
conclusion ; for his own death had those impressions
in it. He was reputed, he was executed as a malefactor, and no doubt many of them who concurred
to his death, did believe him to be so. Of sudden
death there are scarce examples to be found in the
Scriptures upon good men, for death in battle cannot
be called sudden death. But God governs not by
examples, but by rules ; and therefore make no ill
conclusion upon sudden death nor upon distempers
neither, though perchance accompanied with some
words of diffidence and distrust in the mercies of
God : ' The tree lies as it falls,' it's true, but it is
not the last stroke that fells the tree, nor the last

word nor gasp that qualifies the soul. Still pray we for a peaceable life, against violent death, and for time of repentance against sudden death, and for sober and modest assurance against distempered and diffident death, but never make ill conclusions upon persons overtaken with such deaths ; *Domini Domini sunt exitus mortis*, ' to God the Lord belong the issues of death.' And he received Samson, who went out of this world in such a manner (consider it actively, consider it passively in his own death, and in those whom he slew with himself) as was subject to interpretation hard enough. Yet the Holy Ghost hath moved St. Paul to celebrate Samson in his great catalogue, and so doth all the Church. Our critical day is not the very day of our death, but the whole course of our life. I thank him that prays for me when the bell tolls, but I thank him much more that catechizes me, or preaches to me, or instructs me how to live. *Fac hoc et vives*, there's my security, the mouth of the Lord hath said it, ' do this and thou shalt live ' : but though I do it, yet I shall die too, die a bodily, a natural death. But God never mentions, never seems to consider that death, the bodily, the natural death. God doth not say, live well and thou shalt die well, that is, an easy, a quiet death ; but live well here, and thou shalt live well for ever. As the first part of a sentence pieces well with the last, and never respects, never hearkens after the parenthesis that comes between, so doth a good life here flow into an eternal life, without any consideration, what manner of death we die. But whether the gate of my prison be opened with an oiled key (by a gentle and preparing sickness), or the gate be hewn down by a violent death, or the gate be burnt down by a raging and frantic fever, a gate into heaven I shall have, for from the Lord is the cause of my life, and 'with God the Lord are the issues of death.' And further we carry not this second acceptation of the words, as this issue of death is *liberatio in morte*, God's care that the soul be safe, what agonies soever the body suffers in the hour of death.

But pass to our third part and last part ; as this issue of death is *liberatio per mortem*, a deliverance by the death of another, by the death of Christ. *Sufferentiam Job audiisti, et vidisti finem Domini*, says St. James 5. 11. ' You have heard of the patience of Job,' says he. All this while you have done that, for in every man, calamitous, miserable man, a Job speaks ; Now see the end of the Lord, saith that Apostle, which is not that end that the Lord proposed to himself (salvation to us) nor the end which he proposes to us (conformity to him), but see the end of the Lord, says he, the end, that the Lord himself came to, death and a painful and a shameful death. But why did he die ? and why die so ? *Quia Domini Domini sunt exitus mortis* (as St. Augustine interpreting this text answers that question), because to this ' God our Lord belonged the issues of death.' *Quid apertius diceretur ?* says he there, what can be more obvious, more manifest than this sense of these words. In the former part of this verse, it is said ; 'He that is our God, is the God of salvation,' *Deus salvos faciendi*, so he reads it, the God that must save us. Who can that be, says he, but Jesus ? for therefore that name was given him, because he was to save us. And to this Jesus, says he, this Saviour, 'belong the issues of death' ; *Nec oportuit eum de hac vita alios exitus habere quam mortis.* Being come into this life in our mortal nature, he could not go out of it any other way but by death. *Ideo dictum*, says he, therefore it is said, 'To God the Lord belong the issues of death' ; *ut ostenderetur moriendo nos salvos facturum*, to show that his way to save us was to die. And from this text doth St. Isidore prove, that Christ was truly Man (which as many sects of heretics denied, as that he was truly God) because to him, though he were *Dominus Dominus* (as the text doubles it) God the Lord, yet to him, 'to God the Lord belonged the issues of death,' *oportuit eum pati* ; more can not be said, than Christ himself says of himself ; 'These things Christ ought to suffer,' he had no other way but by death : so then this part of our Sermon must needs be a Passion Sermon ; since all his life was a continual passion, all our Lent may well be a continual Good Friday. Christ's painful life took off none of the pains of his death, he felt not the less then for having felt so much before. Nor will anything that shall be said before, lessen, but rather enlarge the devotion, to that which shall be said of his passion at the time of due solemnization thereof. Christ bled not a drop the less at the last, for having bled at his circumcision before, nor will you shed a tear the less then, if you shed some now. And therefore be now content to consider with me how to this God the Lord belonged the issues of death. That God, this Lord, the Lord of life could die, is a strange contemplation ; that the Red Sea could be dry, that the sun could stand still, that an oven could be seven times heat and not burn, that lions could be hungry and not bite, is strange, miraculously strange, but supermiraculous that God could die ; but that God would die is an exaltation of that. But even of that also it is a superexaltation, that God should die, must die, and *non exitus* (said St. Augustine), God the Lord had no issue but by death, and *oportuit pati* (says Christ himself), ' all this Christ ought to suffer,' was bound to suffer ; *Deus ultionum Deus*, says David, God is the ' God of revenges,' he would not pass over the sin of man unrevenged, unpunished. But then *Deus ultionum libere egit* (says that place), the God of revenges works freely, he punishes, he spares whom he will. And would he not spare himself ? he would not : *Dilectio fortis ut mors*, ' love is strong as death,' stronger, it drew in death that naturally is not welcome. *Si possibile*, says Christ, ' If it be possible, let this cup pass,' when his love expressed in a former decree with his Father, had made it impossible. ' Many waters quench not love ' ; Christ tried many ; he was baptized out of his love, and his love determined not there. He mingled blood with water in

119

his agony and that determined not his love ; he wept pure blood, all his blood at all his eyes, at all his pores, in his flagellation and thorns (to the Lord our God belonged the issues of blood) and these expressed, but these did not quench his love. He would not spare, nay he could not spare himself. There was nothing more free, more voluntary, more spontaneous than the death of Christ. 'Tis true, *libere egit*, he died voluntarily, but yet when we consider the contract that had passed between his Father and him, there was an *oportuit*, a kind of necessity upon him. All this Christ ought to suffer. And when shall we date this obligation, this *oportuit*, this necessity ? when shall we say that begun ? Certainly this decree by which Christ was to suffer all this, was an eternal decree, and was there anything before that, that was eternal ? Infinite love, eternal love ; be pleased to follow this home, and to consider it seriously, that what liberty soever we can conceive in Christ, to die or not to die ; this necessity of dying, this decree is as eternal as that liberty ; and yet how small a matter made he of this necessity and this dying ? His Father calls it but a bruise, and but a bruising of his heel (the serpent shall bruise his heel) and yet that was, that the serpent should practise and compass his death. Himself calls it but a baptism, as though he were to be the better for it. 'I have a baptism to be baptized with,' and he was in pain till it was accomplished, and yet this baptism was his death. The Holy Ghost calls it joy (' for the joy which was

set before him he endured the cross ') which was not
a joy of his reward after his passion, but a joy that
filled him even in the midst of those torments, and
arose from him ; when Christ calls his *Calicem*, a cup,
and no worse (' can ye drink of my Cup ? ') he speaks
not odiously, not with detestation of it. Indeed it
was a cup, *salus mundo*, a health to all the world. And
quid retribuam, says David, ' what shall I render to the
Lord ? ' Answer you with David, *accipiam Calicem*,
' I will take the cup of salvation,' take it, that cup
is salvation, his passion, if not into your present
imitation, yet into your present contemplation. And
behold how that Lord that was God, yet could die,
would die, must die, for your salvation. That Moses
and Elias talked with Christ in the Transfiguration,
both St. Matthew and St. Mark tell us, but what
they talked of only St. Luke, *Dicebant excessum ejus*,
says he, ' they talked of his decease, of his death
which was to be accomplished at Jerusalem.' The
word is of his exodus, the very word of our text,
exitus, his issue by death. Moses who in his *Exodus*
had prefigured this issue of our Lord, and in passing
Israel out of Egypt through the Red Sea, had foretold
in that actual prophecy, Christ passing of mankind
through the sea of his blood. And Elias, whose
exodus and issue out of this world was a figure of
Christ's ascension, had no doubt a great satisfaction
in talking with our blessed Lord *de excessu ejus*, of
the full consummation of all this in his death, which
was to be accomplished at Jerusalem. Our meditation

of his death should be more visceral and affect us more because it is of a thing already done. The ancient Romans had a certain tenderness and detestation of the name of death, they could not name death, no, not in their wills. There they could not say *Si mori contigerit*, but *si quid humanitas contingat*, not if, or when I die, but when the course of nature is accomplished upon me. To us that speak daily of the death of Christ (' he was crucified, dead and buried ') can the memory or the mention of our own death be irksome or bitter ? There are in these latter times amongst us, that name death freely enough, and the death of God, but in blasphemous oaths and execrations. Miserable men, who shall therefore be said never to have named Jesus, because they have named him too often. And therefore hear Jesus say, *Nescivi vos*, ' I never knew you,' because they made themselves too familiar with him. Moses and Elias talked with Christ of his death, only, in a holy and joyful sense of the benefit which they and all the world were to receive by that. Discourses of Religion should not be out of curiosity, but of edification. And then they talked with Christ of his death at that time, when he was in the greatest height of glory that ever he admitted in this world, that is, his transfiguration. And we are afraid to speak to the great men of this world of their death, but nourish in them a vain imagination of immortality, and immutability. But *bonum est nobis esse hic* (as St. Peter said there), ' It is good to dwell here,' in this con-

sideration of his death, and therefore transfer we our
tabernacle (our devotions) through some of those steps
which God the Lord made to his issue of death that
day. Take in the whole day from the hour that
Christ received the passover upon Thursday, unto the
hour in which he died the next day. Make this
present day that day in thy devotion, and consider
what he did, and remember what you have done.
Before he instituted and celebrated the Sacrament
(which was after the eating of the passover) he
proceeded to that act of humility, to wash his
disciples' feet, even Peter's, who for a while resisted
him. In thy preparation to the holy and blessed
Sacrament, hast thou with a sincere humility sought
a reconciliation with all the world, even with those
that have been averse from it, and refused that
reconciliation from thee ? If so, and not else, thou
hast spent that first part of his last day, in a conformity with him. After the Sacrament he spent the
time till night in prayer, in preaching, in psalms.
Hast thou considered that a worthy receiving of the
Sacrament consists in a continuation of holiness after,
as well as in a preparation before ? If so, thou hast
therein also conformed thyself to him, so Christ
spent his time till night. At night he went into the
garden to pray, and he prayed *prolixius*, he spent
much time in prayer. How much ? Because it is
literally expressed, that he prayed there three several
times, and that returning to his disciples after his
first prayer, and finding them asleep, said, ' Could

ye not watch with me one hour?' it is collected that
he spent three hours in prayer. I dare scarce ask
thee whither thou wentest, or how thou disposedst
of thyself, when it grew dark and after last night.
If that time were spent in a holy recommendation of
thyself to God, and a submission of thy will to his,
it was spent in a conformity to him. In that time
and in those prayers was his agony and bloody sweat.
I will hope that thou didst pray; but not every
ordinary and customary prayer, but prayer actually
accompanied with shedding of tears, and dispositively
in a readiness to shed blood for his glory in necessary
cases, puts thee into a conformity with him. About
midnight he was taken and bound with a kiss. Art
thou not too conformable to him in that? Is not
that too literally, too exactly thy case? at midnight
to have been taken and bound with a kiss? from
thence he was carried back to Jerusalem, first to
Annas, then to Caiaphas, and (as late as it was) then
he was examined and buffeted, and delivered over
to the custody of those officers, from whom he
received all those irrisions, and violences, the covering
of his face, the spitting upon his face, the blasphemies
of words, and the smartness of blows which that
Gospel mentions. In which compass fell that
Gallicinium, that crowing of the cock which called
up Peter to his repentance. How thou passedst all
that time last night thou knowest. If thou didst
anything that needed Peter's tears, and hast not shed
them, let me be thy cock, do it now. Now thy

Master (in the unworthiest of his servants) looks back
upon thee, do it now. Betimes, in the morning, so
soon as it was day, the Jews held a counsel in the
high priest's hall, and agreed upon their evidence
against him, and then carried him to Pilate, who was
to be his judge ; didst thou accuse thyself when
thou wakedst this morning, and wast thou content
even with false accusations (that is) rather to suspect
actions to have been sin, which were not, than to
smother and justify such as were truly sins ? then
thou spentest that hour in conformity to him : Pilate
found no evidence against him, and therefore to ease
himself, and to pass a compliment upon Herod,
tetrarch of Galilee, who was at that time at Jerusalem
(because Christ being a Galilean was of Herod's
jurisdiction) Pilate sent him to Herod, and rather as
a madman than a malefactor, Herod remanded him
(with scorns) to Pilate to proceed against him ; and
this was about eight of the clock. Hast thou been
content to come to this inquisition, this examination,
this agitation, this cribration, this pursuit of thy
conscience, to sift it, to follow it from the sins of
thy youth to thy present sins, from the sins of thy
bed, to the sins of thy board, and from the substance
to the circumstance of thy sins ? That's time spent
like thy Saviour's. Pilate would have saved Christ,
by using the privilege of the day in his behalf, because
that day one prisoner was to be delivered, but they
chose Barabbas. He would have saved him from
death, by satisfying their fury, with inflicting other

torments upon him, scourging and crowning with thorns, and loading him with many scornful and ignominious contumelies ; but they regarded him not, they pressed a crucifying. Hast thou gone about to redeem thy sin, by fasting, by alms, by disciplines and mortifications, in way of satisfaction to the justice of God ? that will not serve, that's not the right way, we press an utter crucifying of that sin that governs thee ; and that conforms thee to Christ. Towards noon Pilate gave judgement, and they made such haste to execution, as that by noon he was upon the cross. There now hangs that sacred body upon the cross, rebaptized in his own tears and sweat, and embalmed in his own blood alive. There are those bowels of compassion, which are so conspicuous, so manifested, as that you may see them through his wounds. There those glorious eyes grew faint in their light : so as the sun, ashamed to survive them, departed with his light too. And then that Son of God, who was never from us, and yet had now come a new way unto us in assuming our nature, delivers that soul (which was never out of his Father's hands) by a new way, a voluntary emission of it into his Father's hands. For though to this ' God our Lord, belonged these issues of death,' so that considered in his own contract, he must necessarily die, yet at no breach or battery, which they had made upon his sacred Body, issued his soul, but *emisit*, he ' gave up the ghost,' and as God breathed a soul into the first Adam, so this second Adam breathed his soul into

God, into the hands of God. There we leave you in that blessed dependency, to hang upon him that hangs upon the cross, there bathe in his tears, there suck at his wounds, and lie down in peace in his grave, till he vouchsafe you a resurrection, and an ascension into that Kingdom, which he hath purchased for you, with the inestimable price of his incorruptible blood. Amen.

Of the Spirit of Grace

JEREMY TAYLOR

✠

But ye are not in the flesh, but in the Spirit, if so be that the Spirit of God dwell in you. Now if any man have not the Spirit of Christ he is none of His : and if Christ be in you, the body is dead because of sin, but the spirit is life because of righteousness.—ROM. viii. 9, 10.

OF THE SPIRIT OF GRACE

JEREMY TAYLOR

THE day in which the Church commemorates the
descent of the Holy Ghost upon the apostles,
was the first beginning of the gospel of Jesus Christ.
This was the first day that the religion was professed ;
now the apostles first opened their commission, and
read it to all the people. ' The Lord gave His spirit,'
or, ' the Lord gave His word, and great was the
company of the preachers ' ; for so I make bold to
render that prophecy of David. Christ was the
' Word ' of God, *Verbum æternum* ; but the Spirit
was the Word of God, *Verbum patefactum* : Christ
was the Word manifested ' in ' the flesh ; the Spirit
was the Word manifested ' to ' flesh, and set in
dominion over, and in hostility against, the flesh.
The gospel and the Spirit are the same thing ; not
in substance ; but ' the manifestation of the Spirit '
is ' the gospel of Jesus Christ ' : and because He
was this day manifested, the gospel was this day
first preached, and it became a law to us, called
' the law of the Spirit of life ' ; that is, a law taught
us by the Spirit, leading us to life eternal.

But the gospel is called ' the Spirit.'

1. Because it contains in it such glorious mysteries which were revealed by the immediate inspirations of the Spirit, not only in the matter itself, but also in the manner and powers to apprehend them. For what power of human understanding could have found out the incarnation of a God; that two natures, a finite and an infinite, could have been concentred into one *hypostasis* or person; that a virgin should be a mother; that dead men should live again; that the

Κόνις ὀστέων λυθεύτων,

' the ashes of dissolved bones,' should become bright as the sun, blessed as the angels, swift in motion as thought, clear as the purest noon; that God should so love us as to be willing to be reconciled to us, and yet that Himself must die that He might pardon us; that God's most holy Son should give us His body to eat, and His blood to crown our chalices, and His spirit to sanctify our souls, to turn our bodies into temperance, our souls into minds, our minds into spirit, our spirit into glory; that He who can give us all things, who is Lord of men and angels and King of all the creatures, should pray to God for us without intermission; that He who reigns over all the world, should at the day of judgment ' give up the kingdom to God the Father,' and yet after this resignation Himself and we with Him should for ever reign the more gloriously; that we should be justified by faith in Christ, and that charity should be a part of faith, and that both should work as acts of duty and as acts of relation ; that God should crown the imperfect endeavours of His saints with glory, and that a human act should be rewarded with an eternal inheritance ; that the wicked for the transient pleasure of a few minutes should be tormented with an absolute eternity of pains ; that the waters of baptism, when they are fallowed by the Spirit, shall purge the soul from sin ; and that the spirit of a man should be nourished with the consecrated and mysterious elements, and that any such nourishment should bring a man up to heaven ; and after all this, that all Christian people, all that will be saved, must be ' partakers of the divine nature,' of the nature, the infinite nature, of God, and must dwell in Christ, and Christ must dwell in them, and they must be in the Spirit, and the Spirit must be for ever in them ? These are articles of so mysterious a philosophy that we could have inferred them from no premises, discoursed them upon the stock of no natural or scientifical principles ; nothing but God and God's Spirit could have taught them to us : and therefore the gospel is *Spiritus patefactus*, ' the manifestation of the Spirit,' *ad œdificationem*, as the apostle calls it, ' for edification,' and building us up to be a holy temple to the Lord.

2. But when we had been taught all these mysterious articles, we could not by any human power have understood them unless the Spirit of God had given

us a new light, and created in us a new capacity, and made us to be a new creature, of another definition. *Animalis homo*, ψυχικὸς, that is, as St. Jude expounds the word, πνεῦμα μὴ ἔχων, ' the animal ' or ' the natural man,' the man that ' hath not the Spirit,' ' cannot discern the things of God, for they are spiritually discerned,' that is, not to be understood but by the light proceeding from the Sun of righteousness, and by that eye whose bird is the holy Dove, whose candle is the gospel.

> Scio incapacem te sacramenti, impie,
> Non posse cœcis sensibus mysterium
> Haurire nostrum ; nil diurnum nox capit.

He that shall discourse Euclid's elements to a swine, or preach, as venerable Bede's story reports of him, to a rock, or talk metaphysics to a boar, will as much prevail upon his assembly as St. Peter and St. Paul could do upon uncircumcised hearts and ears, upon the indisposed Greeks and prejudicate Jews. An ox will relish the tender flesh of kids with as much gust and appetite, as an unspiritual and unsanctified man will do the discourses of angels, or of an apostle, if he should come to preach the secrets of the gospel. And we find it true by sad experience. How many times doth God speak to us by His servants the prophets, by His Son, by His apostles, by sermons, by spiritual books, by thousands of homilies, and arts of counsel and insinuation ; and we sit as unconcerned as the pillars of a church, and hear the sermons as the Athenians did a story, or as we read a gazette ? And if ever it come to pass that we tremble, as Felix did, when we hear a sad story of death, of 'righteousness and judgment to come,' then we put it off to another time, or we forget it, and think we had nothing to do but to give the good man a hearing ; and as Anacharsis said of the Greeks, they used money for nothing but to cast account withal ; so our hearers make use of sermons and discourses evangelical, but to fill up void spaces of their time, to help to tell an hour with, or pass it without tediousness. The reason of this is, a sad condemnation to such persons ; they have not yet entertained the Spirit of God, they are in darkness ; they were washed in water, but never baptized with the Spirit ; for these things 'are spiritually discerned.' They would think the preacher rude if he should say, they are not Christians, they are not within the covenant of the gospel ; but it is certain that 'the Spirit of manifestation' is not yet upon them, and that is the first effect of the Spirit whereby we can be called sons of God or relatives of Christ. If we do not apprehend and greedily suck in the precepts of this holy discipline as aptly as merchants do discourse of gain or farmers of fair harvests, we have nothing but the name of Christians, but we are no more such really than mandrakes are men or sponges are living creatures.

3. The gospel is called 'Spirit,' because it consists of spiritual promises and spiritual precepts, and makes

all men that embrace it truly to be spiritual men;
and therefore St. Paul adds an epithet beyond this,
calling it ' a quickening Spirit,' that is, puts life into
our spirits, which the law could not. The law bound
us to punishment, but did not help us to obedience,
because it gave not the promise of eternal life to its
disciples. The Spirit, that is, the gospel, only does
this; and this alone is it which comforts afflicted
minds, which puts activeness into wearied spirits,
which inflames our cold desires, and does ἀναζωπυρεῖν,
blows up sparks into live coals, and coals up to
flames, and flames to perpetual burnings. And it is
impossible that any man who believes and considers
the great, the infinite, the unspeakable, the unimaginable, the never-ceasing joys that are prepared
for all the sons and daughters of the gospel, should
not desire them; and unless he be a fool, he cannot
but use means to obtain them, effective, hearty
pursuances. For it is not directly in the nature of
a man to neglect so great a good; there must be
something in his manner, some obliquity in his will,
or madness in his intellectuals, or incapacity in his
naturals, that must make him sleep such a reward
away, or change it for the pleasure of a drunken fever,
or the vanity of a mistress, or the rage of a passion,
or the unreasonableness of any sin. However, this
promise is the life of all our actions, and the Spirit
that first taught it is the life of our souls.

4. But beyond this is the reason which is the consummation of all the faithful. The gospel is called

the Spirit, because by and in the gospel God hath
given to us not only 'the Spirit of manifestation,'
that is, of instruction and of catechism, of faith and
confident assent; but the 'Spirit of confirmation,'
or 'obsignation,' to all them that believe and obey
the gospel of Christ : that is, the power of God is
come upon our hearts, by which in an admirable
manner we are made sure of a glorious inheritance ;
made sure, I say, in the nature of the thing ; and our
own persuasions also are confirmed with an excellent,
a comfortable, a discerning, and a reasonable hope ;
in the strength of which, and by whose aid, as we
do not doubt of the performance of the promise, so
we vigorously pursue all the parts of the condition,
and are enabled to work all the work of God, so as
not to be affrighted with fear, or seduced by vanity,
or oppressed by lust, or drawn off by evil example, or
abused by riches, or imprisoned by ambition and
secular designs. This the Spirit of God does work
in all His servants ; and is called 'the Spirit of
obsignation,' or 'the confirming Spirit,' because it
confirms our hope, and assures our title to life
eternal ; and by means of it, and other its collateral
assistances, it also confirms us in our duty, that we
may not only profess in word, but live lives according
to the gospel. And this is the sense of 'the Spirit'
mentioned in the text ; 'Ye are not in the flesh, but
in the Spirit, if so be that the Spirit of God dwell in
you' : that is, if ye be made partakers of the gospel,
or of 'the Spirit of manifestation' ; if ye be truly

entitled to God, and have received the promise of
the Father, then are ye not carnal men ; ye are
'spiritual,' ye are 'in the Spirit': if ye have the
Spirit in one sense to any purpose, ye have it also in
another : if the Spirit be in you, you are in it ; if
it hath given you hope, it hath also enabled and
ascertained your duty.   For 'the Spirit of manifestation' will but upbraid you in the shame and horrors
of a sad eternity if you have not 'the Spirit of
obsignation': if the Holy Ghost be not come upon
you to great purposes of holiness, all other pretences
are vain, ye are still in the flesh, which shall never
inherit the kingdom of God.

'In the Spirit': that is, in the power of the
Spirit.   So the Greeks call him ἔνθεον, who is
'possessed by a spirit,' whom God hath filled with
a celestial immission ; he is said to be in God, when
God is in him.   And it is a similitude taken from
persons encompassed with guards ; they are *in custodia*,
that is, in their power, under their command, moved
at their dispose ; they rest in their time, and receive
laws from their authority, and admit visitors whom
they appoint, and must be employed as they shall
suffer : so are men who are in the Spirit ; that is,
they believe as He teaches, they work as He enables,
they choose what He calls good, they are friends
of His friends, and they hate with His hatred : with
this only difference, that persons in custody are
forced to do what their keepers please, and nothing
is free but their wills ; but they that are under the

command of the Spirit do all things which the Spirit commands, but they do them cheerfully ; and their will is now the prisoner, but it is *in libera custodia*, the will is where it ought to be, and where it desires to be, and it cannot easily choose anything else because it is extremely in love with this ; as the saints and angels in their state of beatific vision cannot choose but love God, and yet the liberty of their choice is not lessened because the object fills all the capacities of the will and the understanding. Indifference to an object is the lowest degree of liberty, and supposes unworthiness or defect in the object or the apprehension ; but the will is then the freest and most perfect in its operation when it entirely pursues a good with so certain determination and clear election that the contrary evil cannot come into dispute or pretence. Such in our proportions is the liberty of the sons of God ; it is a holy and amiable captivity to the Spirit : the will of man is in love with those chains which draw us to God, and loves the fetters that confine us to the pleasures and religion of the kingdom. And as no man will complain that his temples are restrained and his head is prisoner when it is encircled with a crown ; so when the Son of God hath made us free, and hath only subjected us to the service and dominion of the Spirit, we are free as princes within the circles of their diadem, and our chains are bracelets, and the law is a law of liberty, and ' His service is perfect freedom ' ; and the more we are subjects the more we shall ' reign as kings ' ;

and the faster we run, the easier is our burden ; and Christ's yoke is like feathers to a bird, not loads, but helps to motion ; without them the body falls ; and we do not pity birds when in summer we wish them unfeathered and callow, or bald as eggs, that they might be cooler and lighter. Such is the load and captivity of the soul when we do the work of God, and are His servants, and under the government of the Spirit. They that strive to be quit of this subjection, love the liberty of outlaws, and the licentiousness of anarchy, and the freedom of sad widows and distressed orphans : for so rebels, and fools, and children, long to be rid of their princes, and their guardians, and their tutors, that they may be accursed without law, and be undone without control, and be ignorant and miserable without a teacher and without discipline. He that is in the Spirit is under tutors and governors until the time appointed of the Father, just as all great heirs are ; only the first seizure the Spirit makes is upon the will. He that loves the yoke of Christ and the discipline of the gospel, he is in the Spirit, that is, in the Spirit's power.

Upon this foundation the apostle hath built these two propositions :

1. Whosoever hath not the Spirit of Christ, he is none of His ; he does not belong to Christ at all ; he is not partaker of His Spirit, and therefore shall never be partaker of His glory.

2. Whosoever is in Christ is dead to sin, and lives

to the Spirit of Christ : that is, lives a spiritual, a holy, and a sanctified life.

These are to be considered distinctly.

I. All that belong to Christ have the Spirit of Christ. Immediately before the ascension our blessed Saviour bid His disciples ' tarry in Jerusalem till they should receive the promise of the Father ' : whosoever stay at Jerusalem, and are in the actual communion of the Church of God, shall certainly receive this promise ; ' for it is made to you and to your children,' said St. Peter, ' and to as many as the Lord our God shall call.' All shall receive the Spirit of Christ, the promise of the Father, because this was the great instrument of distinction between the law and the gospel. In the law, God gave His Spirit, first, to some ; secondly, to them extra-regularly ; thirdly, without solemnity ; fourthly, in small portions, like the dew upon Gideon's fleece ; a little portion was wet sometimes with the dew of heaven when all the earth besides was dry. And the Jews called it *filiam vocis*, ' the daughter of a voice,' still, and small, and seldom, and that by secret whispers, and sometimes inarticulate, by way of enthusiasm rather than of instruction ; and God spake by the prophets, transmitting the sound as through an organ pipe, things which themselves oftentimes understood not. But in the gospel the Spirit is given without measure : first poured forth upon our Head, Christ Jesus ; then descending upon the beard of Aaron, the fathers of the Church ; and thence falling, like the tears of

the balsam of Judea, upon the foot of the plant, upon
the lowest of the people. And this is given regularly
to all that ask it, to all that can receive it, and by a
solemn ceremony, and conveyed by a sacrament; and
is now not the ' daughter of a voice ' but the mother
of many voices, of divided tongues and united hearts,
of the tongues of prophets and the duty of saints, of
the sermons of apostles and the wisdom of governors;
it is the parent of boldness and fortitude to martyrs,
the fountain of learning to doctors, an ocean of all
things excellent to all who are within the ship and
bounds of the Catholic Church: so that old men
and young men, maidens and boys, the scribe and
the unlearned, the judge and the advocate, the priest
and the people, are full of the Spirit if they belong
to God. Moses's wish is fulfilled, and all the Lord's
people are prophets in some sense or other.

In the wisdom of the ancient it was observed, that
there are four great cords which tie the heart of man
to inconvenience and a prison, making it a servant of
vanity and an heir of corruption: Pleasure and Pain;
Fear and Desire.

> —Πρὸς τὸ τετράχορδον δ' ὅλον,
> τὴν ἡδονὴν, ἐπιθυμίαν, λύπην, φόβον,
> ἀσκήσεως γε καὶ μάχης πολλῆς δέοι.

These are they that exercise all the wisdom and
resolutions of man, and all the powers that God
hath given him;

> οὗτοι γὰρ, οὗτοι καὶ διὰ σπλάγχνων ἀεὶ
> χωροῦσι καὶ κυκῶσιν ἀνθρώπων κέαρ,

said Agathon. These are those evil spirits that possess the heart of man, and mingle with all his actions; so that either men are tempted to lust, by pleasure; or secondly, to baser arts, by covetousness; or thirdly, to impatience, by sorrow; or fourthly, to dishonourable actions, by fear: and this is the state of man by nature, and under the law, and for ever, till the Spirit of God came, and by four special operations cured these four inconveniences, and restrained or sweetened these unwholesome waters.

1. God gave us His Spirit that we might be insensible of worldly pleasures, having our souls wholly filled with spiritual and heavenly relishes. For when God's Spirit hath entered into us, and possessed us as His temple or as His dwelling, instantly we begin to taste Manna, and to loathe the diet of Egypt; we begin to consider concerning heaven, and to prefer eternity before moments, and to love the pleasures of the soul above the sottish and beastly pleasures of the body. Then we can consider that the pleasures of a drunken meeting cannot make recompense for the pains of a surfeit and that night's intemperance, much less for the torments of eternity; then we are quick to discern that the itch and scab of lustful appetites is not worth the charges of a chirurgeon; much less can it pay for the disgrace, the danger, the sickness, the death, and the hell, of lustful persons. Then we wonder that any man should venture his head to get a crown unjustly, or that for the hazard of a

victory he should throw away all his hopes of heaven certainly.

A man that hath tasted of God's Spirit can instantly discern the madness that is in rage, the folly and the disease that is in envy, the anguish and tediousness that is in lust, the dishonour that is in breaking our faith and telling a lie ; and understands things truly as they are ; that is, that charity is the greatest nobleness in the world ; that religion hath in it the greatest pleasures ; that temperance is the best security of health ; that humility is the surest way to honour. And all these relishes are nothing but antepasts of heaven, where the quintessence of all these pleasures shall be swallowed for ever ; where the chaste shall follow the Lamb, and the virgins sing there where the mother of God shall reign, and the zealous converters of souls and labourers in God's vineyard shall worship eternally ; where St. Peter and St. Paul do wear their crowns of righteousness ; and the patient persons shall be rewarded with Job, and the meek persons with Christ and Moses, and all with God : the very expectation of which, proceeding from a hope begotten in us by ' the Spirit of manifestation,' and bred up and strengthened by ' the Spirit of obsignation,' is so delicious an entertainment of all our reasonable appetites, that a spiritual man can no more be removed or enticed from the love of God and of religion, than the moon from her orb, or a mother from loving the son of her joys and of her sorrows.

143

This was observed by St. Peter : ' As new-born
babes, desire the sincere milk of the word, that ye
may grow thereby ; if so be that ye have tasted that
the Lord is gracious.' When once we have tasted
the grace of God, the sweetness of His Spirit, then
no food but ' the food of angels,' no cup but ' the
cup of salvation,' the ' divining cup,' in which we
drink salvation to our God, and call upon the name
of the Lord with ravishment and thanksgiving. And
there is no greater eternal testimony that we are in
the Spirit and that the Spirit dwells in us, than if
we find joy and delight and spiritual pleasures in the
greatest mysteries of our religion ; if we communicate
often, and that with appetite, and a forward choice,
and an unwearied devotion, and a heart truly fixed
upon God and upon the offices of a holy worship.
He that loathes good meat is sick at heart, or near
it ; and he that despises, or hath not a holy appetite
to, the food of angels, the wine of elect souls, is fit
to succeed the prodigal at his banquet of sin and
husks, and to be partaker of the table of devils ; but
all they who have God's Spirit love to feast at the
supper of the Lamb, and have no appetites but what
are of the Spirit or servants to the Spirit. I have
read of a spiritual person who saw heaven but in a
dream, but such as made great impression upon him,
and was represented with vigorous and pertinacious
phantasms not easily disbanding ; and when he
awaked he knew not his cell, he remembered not
him that slept in the same dorter, nor could tell how

night and day were distinguished, nor could discern oil from wine; but called out for his vision again; *Redde mihi campos meos floridos, columnam auream, comitem Hieronymum, assistentes angelos,* 'give me my fields again, my most delicious fields, my pillar of a glorious light, my companion St. Hierome, my assistant angels.' And this lasted till he was told of his duty and matter of obedience, and the fear of a sin had disencharmed him, and caused him to take care lest he lose the substance out of greediness to possess the shadow.

And if it were given to any of us to see paradise or the third heaven, as it was to St. Paul, could it be that ever we should love anything but Christ, or follow any guide but the Spirit, or desire anything but heaven, or understand anything to be pleasant but what shall lead thither? Now what a vision can do, that the Spirit doth certainly to them that entertain Him. They that have Him really and not in pretence only, are certainly great despisers of the things of the world. The Spirit doth not create or enlarge our appetites of things below; spiritual men are not designed to reign upon earth, but to reign over their lusts and sottish appetites. The Spirit doth not inflame our thirst of wealth, but extinguishes it, and makes us to 'esteem all things as loss, and as dung, so that we may gain Christ'; no gain then is pleasant but godliness, no ambition but longings after heaven, no revenge but against ourselves for sinning; nothing but God and Christ: *Deus meus, et omnia :* and, *date nobis animas, cætera vobis tollite*, as the king of Sodom said to Abraham ; ' Secure but the souls to us, and take our goods.' Indeed, this is a good sign that we have the Spirit.

St. John spake a hard saying, but by the Spirit of manifestation we are all taught to understand it, ' Whosoever is born of God doth not commit sin, for His seed remaineth in him ; and he cannot sin, because he is born of God.' The seed of God is the Spirit, which hath a plastic power to efform us *in similitudinem filiorum Dei*, ' into the image of the sons of God ' ; and as long as this remains in us, while the Spirit dwells in us, we cannot sin ; that is, it is against our natures, our reformed natures, to sin. And as we say, we cannot endure such a potion, we cannot suffer such a pain ; that is, we cannot without great trouble, we cannot without doing violence to our nature ; so all spiritual men, all that are born of God, and the seed of God remains in them, they ' cannot sin ' ; cannot without trouble, and doing against their natures, and their most passionate inclinations. A man, if you speak naturally, can masticate gums, and he can break his own legs, and he can sip up by little draughts mixtures of aloes and rhubarb, of henbane or the deadly night-shade ; but he cannot do this naturally or willingly, cheerfully or with delight. Every sin is against a good man's nature ; he is ill at ease when he hath missed his usual prayers, he is amazed if he have fallen into an error, he is infinitely ashamed of his imprudence ; he remembers a sin as he thinks of an enemy or the horrors of a midnight apparition : for all his capacities, his understanding, and his choosing faculties, are filled up with the opinion and persuasions, with the love and with the desires of God. And this, I say, is the great benefit of the Spirit, which God hath given to us an antidote against worldly pleasures. And, therefore, St. Paul joins them as consequent to each other : ' For it is impossible for those who were once enlightened, and have tasted of the heavenly gift, and were made partakers of the Holy Ghost, and have tasted the good word of God, and the powers of the world to come,' etc. First, we are enlightened in baptism, and by ' the Spirit of manifestation,' the revelations of the gospel ; then we relish and taste interior excellencies, and we receive the Holy Ghost, ' the Spirit of confirmation,' and He gives us a taste of the powers of the world to come, that is, of the great efficacy that is in the article of eternal life to persuade us to religion and holy living ; then we feel that as the belief of that article dwells upon our understanding, and is incorporated into our wills and choice, so we grow powerful to resist sin by the strengths of the Spirit, to defy all carnal pleasure, and to suppress and mortify it by the powers of this article ; those are ' the powers of the world to come.'

2. The Spirit of God is given to all who truly belong to Christ, as an antidote against sorrows, against impatience, against the evil accidents of the

world, and against the oppression and sinking of our
spirits under the cross. There are in Scripture noted
two births besides the natural ; to which also by
analogy we may add a third. The first is, to be
' born of water and the Spirit.' It is ἐν διὰ δυοῖν, one
thing signified by a divided appellative, by two
substantives, ' Water and the Spirit,' that is *Spiritus
aqueus*, the ' Spirit moving upon the waters of
baptism.' The second is, to be born of Spirit and
fire ; for so Christ was promised to ' baptize us
with the Holy Ghost and with fire,' that is, *cum
Spiritu igneo*, ' with a fiery Spirit,' the Spirit as it
descended in Pentecost in the shape of fiery tongues.
And as the watery Spirit washed away the sins of
the Church, so the Spirit of fire enkindles charity
and the love of God. Τὸ πῦρ καθαίρει, τὸ ὕδωρ ἁγνίζει,
says Plutarch ; the Spirit is the same under both
the titles, and it enables the Church with gifts and
graces. And from these there is another operation
of the new birth, but the same Spirit, the Spirit
of rejoicing, or *Spiritus exultans, Spiritus lætitiæ* ;
' Now the God of hope fill you with all ' joy ' and
peace in believing, that ye may abound in hope
through the power of the Holy Ghost.' There is a
certain joy and spiritual rejoicing that accompanies
them in whom the Holy Ghost doth dwell ; a joy
in the midst of sorrow : a joy given to allay the
sorrows of secular troubles, and to alleviate the
burden of persecution. This St. Paul notes to this
purpose : ' And ye became followers of us, and of

the Lord, having received the word in much affliction, with joy of the Holy Ghost.' Worldly afflictions and spiritual joys may very well dwell together ; and if God did not supply us out of His storehouses, the sorrows of this world would be mere and unmixed, and the troubles of persecution would be too great for natural confidences. For who shall make him recompense that lost his life in a duel, fought about a draught of wine, or a cheaper woman ? What arguments shall invite a man to suffer torments in testimony of a proposition of natural philosophy ? And by what instruments shall we comfort a man who is sick and poor, and disgraced, and vicious, and lies cursing, and despairs of anything hereafter ? That man's condition proclaims what it is to want the Spirit of God, ' the Spirit of comfort.' Now this Spirit of comfort is the hope and confidence, the certain expectation, of partaking in the inheritance of Jesus ; this is the faith and patience of the saints ; this is the refreshment of all wearied travellers, the cordial of all languishing sinners, the support of the scrupulous, the guide of the doubtful, the anchor of timorous and fluctuating souls, the confidence and the staff of the penitent. He that is deprived of his whole estate for a good conscience, by the Spirit he meets this comfort, that he shall find it again with advantage in the day of restitution : and this comfort was so manifest in the first days of Christianity, that it was no infrequent thing to see holy persons court a martyrdom with a fondness as great as is our

impatience and timorousness in every persecution.
Till the Spirit of God comes upon us, we are
ὀλιγόψυχοι.

> —Inopes non atque pusilli
> Finxerunt animi ; . . .

we have 'little souls,' little faith, and as little
patience ; we fall at every stumbling-block, and sink
under every temptation ; and our hearts fail us, and
we die for fear of death, and lose our souls to preserve
our estates or our persons, till the Spirit of God
'fills us with joy in believing': and a man that is
in a great joy, cares not for any trouble that is less
than his joy ; and God hath taken so great care to
secure this to us, that He hath turned it into a
precept, 'Rejoice evermore'; and, 'Rejoice in the
Lord always, and again I say rejoice.' But this
rejoicing must be only in the hope that is laid up
for us, ἐν ἐλπίδι χαίροντες, so the apostle, 'rejoicing
in hope.' For although God sometimes makes a
cup of sensible comfort to overflow the spirit of a
man, and thereby loves to refresh his sorrows ; yet
that is from a secret principle not regularly given,
not to be waited for, not to be prayed for, and it may
fail us if we think upon it : but the hope of life
eternal can never fail us, and the joy of that is great
enough to make us suffer anything, or to do anything.

> . . . Ibimus, ibimus,
> Utcunque præcedes, supremum
> Carpere iter comites parati ;

to death, to bands, to poverty, to banishment, to
tribunals any whither in hope of life eternal : as long
as this anchor holds, we may suffer a storm, but
cannot suffer shipwreck. And I desire you by the
way to observe how good a God we serve, and how
excellent a religion Christ taught, when one of His
great precepts is that we should ' rejoice and be
exceeding glad ' : and God hath given us the spirit
of rejoicing, not a sullen melancholy spirit, not the
spirit of bondage or of a slave, but the Spirit of His
Son, consigning us by a holy conscience to ' joys
unspeakable and full of glory.' And from hence
you may also infer that those who sink under a
persecution, or are impatient in a sad accident, they
put out their own fires which the Spirit of the Lord
hath kindled, and lose those glories which stand
behind the cloud.

The Life of Faith

RICHARD BAXTER

✦

*Now faith is the substance of things hoped for, the
evidence of things not seen.*—HEB. xi. 1.

THE LIFE OF FAITH

RICHARD BAXTER

THOUGH the wicked are distinguished into Hypocrites and Unbelievers, yet Hypocrites themselves
are Unbelievers too. They have no faith which they
can justify, by its prevailing efficacy and works : and
therefore have no faith by which they can be justified.
Because their discovery is needful to their recovery,
and all our salvation depends on the sincerity of our
faith, I have chosen this Text, which is a Description
of faith, that the opening of it may help us for the
opening of our hearts, and resolving the great
Question, on which our endless life depends.

To be a Christian and to be a Believer in Christ,
are words in Scripture of the same signification. If
you have not faith, you are not Christians. This
faith hath various offices and objects. By it we are
justified, sanctified and saved. We are justified, not
by believing that we are justified, but by believing
that we may be justified. Not by receiving justification immediately, but by receiving Christ for our
justification : not by mere accepting the pardon in
itself, but by first receiving him that procureth and

bestoweth it, on his terms: Not by mere accepting health, but by receiving the Physician and his remedies, for health.

Faith is the practical Believing in God as promising, and Christ as procuring justification and salvation. Or, the practical belief and acceptance of life, as procured by Christ, and promised by God in the Gospel.

The everlasting fruition of God in Heaven, is the ultimate object. No man believeth in Christ as Christ, that believeth not in him for eternal life. As faith looks at Christ as the necessary means, and at the Divine benignity as the fountain, and at his Veracity as the foundation or formal object, and at the promise, as the true signification of his will; so doth it ultimately look at our salvation (begun on earth, and perfected in Heaven) as the end, for which it looketh at all the rest.

No wonder therefore if the holy Ghost here speaking on the Dignity and Power of faith, do principally insist on that part of its Description, which is taken from this final object.

As Christ himself in his Humiliation was rejected by the Gentiles, and a stumbling stone to the Jews, *despised and not esteemed*, Isa. liii. 2, 3, *having made himself of no reputation*, Phil. ii. 7. So faith in Christ as incarnate and crucified, is despised and counted foolishness by the world. But as Christ in his Glory, and the glory of believers, shall force them to an awful admiration; so faith itself as exercised on that Glory, is more glorious in the eyes of all. Believers are never so reverenced by the world, as when they converse in Heaven, and the *Spirit of Glory resteth on them*, I Pet. iv. 14.

How faith by beholding this glorious end, doth move all the faculties of the soul, and subdue the inclinations and interests of the flesh, and make the greatest sufferings tolerable, is the work of the holy Ghost in this Chapter to demonstrate, which beginning with the Description, proceeds to the proof by a cloud of witnesses. There are two sorts of persons (and employments) in the world, for whom there are two contrary ends hereafter. One sort subject their Reason to their sensuality or carnal interest. The other subject their senses to their Reason, cleared, conducted and elevated by faith. Things present or possessed, are the riches of the sensual ; and the bias of their hearts and lives : things absent but hoped for, are the riches of believers, which actuate their chief endeavours.

This is the sense of the Text which I have read to you ; which setting things hoped for in opposition to things present, and things unseen to those that sense doth apprehend, assureth us that faith (which fixeth on the first) doth give to its object a subsistence, presence, and evidence, that is, it seeth that which supplyeth the want of presence and visibility. The ὑπόστασις, is that which *quoad effectum* is equal to a present subsistence. And the ἐλέγχη, the evidence is somewhat which *quoad effectum* is equal to visibility.

THE LIFE OF FAITH

As if he had said, [Though the glory promised to
believers, and expected by them, be yet to come,
and only hoped for, and be yet unseen and only
believed, yet is the sound believer as truely affected
with it, and acted by its attractive force, as if it
were present and before his eyes] as a man is by an
inheritance, or estate in reversion, or out of sight, if
well secured, and not only by that which is present
to his view. The Syriac Interpreter instead of a
Translation, gives us a true exposition of the words ;
viz. [Faith is a certainty of those things that are in
hope, as if they did already actually exist, and the
revelation of those things that are not seen.]

Or you may take the sense in this Proposition,
which I am next to open further, and apply, viz.
[That the nature and use of faith is to be as it were
instead of presence, possession and sight : or to make
the things that will be, as if they were already in
existence ; and the things unseen which God
revealeth, as if our bodily eyes beheld them.]

Not that faith doth really change its object.
Nor doth it give the same Degree of apprehensions
and affections as the sight of present things would
do. But Things Invisible are the Objects of our
Faith.

And Faith is effectual instead of sight to all these
uses : 1. The apprehension is as Infallible, because
of the objective certainty (though not so satisfactory
to our imperfect souls), as if the things themselves
were seen. 2. The will is determined by it in its

necessary consent and choice. 3. The affections are moved in the necessary degree. 4. It ruleth in our lives, and bringeth us through duty, and suffering, for the sake of the Happiness which we Believe.

This Faith is a grounded wise and justifiable act : an infallible knowledge ; and often called so in Scripture, Job vi. 69, 1 Cor. xv. 58, Rom. viii. 28, etc. And the constitutive and efficient causes will justify the Name.

And that Faith may be so powerful as to serve instead of sight and presence, Believers have the Spirit of Christ within them, to excite and actuate it, and help them against all temptations to unbelief, and to work in them all other graces that concur to promote the works of Faith ; and to mortify those sins that hinder our believing, and are contrary to a heavenly life : So that as the exercise of our sight, and taste, and hearing, and feeling, is caused by our natural life, so the exercise of Faith and Hope, and Love, upon things unseen, is caused by the holy Spirit, which is the principle of our new life. *We have received the Spirit, that we might know the things that are given us of God*, 1 Cor. ii. 12.

And the work of Faith is much promoted by the spiritual experiences of Believers. When they find a considerable part of the holy Scripture verified on themselves, it much confirmeth their Faith as to the whole. They are really possessed of that heavenly disposition, called, the Divine Nature, and have felt the power of the Word upon their hearts, renewing them to the Image of God, mortifying their most dear and strong corruptions, shewing them a greater beauty and desirableness in the Objects of Faith, than is to be found in sensible things : They have found many of the Promises made good upon themselves, in the answers of prayers, and in great deliverances, which strongly persuadeth them to believe the rest that are yet to be accomplished. And experience is a very powerful and satisfying way of conviction. He that feeleth, as it were, the first fruits, the earnest, and the beginnings of Heaven already in his soul, will more easily and assuredly believe that there is a Heaven hereafter.

And it exceedingly helpeth our Belief of the life that's yet unseen, to find that Nature affordeth us undeniable Arguments to prove a future Happiness and Misery, Reward and Punishment, in the general ; yea and in special, that the Love and Fruition of God is this Reward ; and that the effects of his displeasure are this Punishment : Nothing more clear and certain then that there is a God (He must be a fool indeed that dare deny it, Ps. xiv. 1) as also that this God is the Creator of the rational nature, and hath the absolute right of Sovereign Government : and therefore that the rational Creature oweth him the most full and absolute obedience, and deserveth punishment if he disobey. And its most clear that infinite goodness should be loved above all finite imperfect created good : And its clear that the rational nature is so formed, that without the hopes and fears of another life, the world neither is, nor ever was, nor (by ordinary visible means) can be well governed (supposing God to work on man according to his nature). And it is most certain that it consisteth not with infinite wisdom, power and goodness, to be put to rule the world in all ages, by fraud and falsehood. And it is certain that Heathens do for the most part through the world, by the light of nature acknowledge a life of joy, or misery to come : and the most hardened Atheists or Infidels must confess, that [for ought they know there may be such a life] : it being impossible they should know or prove the contrary. And it is most certain that the mere probability or possibility of a Heaven and Hell (being matters of such unspeakable concernment) should in reason command our utmost diligence to the hazard or loss of the transitory vanities below : and consequently that a holy diligent preparation for another life is naturally the duty of the reasonable creature. And it's as sure that God hath not made our nature in vain ; nor set us on a life of vain employments nor made it our business in the world to seek after that which can never be attained.

These things and much more do shew that nature affordeth us so full a testimony of the life to come that's yet invisible, that it exceedingly helpeth us in believing the supernatural revelation of it, which is more full.

Lastly, even the enemy of faith himself doth against his will confirm our faith by the violence and rage of malice, that he stirreth up in the ungodly against the life of faith and holiness ; and by the importunity of his oppositions and temptations, discovering that it is not for nothing that he is so maliciously solicitous, industrious, and violent.

And thus you see how much faith hath, that should fully satisfy a rational man, instead of presence, possession and sight.

If any shall here say, [But why would not God let us have a sight of Heaven or Hell, when he could not but know that it would more generally and certainly have prevailed for the conversion and salvation of the world : Doth he envy us the most effectual means].

I answer, Who art thou O man that disputest against God ? Shall the thing formed say to him that formed it, Why hast thou made me thus ? Must God come down to the bar of man, to render an account of the reason of his works ? Why do ye not also ask him a reason of the nature, situation, magnitude, order, influences, etc., of all the Stars, and Superior Orbs, and call him to an account for all his works ? when yet there are so many things in your own bodies, of which you little understand the reason. Is it not intolerable impudency, for such worms as we, so low, so dark, to question the eternal God, concerning the reason of his Laws and dispensations ? Do we not shamefully forget our ignorance and our distance ?

But if you must have a Reason, let this suffice

you : It is fit that the Government of God be suited
to the nature of the reasonable subject. And Reason
is made to apprehend more then we see, and by
reaching beyond sense, to carry us to seek things
higher and better than sense can reach. If you would
have a man understand no more than he sees, you
would almost equalize a wise man and a fool, and
make a man too like a beast. Even in worldly
matters, you will venture upon the greatest cost and
pains for the things that you see not, nor ever saw.
He that hath a journey to go to a place that he never
saw, will not think that a sufficient reason to stay at
home. The Merchant will sail a thousand miles
to a Land, and for a Commodity, that he never saw.
Must the Husbandman see the Harvest before he
plough his Land and sow his Seed. Must the sick
man feel, that he hath health before he use the means
to get it ? Must the Soldier see that he hath the
victory before he fight ? You would take such
conceits in worldly matters to be the symptoms of
distraction : And will you cherish them where they
are most pernicious ? Hath God made man for
any end, or for none ? If none, he is made in vain :
If for any, no reason can expect that he should see
his end, before he use the means, and see his home
before he begin to travel towards it. When Children
first go to School, they do not see or enjoy the learning
and wisdom which by time and labour they must
attain. You will provide for the Children which
you are like to have before you see them. To look

that sight which is our fruition itself, should go before a holy life, is to expect the end before we will use the necessary means. You see here in the government of the world, that it is things unseen that are the instruments of rule, and motives of obedience. Shall no man be restrained from felony or murders, but he that seeth the Assizes or the Gallows? It is enough that he foreseeth them, as being made known by the Laws.

It would be no discrimination of the good and bad, the wise and foolish, if the reward and punishment must be seen; what thief so mad as to steal at the Gallows, or before the Judge? The basest habits would be restrained from acting, if the reward and punishment were in sight. The most beastly drunkard would not be drunk; the filthy fornicator would forbear his lust; the malicious enemy of godliness would forbear their calumnies and persecutions, if Heaven and Hell were open to their sight. No man will play the adulterer in the face of the Assembly: The chaste and unchaste seem there alike: And so they would do if they saw the face of the most dreadful God. No thanks to any of you all to be godly if Heaven were to be presently seen; or to forbear your sin, if you saw Hell fire, God will have a meeter way of trial: You shall believe his promises, if ever you will have the benefit, and believe his threatenings, if ever you will escape the threatened evil.

This being the Nature and Use of Faith, to

apprehend things absent as if they were present, and things unseen as if they were visible before our eyes ; you may hence understand the nature of Christianity, and what it is to be a true Believer. Verily, it is another matter than the dreaming, self-deceiving world imagineth. Hypocrites think that they are Christians indeed, because they have entertained a superficial opinion, that there is a Christ, an immortality of souls, a Resurrection, a Heaven and a Hell ; though their Lives bear witness, that this is not a living, and effectual faith ; but it is their sensitive faculties and interest that are predominant, and are the bias of their hearts. Alas a little observation may tell them, that notwithstanding their most confident pretentions to Christianity, they are utterly unacquainted with the Christian life. Would they live as they do, in worldly cares, and pampering of the flesh, and neglect of God and the life to come, if they saw the things which they say they do believe ? Could they be sensual, ungodly and secure, if they had a faith that served instead of sight ?

A Believer is one that judgeth of the man by his invisible inside, and not by outward appearances with a fleshly worldly judgment. He seeth by faith a greater ugliness in sin, than in any the most deformed monster. When the unbeliever saith, what harm is it to please my flesh, in ease, or pride, or meat and drink, or lustful wantonness ? the believer takes it as the question of a fool, that should ask [what harm is it to take a dram of Mercury or Arsenic ?]. He seeth the vicious evil, and foreseeth the consequent penal evil, by the eye of faith. And therefore it is that he pitieth the ungodly, when they pity not themselves, and speaks to them oft with a tender heart in compassion of their misery, and perhaps weeps over them (as Paul, Phil. iii. 18, 19) when he cannot prevail ; when they weep not for themselves, but hate his love, and scorn his pity, and bid him keep his lamentations for himself ; because they see not what he sees.

He seeth also the inward beauty of the Saints (as it shineth forth in the holiness of their lives) and through all their sordid poverty and contempt, beholdeth the image of God upon them. For he judgeth not of sin or holiness as they now appear to the distracted world ; but as they will be judged of at the day which he foreseeth ; when sin will be the shame, and holiness the honoured and desired state.

He can see Christ in his poor despised members, and love God in those that are made as the scorn and offscouring of all things, by the malignant unbelieving world. He admireth the excellency and happiness of those, that are made the laughing-stock of the ungodly : and accounteth the Saints the most excellent on earth, Ps. xvi. 2, and had rather be one of their communion in rags, than sit with Princes that are naked within, and void of the true and durable glory. He judgeth of men as he perceiveth them to have more or less of Christ. The worth of a man is not obvious to the sense. You see his stature, complexion and his clothes; but as you see not his Learning or skill in any Art whatsoever, so you see not his grace and heavenly mind. As the soul itself, so the sinful deformity, and the holy beauty of it, are to us invisible, and perceived only by their fruits, and by the eye of faith, which seeth things as God reveals them. And therefore in the eyes of a true believer, *a vile person is contemned ; but he honoureth those that fear the Lord*, Ps. xv. 4.

A true Believer doth seek a Happiness which he never saw, and that with greater estimation and resolution, than he seeks the most excellent things that he hath seen. In all his prayers, his labours and his sufferings, it is an unseen Glory that he seeks : He seeth not the Glory of God, nor the Glorified Redeemer, not the world of Angels, and perfected spirits of the just : but he knoweth by faith, that such a God, such a Glory, such a world as this there is, as certain as if his eyes had seen it. And therefore he provides, he lives, he hopes, he waits, for this unseen state of spiritual bliss, contemning all the wealth and glory, that sight can reach in comparison thereof. He believeth what he shall see ; and therefore strives that he may see it. It's something above the Sun, and all that mortal eyes can see, which is the end, the hope, the portion of a believer, without which all is nothing to him ; and for which he trades and travels here, as worldlings do for worldly things : Matt. vi. 20, 21 ; Col. iii. 1 ; Phil. iii. 20.

A true Believer doth all his life prepare for a day that is yet to come, and for an account of all the passages of his life, though he hath nothing but the word of God, to assure him of it. And therefore he lives as one that is hasting to the presence of his Judge ; and he contriveth his affairs, and disposeth of his worldly riches, as one that looks to hear of it again, and as one that remembereth the *Judge is at the door*, James v. 9.

By this time you may see that the Life of Faith is quite another thing, than the lifeless opinion of multitudes that call themselves believers. To say [I believe there is a God, a Christ, a Heaven, a Hell,] is as easy as it is common. But the faith of the ungodly is but an uneffectual dream. To dream that you are fighting, wins no victories : To dream that you are eating, gets no strength. To dream that you are running, rids no ground : To dream that you are ploughing, or sowing, or reaping, procureth but a fruitless harvest. And to dream that you are Princes, may consist with beggary. If you do any more than dream of Heaven and Hell, how is it that you stir not, and make it not appear by the diligence of your lives, and the fervour of your duties, and the seriousness of your endeavours, that such wonderful unexpressible overpowering things are indeed the matters of your belief ? As you love your souls take heed lest you take an image of faith to be the thing itself. Faith sets on work the powers of the soul, for the obtaining of that joy and the escaping of that misery which you believe. But the image of faith in self-deceivers, neither warms nor works : it conquereth no difficulties ; it stirs not up to faithful duty. It is blind, and therefore seeth not God ; and how then should he be feared and loved ? It seeth not Hell ; and therefore the senseless soul goes on as fearlessly and merrily to the unquenchable fire, as if he were in the safest way. This Image of faith, annihilateth the most potent objects, as to any due impression on the soul. God is as no God, and Heaven as no Heaven, to these Imaginary Christians. If a Prince be in the room, an Image reverenceth him not : If music and feasting be there, an Image finds no pleasure in them. If fire and sword be there, an Image fears them not. You may perceive by the senseless neglectful carriage of ungodly men, that they see not by faith the God that they should love and fear ; the Heaven that they should seek and wait for ; or the Hell that they should with all possible care avoid. He is indeed the true Believer that (allowing the difference of degrees) doth pray as if he saw the Lord ; and speak and live as always in his presence ; and redeem his time as if he were to die to-morrow, or as one that seeth death approach, and ready to lay hands upon him ; that begs and cries to God in prayer, as one that foreseeth the day of judgment ; and the endless joy or misery that followeth : that bestirreth him for everlasting life, as one that seeth Heaven and Hell, by the eye of faith. Faith is a serious apprehension, and causeth a serious conversation : for it is instead of sight and presence.

A sound belief of the things unseen will habitually incline your wills to embrace them, with consent, and complacence, and resolution, above and against those worldly things, that would be set above them, and preferred before them. If you are true believers, you have made your choice, you have fixed your hopes, you have taken up your resolutions ; that God must be your portion, or you can have none that's worth the having : that Christ must be your Saviour, or you cannot be saved : and therefore you are at a point with all things else : they may be your Helps, but not your Happiness : you are resolved on what Rock to build, and where to cast anchor ; and at what port and prize your life shall aim. You are resolved what to seek, and trust to God or none : Heaven or nothing : Christ or none ; is the voice of your rooted, stable resolutions. Though you are full of fears sometimes whether you shall be accepted, and have a part in Christ, or no ? and whether ever you shall attain the Glory which you aim at ; yet you are off all other hopes ; having seen an end of all perfections, and read vanity and vexation written upon all creatures, even on the most flattering state on earth, and are unchangeably resolved not to change your master, and your hopes, and your holy course, for any other life or hopes. What ever come of it

you are resolved that here you will venture all :
Knowing that you have no other game to play, at
which you are not sure to lose, and that you can lay
out your love, and care, and labour on nothing else
that will answer your expectations ; nor make any
other bargain whatsoever, but what you are sure to
be utterly undone by : Ps. lxxiii. 25, and iv. 6, 7 ;
Matt. vi. 20, 21, and xiii. 45, 46 ; Luke, xviii. 33.

And now I have gone before you with the light,
and shewed you what a Believer is, will you presently
consider how far your hearts and lives agree to this
description ? To know [Whether you live by faith
or not] is consequentially to know, Whether God or
the world be your portion and felicity ; and so
whether you are the heirs of Heaven or Hell. And
is not this a Question that you are most nearly
concerned in ? O therefore for your souls sakes, and
as ever you love your everlasting peace, *Examine
yourselves, whether you are in the faith or not ? Know
you not that Christ is in you* (by faith) *except you be
reprobates ?* 2 Cor. xiii. 5 ; will you hearken now
as long to your consciences, as you have done to me ?
As you have heard me telling you, What is the nature
of a living, saving faith ; will you hearken to your
consciences, while they impartially tell you, Whether
you have this life of faith, or not ? It may be known
if you are willing, and diligent, and impartial : If you
search on purpose as men that would know whether
they are alive or dead, and whether they shall live
or die for ever : and not as men that would be

flattered and deceived, and are resolved to think well of their state, be it true or false.

Having enquired whether you are Believers, I am next to ask you, what you will be for the time to come ? will you live upon things seen or unseen ? While you arrogate the name and honour of being Christians, will you bethink you what Christianity is ? and will you be indeed what you say you are, and would be thought to be ? Oh that you would give credit to the Word of God ? that the God of Heaven might be but heartily believed by you ! And that you would but take his Word to be as sure as sense ? and what he hath told you is or will be, to be as certain as if you saw it with your eyes ? Oh what manner of persons would you then be ? how carefully and fruitfully would you speak and live ? How impossible were it then that you should be careless and profane ? And here that I may by seriousness bring you to be serious in so serious a business, I shall first put a few suppositions to you, about the invisible objects of faith ; and then I shall put some applicatory Questions to you, concerning your own resolutions and practice thereupon.

Suppose you saw the Lord in glory continually before you ; When you are hearing, praying, talking, jesting, eating, drinking, and when you are tempted to any wilful sin : Suppose you saw the Lord stand over you, as verily as you see a man ! Would you be godly or ungodly after it ? As sure as you live,

171

and see one another, God always seeth you : He seeth your secret filthiness, and deceit, and malice, which you think is hid : he seeth you in the dark : the locking of your doors, the drawing of your curtains : the setting of the Sun, or the putting out of the candle, doth hide nothing from him that is Omniscient : Ps. xciv. 8, 9. The lust and filthiness, and covetousness, and envy, and vanity of your very thoughts are as open to his view as the Sun at noon. And therefore you may well suppose him present that cannot be absent ; and you may suppose you saw him that still seeth you, and whom you must see. Oh what a change, a glimpse of the glory of his Majesty, would make in this Assembly ! Oh what amazements, what passionate workings of soul would it excite ! Were it but an Angel that did thus appear to you, what manner of hearers would you be ? How serious ? how affectionate ? how sensible ? And yet are you Believers, and have none of this ? when faith makes unseen things to be as seen ? If thou have faith indeed, thou seest him that is invisible : thou speakest to him : thou hearest him in his Word : thou seest him in his Works : thou walkest with him : he is the life of thy comforts, thy converse and thy life.

Suppose you saw the Everlasting Glory which Christ hath purchased and prepared for his Saints : That you had been once with Paul rapt up into the third heavens, and seen the things that are unutterable : Would you not after that have rather lived like Paul,

and undergone his sufferings and contempt, then to
have lived like the brain-sick brutish world ? If
you had seen what Stephen saw before his death,
the Glory of God, and Christ standing at his right hand,
Acts vii. 55, 56 ; If you had seen the thousands and
millions of holy Glorious spirits, that are continually
attending the Majesty of the Lord ; If you had seen
the glorified spirits of the just, that were once in
flesh, despised by the blind ungodly world, while
they waited on God in faith, and holiness, and hope,
for that blessed crown which now they wear : If
you had felt one moment of their joys ; If you had
seen them shine as the Sun in glory, and made like
unto the Angels of God ; If you had heard them
sing the song of the Lamb, and the joyful Hallelujah's,
and praise to their eternal King : What would you
be, and what would you resolve on after such a sight
as this ? If the rich man (Luke xvi) had seen Lazarus
in Abraham's bosom in the midst of his bravery, and
honour, and feasting, and other sensual delights, as
afterwards he saw it when he was tormented in the
flames of hell, do you think such a sight would not
have cooled his mirth and jollity, and helped him to
understand the nature and value of his earthly felicity ;
and have proved a more effectual argument than a
despised Preacher's words ? as least to have brought
him to a freer exercise of his Reason, in a sober
consideration of his state and ways ? Had you seen
one hour what Abraham, David, Paul, and all the
Saints now see, while sin and flesh doth keep us

here in the dark, what work do you think yourselves
it would make upon your hearts and lives ?

Suppose you saw the face of Death, and that you
were now lying under the power of some mortal
sickness, Physicians having forsaken you and said,
There is no hope : Your friends weeping over you,
and preparing your winding-sheet and coffin, digging
your graves, and casting up the skulls, and bones,
and earth, that must again be cast in to be your
covering and company : Suppose you saw a Messenger
from God to tell you that you must die to-morrow ;
or heard but what one of your predecessors heard,
*Thou fool, this night shall thy soul be required of thee : then
whose shall these things be that thou hast provided ?* Luke
xii. 20. How would such a Message work with
you ? Would it leave you as you are ? If you heard
a voice from God this night in your chamber in the
dark, telling you, that This is the last night that
you shall live on earth, and before to-morrow your
souls must be in another world, and come before
the dreadful God : What would be the effect of
such a Message ? And do you not verily Believe
that all this will very shortly be ? Nay do you not
know without Believing, that you must die, and
leave your worldly Glory ? and that all your pleasures
and contents on earth, will be as if they had never
been (and much worse) ! O wonderful ! that a
change so sure, so great, so near, should no more
affect you, and no more be forethought on, and no
more prepared for ! and that you be not awakened

by so full and certain a foreknowledge, to be in good sadness for eternal life, as you seem to be when death is at hand !

Once more ; suppose that in your temptations you saw the tempter appearing to you, and pleading with you as he doth by his inward suggestions, or by the mouths of his instruments. If you saw him and heard him hissing you on to sin, persuading you to gluttony, drunkenness, or uncleanness ? If the Devil appeared to you, and led you to the place of lust, and offered you the harlot, or the cup of excess, and urged you to swear, or curse, or rail, or scorn at a holy life ; would not the sight of the angler mar his game, and cool your courage, and spoil your sport, and turn your stomachs ? would you be drunk, or filthy, if you saw him stand by you ? Think on it the next time you are tempted. Stout men have been appalled by such a sight. And do you not Believe that it is he indeed that tempteth you ? As sure as if your eyes beheld him, it's he that prompteth men to jeer at godliness ; and puts your wanton ribbald speeches, and oaths, and curses into your mouths : He is the Tutor of the enemies of grace, that teacheth them *docte delirare, ingeniose insanire,* ingeniously to quarrel with the way of life, and learnedly to confute the arguments that would have saved them ; and subtilly to dispute themselves out of the hands of mercy, and gallantly to scorn to stoop to Christ, till there be no remedy ; and with plausible eloquence to commend the plague and sickness of their souls ; and irrefragably maintain it, that the way to hell will lead to heaven ; and to justify the sins that will condemn them ; and honourably and triumphantly to overcome their friends, and to serve the Devil in mood and figure ; and valiantly to cast themselves into hell, in despite of all the laws and reproofs of God or man that would have hindered them. It being most certain that this is the Devils work, and you durst not do it if he moved you to it with open face, how dare you do it when faith would assure you, that its as verily he, as if you saw him ?

And O that now we might all consent to addict ourselves to the Life of Faith : and 1. That we live not too much on visibles ; 2. That we live on the things invisible.

1. One would think that worldliness is a disease that carryeth with it a cure for itself ; and that the rational nature should be loth to Love at so dear a rate, and to labour for so poor a recompense. It is pity that Gehezi's leprosy, and Judas's death, should no more prevent a succession of Gehezi's and Judas's in all generations. Our Lord went before us most eminently in a contempt of earth : His Kingdom was not of this world. No men are more unlike him than the worldlings. I know necessity is the pretence : But it is the dropsy of Covetousness that causeth the thirst which they call Necessity : And therefore the cure is *non addere opibus, sed imminuere cupiditatem* : The disease must not be fed but healed. *Satis est divitiarum non amplius velle.* It hath lately

been a controversy, Whether this be not the golden age ? that it is *ætas ferrea* we have felt ; our demonstrations are undeniable : that it is *ætas aurata*, we have sufficient proof : and while gold is the god that rules the most, we will not deny it to be *ætas aurea*, in the Poets sense.

> Aurea nunc vere sunt secula : plurimus auro
> Vænit honos : auro conciliatur amor.

This prevalency of things seen, against things unseen, is the Idolatry of the world ; the subversion of nature ; the perversion of our faculties and actions ; making the soul a drudge to flesh, and God to be used as a servant to the world. It destroyeth Piety, Justice and Charity : It turneth J U S by perversion into V I S ; or by reversion into S U I. No wonder then if it be the ruin of societies, when

> Gens sine justitia, sine remige navis in unda.

2. Consider that it is the unseen things that are only Great and Necessary, that are worthy of a man, and answer the excellency of our nature, and the ends of our lives and all our mercies. All other things are inconsiderable toys, except as they are dignified by their relation to these. Whether a man step into eternity from a Palace or a prison, a Lordship or a Lazarus state, is little to be regarded. All men in the world, whose designs and business take up with any thing short of Heaven, are in the

main of one condition, and are but in several degrees
and forms in the School of folly. If the intendment
of your lives fall short of God, it matters not much
what it is you seek, as to any great difference. If
lesser children play for pins, and bigger boys for
points and pence, and aged children for lands and
money, for titles of honour, and command ; What
difference is there between these, in point of wisdom
and felicity ? but that the little ones have more
innocent delights, and at a cheaper rate, than the aged
have, without the vexatious cares and dangers that
attend more grave and serious dotage. As Holiness
to the Lord is written upon all that is faithfully
referred to his Will and Glory ; so Vanity and Sin
is written upon all that is but made provision for
the flesh, and hath no higher end than Self. To go
to Hell with greater stir, and attendance, and repute,
with greater pomp and pleasure than the poor, is a
poor consolation, a pitiful felicity !

3. Faith is the wisdom of the soul : and unbelief
and sensuality are its blindness, folly and brutishness.
How short is the Knowledge of the wisest unbelievers ?
They know not much of what is past (and less they
would know, if Historians were not of more credit
with them, than the Word of God) : But alas, how
little do they know of what is to come ? sense tells
them where they are, and what they are now doing :
but it tells them not where they shall be to-morrow.
But Faith can tell a true Believer, What will be when
this world is ended, and where he shall live to all

eternity, and what he shall be doing, what thoughts he shall be thinking, what affections shall be the temper and employment of his soul : what he shall see, and feel, and enjoy ; and with what company he shall converse for ever. If the pretenders to Astrological prediction, could but foretell the changes of men's lives, and the time and manner of their deaths, what resort would be to them ? and how wise would they be esteemed ? But what is all this to the infallible predictions of the All-knowing God, that hath given us a prospect into another world, and shewed us what will be for ever, more certainly than you know what a day may bring forth.

So necessary is foreknowledge in the common affairs of men, that without it the actions of the world would be but mad tumultuary confusion : What would you think of that man's understanding, or how would you value the employments of his life, that looked no further in all his actions, than the present hour, and saw no more than the things in hand ? What would you call him that so spends the day, as one that knoweth not there will be any night : and so past the night, as one that looked not for day ? That knew not in the Spring there would be an Harvest, or in Summer, that there would be any Winter : or in Youth, that there would be Age or Death ? The silly brutes that have no fore-knowledge, are furnished with an instinct that supplyeth the want of it, and also have the help of man's foreknowledge, or else their kind would be soon extinct. The Bees labour in Summer, as if they foresaw the Winter's need. And can that man be wise, that foreseeth not his everlasting state? Indeed he that knoweth not what is to come, hath no true knowledge of what is present : For the worth and use of present things, is only in their respect to things eternal : And there is no means, where there is no End. What wisdom then remains in Unbelievers, when all their lives are misemployed, because they know not the End of life? and when all their actions are utterly debased, by the baseness of those brutish ends, to which they serve and are referred. Nothing is truly wise or honourable, that is done for small and worthless things. To draw a curious picture of a shadow, or elegantly write the history of a dream, may be an ingenuous kind of foolery ; but the End will not allow it the name of Wisdom : And such are all the actions of the world (though called Heroic, Valiant and Honourable) that aim at transitory trifles, and tend not to the everlasting End. A bird can neatly build her nest, but is not therefore counted Wise. How contrary is the judgment of the world to Christ's? When the same description that he giveth of a fool, is it that worldlings give of a wise and happy man, [*One that layeth up riches for himself, and is not rich towards God*], Luke xii. 20, 21. Will you persuade us that the man is Wise, that can climb a little higher than his neighbours, that he may have the greater fall? That is attended in his way to Hell with greater pomp

and state than others ? That can sin more Syllo-
gistically and Rhetorically than the vulgar ; and
more prudently and gravely run into damnation ;
and can learnedly defend his madness, and prove
that he is safe at the brink of Hell ? Would you
persuade us that he is Wise, that contradicts the
God and Rule of Wisdom, and that parts with
Heaven for a few merry hours, and hath not wit to
save his soul ? When they see the end, and are
arrived at eternity, let them boast of their Wisdom,
as they find cause : We will take them then for
more competent Judges. Let the Eternal God be
the portion of my soul ; let Heaven be my inheritance
and hope ; let Christ be my Head, and the promise
my security, let Faith be my Wisdom, and Love be
my very Heart and will, and patient persevering
Obedience be my life ; and then I can spare the
wisdom of the world, because I can spare the trifles
that it seeks, and all that they are like to get by it.

What abundance of complaints and calamity would
foresight prevent ? Had the events of this one year
been (conditionally) foreseen, the actions of thousands
would have been otherwise ordered, and much sin
and shame have been prevented. What a change
would it make on the judgments of the world ? how
many words would be otherwise spoken ? and how
many deeds would be otherwise done ? and how many
hours would be otherwise spent, if the change that
will be made by Judgment and Execution, were well
foreseen ? And why is it not foreseen, when it is

foreshown ? When the omniscient God, that will certainly perform his Word, hath so plainly revealed it, and so frequently and loudly warns you of it ? Is he wise, that after all these warnings will lie down in everlasting woe, and say, [I little thought of such a day : I did not believe I should ever have seen so great a change ?]

Yea present things as well as future, are unknown to foolish Unbelievers. Do they know who seeth them in their sin ? and what many thousands are suffering for the like, while they see no danger ? Whatever their tongues say, the hearts and lives of fools deny that there is a God that seeth them, and will be their Judge : Ps. xiv. 1. You see then that you must live by Faith, or perish by Folly.

4. Consider that things visible are so transitory, and of so short continuance, that they do but deserve the name of things ; being nothings, and less than nothing, and lighter than vanity itself, compared to the necessary eternal Being, whose name is I AM. There is but a few days difference between a Prince and no Prince ; a Lord and no Lord ; a man and no man ; a world and no world. And if this be all, let the time that is past inform you how small a difference this is. Rational foresight may teach a Xerces to weep over his numerous Army, as knowing how soon they were all to be dead men. Can you forget that Death is ready to undress you ? and tell you, that your sport and mirth is done ? and that now you have had all that the world can do, for those

that serve it, and take it for their part ? How
quickly can a fever, or the choice of an hundred
Messengers of death, bereave you of all that earth
afforded you, and turn your sweetest pleasures into
gall, and turn a Lord into a lump of clay ? It is
but as a wink, an inch of time, till you must quit the
stage ; and speak, and breathe, and see the face of
man no more. If you foresee this, O live as men
that do foresee it. I never heard of any that stole
his winding-sheet, or sought for a Coffin, or went to
Law for his grave. And if you did but see (as wise
men should) how near your Honours, and Wealth,
and Pleasures do stand unto Eternity, as well as your
Winding-sheets, your Coffins, and your Graves, you
would then value, and desire, and seek them regularly
and moderately, as you do these. O what a fading
flower is your strength ? How soon will all your
gallantry shrink into the shell ? *Si vestra sunt tollite
ea vobiscum.*

But yet this is not the great part of the change.
The *terminus ad quem* doth make it greater : It is
great, for persons of renown and honour, to change
their Palaces for graves, and turn to noisome rotten-
ness and dirt : and their Power and Command
into silent impotency, unable to rebuke the poorest
worm, that saucily feedeth on their hearts or faces.
But if you are Believers, you can look further, and
foresee much more. The largest and most capacious
heart alive, is unable fully to conceive, what a change
the stroke of death will make.

For the Holy soul, so suddenly to pass from prayer to Angelical praise, from sorrow unto boundless joys : from the slanders, and contempt, and violence of men, to the bosom of eternal Love ; from the clamours of a tumultuous world, to the universal harmony and perfect uninterrupted Love and Peace ; O what a blessed change is this ; which Believing now, we shall shortly feel.

For an unholy unrenewed soul, that yesterday was drowned in flesh, and laughed at threatenings, and scorned reproofs, to be suddenly snatched into another world ; and see the Heaven that he hath lost, and feel the Hell which he would not Believe : to fall into the gulf of bottomless eternity, and at once to find, that Joy and Hope are both departed ; that horror and grief must be his company, and Desparation hath locked up the door : O what an amazing change is this ! If you think me troublesome for mentioning such ungrateful things, what a trouble will it be to feel them ? May it teach you to prevent that greater trouble, you may well bear this. Find but a medicine against Death, or any security for your continuance here, or any prevention of the Change, and I have done. But that which unavoidably must be seen, should be foreseen.

But the unseen world is not thus mutable ; Eternal life is begun in the Believer. The Church is built on Christ the Rock ; and the gates of Hell shall not prevail against it. Fix here, and you shall never be removed.

May I now in the conclusion more particularly exhort you, 1. That you will live upon things foreseen ; 2. That you will promote this life of faith in others, according to your several capacities.

Princes and Nobles live not always : You are not the Rulers of the unmovable Kingdom ; but of a boat that is in an hasty stream, or a ship under sail, that will speed both Pilot and Passengers to the shore. *Dixi, estis Dii : at moriemini ut homines.* It was not the least or worst of Kings, that said [*I am a stranger upon earth*], Ps. cxix. 19. *Vermis sum, non homo : I am a worm, and no man*, Ps. xxii. 6. You are the greater worms, and we the little ones : but we must all say with Job, xvii. 13, 14, [*The grave is our house, and we must make our beds in darkness : Corruption is our Father, and the worm our mother and our sister.*] The inexorable Leveller is ready at your backs, to convince you by unresistible argument, that dust you are, and to dust you shall return. Heaven should be as desirable, and Hell as terrible to you as to others. No man will fear you after death : much less will Christ be afraid to judge you : Luke xix. 27. As the Kingdoms and glory of the world were contemned by him in the hour of his temptation, so are they inconsiderable to procure his approbation. Trust not therefore to uncertain riches. Value them but as they will prove at last. As you stand on higher ground than others, it is meet that you should see further. The greater are your advantages, the wiser and better you should be : and therefore should better perceive the difference between things temporal and eternal. It is always dark where these glow-worms shine, and a rotten post doth seem a fire.

Your difficulties also should excite you ; You must go as through a needle's eye to heaven. To live as in heaven, in a crowd of business, and stream of temptations, from the confluence of all worldly things, is so hard, that few such come to heaven. Withdraw yourselves therefore to the frequent serious forethoughts of eternity, and live by faith.

Had time allowed it, I should have come down to some particular instances : As, Let the things unseen be still at hand, to answer every temptation, and shame and repel each motion to sin.

Let them be still at hand, to quicken us to duty, when backwardness and coldness doth surprise us. What, shall we do anything coldly for eternity ?

Let it resolve you what company to delight in ; and what society to be of ; even those with whom you must dwell for ever : What side soever is upper-most on earth, you may foresee which side shall reign forever.

Let the things invisible be your daily solace, and the satisfaction of your souls. Are you slandered by men ? Faith tells you, it is enough that Christ will justify you. O happy day, when he will bring forth our righteousness as the light, and set all straight, which all the false histories, or slanderous tongues or pens in all the world made crooked. Are you frowned on or contemned by men ? Is it not enough that you

186

shall everlastingly be honoured by the Lord? Are you wronged, oppressed, or trodden on by pride or malice? Is not Heaven enough to make you reparation? and eternity long enough for your joys? O pray for your malicious enemies, lest they suffer more than you can wish them.

Lastly, I should have become on the behalf of Christ, a petitioner to you for protection and encouragement to the heirs of the invisible world: For them that preach and them that live this life of faith: not for the honours and riches of the world; but for leave and countenance to work in the Vineyard, and peaceably travel through the world as strangers, and live in the Communion of Saints, as they believe. But though it be for the beloved of the Lord, the apple of his eye, the people that are sure to prevail and reign with Christ for ever; whose prayers can do more for the greatest Princes, than you can do for them; whose joy is hastened by that which is intended for their sorrow, I shall now lay by any further suit on their behalf.

But for yourselves, O use your seeing and fore-seeing faculties: Be often looking through the prospective of the promise: and live not by sense on present things; but live as if you saw the Glorious things which you say you do believe. That when worldly titles are insignificant words, and fleshly pleasures have an end, and Faith and Holiness will be the marks of honour; and unbelief and ungodliness the badges of perpetual shame, and when you must give account of your Stewardship, and shall be no longer Stewards, you may then be brought by Faith unto Fruition, and see with Joy the Glorious things that you now believe. Write upon your Palaces and goods, that sentence: *Seeing all these things shall be dissolved, What manner of persons ought ye to be in all holy conversation and godliness, looking for and hasting to the coming of the day of God!* 2 Pet. iii. 11.

A Project for The Advancement of Religion & The Reformation of Manners

JONATHAN SWIFT

A PROJECT FOR THE
ADVANCEMENT OF RELIGION
& THE REFORMATION OF MANNERS

JONATHAN SWIFT

AMONG all the schemes offered to the public in this projecting age, I have observed with some displeasure that there have never been any for the improvement of religion and morals ; which, besides the piety of the design from the consequence of such a reformation in a future life, would be the best natural means for advancing the public felicity of the state as well as the present happiness of every individual. For, as much as faith and morality are declined among us, I am altogether confident they might in a short time, and with no very great trouble, be raised to as high a perfection as numbers are capable of receiving. Indeed, the method is so easy and obvious, and some present opportunities so good, that, in order to have this project reduced to practice, there seems to want nothing more than to put those in mind who by their honour, duty, and interest, are chiefly concerned.

But because it is idle to propose remedies before we are assured of the disease, or to be in fear till we are convinced of the danger, I shall first show in general that the nation is extremely corrupted in religion and morals ; and then I will offer a short scheme for the reformation of both.

As to the first, I know it is reckoned but a form of speech when divines complain of the wickedness of the age : however, I believe, upon a fair comparison with other times and countries, it would be found an undoubted truth.

For, first, to deliver nothing but plain matter of fact, without exaggeration or satire, I suppose it will be granted that hardly one in a hundred among our people of quality or gentry appears to act by any principle of religion ; that great numbers of them do entirely discard it, and are ready to own their disbelief of all revelation in ordinary discourse. Nor is the case much better among the vulgar, especially in great towns, where the profaneness and ignorance of handicraftsmen, small traders, servants, and the like, are to a degree very hard to be imagined greater. Then it is observed abroad that no race of mortals have so little sense of religion as the English soldiers ; to confirm which, I have been often told by great officers of the army that in the whole compass of their acquaintance they could not recollect three of their profession who seemed to regard or believe one syllable of the gospel : and the same at least may be affirmed of the fleet. The consequences of all which

upon the actions of men are equally manifest. They
never go about as in former times to hide or palliate
their vices, but expose them freely to view like any
other common occurrences of life, without the least
reproach from the world or themselves. For instance,
any man will tell you he intends to be drunk this
evening, or was so last night, with as little ceremony
or scruple as he would tell you the time of the day.
He will let you know he is going to a wench, or
that he has got the venereal disease, with as much
indifferency as he would a piece of public news. He
will swear, curse, or blaspheme, without the least
passion or provocation. And though all regard for
reputation is not quite laid aside in the other sex,
it is, however, at so low an ebb that very few among
them seem to think virtue and conduct of absolute
necessity for preserving it. If this be not so, how
comes it to pass that women of tainted reputations
find the same countenance and reception in all public
places with those of the nicest virtue, who pay and
receive visits from them without any manner of
scruple ? Which proceeding, as it is not very old
among us, so I take it to be of most pernicious
consequence : it looks like a sort of compounding
between virtue and vice, as if a woman were allowed
to be vicious provided she be not a profligate ; as if
there were a certain point where gallantry ends and
infamy begins ; or that a hundred criminal amours
were not as pardonable as half a score.

Besides those corruptions already mentioned, it

would be endless to enumerate such as arise from the excess of play or gaming : the cheats, the quarrels, the oaths and blasphemies among the men ; among the women the neglect of household affairs, the unlimited freedoms, the indecent passion, and, lastly, the known inlet to all lewdness, when, after an ill run, the person must answer the defects of the purse ; the rule on such occasions holding true in play as it does in law, *quod non habet in crumena luat in corpore.*

But all these are trifles in comparison, if we step into other scenes, and consider the fraud and cozenage of trading men and shopkeepers ; that insatiable gulf of injustice and oppression, the law ; the open traffic for all civil and military employments (I wish it rested there), without the least regard to merit or qualifications ; the corrupt management of men in office ; the many detestable abuses in choosing those who represent the people, with the management of interest and factions among the representatives : to which I must be bold to add, the ignorance of some of the lower clergy, the mean servile temper of others ; the pert, pragmatical demeanour of several young stagers in divinity upon their first producing themselves into the world ; with many other circumstances needless, or rather invidious, to mention ; which, falling in with the corruptions already related, have, however unjustly, almost rendered the whole order contemptible.

This is a short view of the general depravities

among us, without entering into particulars, which
would be an endless labour. Now, as universal and
deep-rooted as these appear to be, I am utterly deceived
if an effectual remedy might not be applied to most
of them : neither am I at present upon a wild
speculative project, but such a one as may be easily
put in execution.

For while the prerogative of giving all employments
continues in the crown, either immediately or by
subordination, it is in the power of the prince to
make piety and virtue become the fashion of the age,
if at the same time he would make them necessary
qualifications for favour and preferment.

It is clear, from present experience, that the bare
example of the best prince will not have any mighty
influence where the age is very corrupt. For when
was there ever a better prince on the throne than the
present queen ? I do not talk of her talent for
government, her love of the people, or any other
qualities that are purely regal ; but her piety, charity,
temperance, conjugal love, and whatever other virtues
do best adorn a private life ; wherein, without
question or flattery, she has no superior : yet neither
will it be satire nor peevish invective to affirm that
infidelity and vice are not much diminished since her
coming to the crown, nor will, in all probability, till
more effectual remedies be provided.

Thus human nature seems to lie under the disadvantage, that the example alone of a vicious prince
will in time corrupt an age ; but the example of a

good one will not be sufficient to reform it, without
farther endeavours. Princes must therefore supply
this defect by a vigorous exercise of that authority
which the law has left them, by making it every
man's interest and honour to cultivate religion and
virtue ; by rendering vice a disgrace and the certain
ruin to preferment or pretensions : all which they
should first attempt in their own courts and families.
For instance, might not the queen's domestics of
the middle and lower sort be obliged, upon penalty
of suspension or loss of their employments, to a
constant weekly attendance at least on the service of
the church ; to a decent behaviour in it ; to receive
the sacrament four times in the year ; to avoid
swearing and irreligious profane discourses ; and to
the appearance, at least, of temperance and chastity ?
Might not the care of all this be committed to the
strict inspection of proper officers ? Might not
those of higher rank and nearer access to her majesty's
person receive her own commands to the same purpose,
and be countenanced or disfavoured according as they
obey ? Might not the queen lay her injunctions on
the bishops, and other great men of undoubted piety,
to make diligent inquiry and give her notice if any
person about her should happen to be of libertine
principles or morals ? Might not all those who enter
upon any office in her majesty's family be obliged
to take an oath parallel with that against simony
which is administered to the clergy ? It is not to
be doubted but that, if these or the like proceedings

were duly observed, morality and religion would soon become fashionable court virtues, and be taken up as the only methods to get or keep employments there ; which alone would have mighty influence upon many of the nobility and principal gentry.

But if the like methods were pursued, as far as possible, with regard to those who are in the great employments of state, it is hard to conceive how general a reformation they might in time produce among us. For if piety and virtue were once reckoned qualifications necessary to preferment, every man thus endowed, when put into great stations, would readily imitate the queen's example in the distribution of all offices in his disposal : especially if any apparent transgression through favour or partiality would be imputed to him for a misdemeanour by which he must certainly forfeit his favour and station ; and there being such great numbers in employment, scattered through every town and country in this kingdom, if all these were exemplary in the conduct of their lives, things would soon take a new face, and religion receive a mighty encouragement ; nor would the public weal be less advanced, since, of nine offices in ten that are ill executed, the defect is not in capacity or understanding, but in common honesty. I know no employment for which piety disqualifies any man ; and if it did, I doubt the objection would not be very seasonably offered at present ; because it is perhaps too just a reflection, that in the disposal of places the question whether a person be fit for what he is recommended to, is generally the last that is thought on or regarded.

I have often imagined that something parallel to the office of censors anciently in Rome would be of mighty use among us, and could be easily limited from running into any exorbitances. The Romans understood liberty at least as well as we, were as jealous of it, and upon every occasion as bold assertors. Yet I do not remember to have read any great complaint of the abuses in that office among them, but many admirable effects of it are left upon record. There are several pernicious vices, frequent and notorious among us, that escape or elude the punishment of any law we have yet invented, or have had no law at all against them ; such as atheism, drunkenness, fraud, avarice, and several others ; which by this institution, wisely regulated, might be much reformed. Suppose, for instance, that itinerary commissioners were appointed to inspect everywhere throughout the kingdom into the conduct at least of men in office, with respect to their morals and religion as well as their abilities ; to receive the complaints and informations that should be offered against them, and make their report here upon oath to the court or the ministry, who should reward or punish accordingly. I avoid entering into the particulars of this or any other scheme, which, coming from a private hand, might be liable to many defects, but would soon be digested by the wisdom of the nation ; and surely £6,000 a year would not be ill laid out among as many commissioners duly qualified, who, in three divisions, should be personally obliged to take their yearly circuits for that purpose.

But this is beside my present design, which was only to show what degree of reformation is in the power of the queen without the interposition of the legislature, and which her majesty is without question obliged in conscience to endeavour by her authority, as much as she does by her practice.

It will be easily granted that the example of this great town has a mighty influence over the whole kingdom ; and it is as manifest that the town is equally influenced by the court, the ministry, and those who, by their employments or their hopes, depend upon them. Now if, under so excellent a princess as the present queen, we would suppose a family strictly regulated, as I have above proposed ; a ministry where every single person was of distinguished piety ; if we should suppose all great offices of state and law filled after the same manner, and with such as were equally diligent in choosing persons who, in their several subordinations, would be obliged to follow the examples of their superiors, under the penalty of loss of favour and place ; will not everybody grant that the empire of vice and irreligion would be soon destroyed in this great metropolis, and receive a terrible blow through the whole island, which has so great an intercourse with it, and so much affects to follow its fashions ?

For if religion were once understood to be the

necessary step to favour and preferment, can it be imagined that any man would openly offend against it who had the least regard for his reputation or his fortune ? There is no quality so contrary to nature which men cannot affect and put on, upon occasion, in order to serve an interest or gratify a prevailing passion. The proudest man will personate humility, the morosest learn to flatter, the laziest will be sedulous and active, where he is in pursuit of what he has much at heart : how ready, therefore, would most men be to step into the paths of virtue and piety, if they infallibly led to favour and fortune !

If swearing and profaneness, scandalous and avowed lewdness, excessive gaming, and intemperance, were a little discountenanced in the army, I cannot readily see what ill consequences could be apprehended. If gentlemen of that profession were at least obliged to some external decorum in their conduct, or even if a profligate life and character were not a means of advancement, and the appearance of piety a most infallible hindrance, it is impossible the corruptions there should be so universal and exorbitant. I have been assured by several great officers that no troops abroad are so ill disciplined as the English ; which cannot well be otherwise while the common soldiers have perpetually before their eyes the vicious example of their leaders ; and it is hardly possible for those to commit any crime, whereof these are not infinitely more guilty, and with less temptation.

It is commonly charged upon the gentlemen of

the army, that the beastly vice of drinking to excess has been lately, from their example, restored among us ; which for some years before was almost dropped in England. But, whoever the introducers were, they have succeeded to a miracle ; many of the young nobility and gentry are already become great proficients, and are under no manner of concern to hide their talent, but are got beyond all sense of shame or fear of reproach.

This might soon be remedied, if the queen would think fit to declare that no young person of quality whatsoever who was notoriously addicted to that or any other vice should be capable of her favour, or even admitted into her presence ; with positive command to her ministers, and others in great office, to treat them in the same manner ; after which all men who had any regard for their reputation, or any prospect of preferment, would avoid their commerce. This would quickly make that vice so scandalous, that those who could not subdue would at least endeavour to disguise it.

By the like methods, a stop might be put to that ruinous practice of deep gaming ; and the reason why it prevails so much is, because a treatment directly opposite in every point is made use of to promote it ; by which means the laws enacted against this abuse are wholly eluded.

It cannot be denied that the want of strict discipline in the universities has been of pernicious consequence to the youth of this nation, who are there almost left entirely to their own management, especially those among them of better quality and fortune ; who, because they are not under a necessity of making learning their maintenance, are easily allowed to pass their time, and take their degrees with little or no improvement ; than which there cannot well be a greater absurdity : for if no advancement of knowledge can be had from those places, the time there spent is at best utterly lost, because every ornamental part of education is better taught elsewhere : and as for keeping youths out of harm's way, I doubt, where so many of them are got together, at full liberty of doing what they please, it will not answer the end. But whatever abuses, corruptions, or deviations from statutes, have crept into the universities through neglect or length of time, they might in a great degree be reformed by strict injunctions from court (upon each particular) to the visitors and heads of houses ; besides the peculiar authority the queen may have in several colleges whereof her predecessors were the founders. And among other regulations it would be very convenient to prevent the excess of drinking ; with that scurvy custom among the lads, and parent of the former vice, the taking of tobacco where it is not absolutely necessary in point of health.

From the universities, the young nobility, and others of great fortunes, are sent for early up to town, for fear of contracting any airs of pedantry by a college education. Many of the younger gentry retire in the inns of court, where they are wholly left to their own discretion. And the consequence of this remissness in education appears, by observing that nine in ten of those who rise in the Church, or the court, the law, or the army, are younger brothers, or new men, whose narrow fortunes have forced them upon industry and application.

As for the inns of court, unless we suppose them to be much degenerated, they must needs be the worst instituted seminaries in any Christian country ; but whether they may be corrected without inter-position of the legislature, I have not skill enough to determine. However, it is certain that all wise nations have agreed in the necessity of a strict education, which consisted, among other things, in the observance of moral duties, especially justice, temperance, and chastity, as well as the knowledge of arts, and bodily exercises ; but all these among us are laughed out of doors.

Without the least intention to offend the clergy, I cannot but think that, through a mistaken notion and practice, they prevent themselves from doing much service, which otherwise might lie in their power, to religion and virtue : I mean, by affecting so much to converse with each other, and caring so little to mingle with the laity. They have their particular clubs, and particular coffeehouses, where they generally appear in clusters : a single divine dares hardly show his person among numbers of fine gentlemen ; or, if he happens to fall into such company, he is silent and suspicious, in continual apprehension that some pert man of pleasure should break an unmannerly jest and render him ridiculous. Now, I take this behaviour of the clergy to be just as reasonable as if the physicians should agree to spend their time in visiting one another, or their several apothecaries, and leave their patients to shift for themselves. In my humble opinion, the clergy's business lies entirely among the laity; neither is there, perhaps, a more effectual way to forward the salvation of men's souls, than for spiritual persons to make themselves as agreeable as they can in the conversations of the world, for which a learned education gives them great advantage, if they would please to improve and apply it. It so happens that the men of pleasure, who never go to church, nor use themselves to read books of devotion, form their ideas of the clergy from a few poor strollers they often observe in the streets, or sneaking out of some person of quality's house, where they are hired by the lady at ten shillings a month: while those of better figure and parts do seldom appear, to correct these notions. And, let some reasoners think what they please, it is certain that men must be brought to esteem and love the clergy, before they can be persuaded to be in love with religion. No man values the best medicine, if administered by a physician whose person he hates or despises. If the clergy were as forward to appear in all companies as other gentlemen, and would a little study the arts of conversation to make themselves agreeable, they might be welcome at every party where there was the least regard for politeness or good sense, and consequently prevent a thousand vicious or profane discourses as well as actions : neither would men of understanding complain that a clergyman was a constraint upon the company because they could not speak blasphemy or obscene jests before him. While the people are so jealous of the clergy's ambition as to abhor all thoughts of the return of ecclesiastical discipline among them, I do not see any other method left for men of that function to take, in order to reform the world, than by using all honest arts to make themselves acceptable to the laity. This, no doubt, is part of that wisdom of the serpent which the author of Christianity directs ; and is the very method used by St. Paul, who became all things to all men, to the Jews a Jew, and a Greek to the Greeks.

How to remedy these inconveniences may be a matter of some difficulty, since the clergy seem to be of an opinion that this humour of sequestering themselves is a part of their duty ; nay, as I remember, they have been told so by some of their bishops in their pastoral letters, particularly by one [1] among them of great merit and distinction, who yet in his own practice has all his lifetime taken a course directly contrary. But I am deceived if an awkward shame and fear of ill usage from the laity have not a greater share in this mistaken conduct than their own

[1] Dr. Burnet, Bishop of Salisbury.

inclinations : however, if the outward profession of
religion and virtue were once in practice and countenance at court, as well as among all men in office or
who have any hopes or dependence for preferment, a
good treatment of the clergy would be the necessary
consequence of such a reformation ; and they would
soon be wise enough to see their own duty and interest
in qualifying themselves for lay conversation, when
once they were out of fear of being choked by ribaldry
or profaneness.

There is one farther circumstance, upon this
occasion, which I know not whether it will be very
orthodox to mention : the clergy are the only set of
men among us who constantly wear a distinct habit
from others ; the consequence of which (not in
reason but in fact) is this, that as long as any
scandalous persons appear in that dress, it will
continue in some degree a general mark of contempt.
Whoever happens to see a scoundrel in a gown
reeling home at midnight (a sight neither frequent
nor miraculous), is apt to entertain an ill idea of the
whole order, and at the same time to be extremely
comforted in his own vices. Some remedy might
be put to this, if those straggling gentlemen who
come up to town to seek their fortunes were fairly
dismissed to the West Indies, where there is work
enough, and where some better provision should be
made for them than I doubt there is at present.
Or what if no person were allowed to wear the habit
who had not some preferment in the Church, or at

least some temporal fortune sufficient to keep him out of contempt? though in my opinion it were infinitely better if all the clergy (except the bishops) were permitted to appear like other men of the graver sort, unless at those seasons when they are doing the business of their function.

There is one abuse in this town which wonderfully contributes to the promotion of vice; that such men are often put into the commission of the peace, whose interest it is that virtue should be utterly banished from among us; who maintain or at least enrich themselves by encouraging the grossest immoralities; to whom all the bawds of the ward pay contribution for shelter and protection from the laws. Thus these worthy magistrates, instead of lessening enormities, are the occasion of just twice as much debauchery as there would be without them. For those infamous women are forced upon doubling their work and industry to answer the double charges of paying the justice and supporting themselves; like thieves who escape the gallows, and are let out to steal in order to discharge the gaoler's fees.

It is not to be questioned but the queen and ministry might easily redress this abominable grievance, by enlarging the number of justices of the peace; by endeavouring to choose men of virtuous principles; by admitting none who have not considerable fortunes; perhaps by receiving into the number some of the most eminent clergy: then by forcing all of them, upon severe penalties, to act when there is occasion, and not permitting any who are offered to refuse the commission ; but in these two last cases, which are very material, I doubt there will be need of the legislature.

The reformation of the stage is entirely in the power of the queen ; and, in the consequences it has upon the minds of the younger people, does very well deserve the strictest care. Besides the indecent and profane passages, besides the perpetual turning into ridicule the very function of the priesthood, with other irregularities, in most modern comedies, which have been often objected to them ; it is worth observing the distributive justice of the authors, which is constantly applied to the punishment of virtue and the reward of vice ; directly opposite to the rules of their best critics, as well as to the practice of dramatic poets in all other ages and countries. For example, a country squire, who is represented with no other vice but that of being a clown and having the provincial accent upon his tongue, which is neither a fault nor in his power to remedy, must be condemned to marry a cast wench or a cracked chambermaid. On the other side, a rakehell of the town, whose character is set off with no other accomplishment but excessive prodigality, profaneness, intemperance, and lust, is rewarded with a lady of great fortune to repair his own, which his vices had almost ruined. And as in a tragedy the hero is represented to have obtained many victories, in order to raise his character in the minds of the

spectators ; so the hero of a comedy is represented
to have been victorious in all his intrigues, for the
same reason. I do not remember that our English
poets ever suffered a criminal amour to succeed upon
the stage till the reign of king Charles II. Ever
since that time the alderman is made a cuckold,
the deluded virgin is debauched, and adultery and
fornication are supposed to be committed behind the
scenes, as part of the action. These and many more
corruptions of the theatre, peculiar to our age and
nation, need continue no longer than while the court
is content to connive at or neglect them. Surely a
pension would not be ill employed on some men of
wit, learning, and virtue, who might have power to
strike out every offensive or unbecoming passage from
plays already written, as well as those that may be
offered to the stage for the future. By which and
other wise regulations the theatre might become
a very innocent and useful diversion, instead of
being a scandal and reproach to our religion and
country.

The proposals I have hitherto made for the advancement of religion and morality, are such as come
within reach of the administration ; such as a pious
active prince, with a steady resolution, might soon
bring to effect. Neither am I aware of any objections
to be raised against what I have advanced ; unless it
should be thought that making religion a necessary
step to interest and favour might increase hypocrisy
among us ; and I readily believe it would. But

if one in twenty should be brought over to true piety by this or the like methods, and the other nineteen be only hypocrites, the advantage would still be great. Besides, hypocrisy is much more eligible than open infidelity and vice ; it wears the livery of religion ; it acknowledges her authority, and is cautious of giving scandal. Nay, a long continued disguise is too great a constraint upon human nature, especially an English disposition : men would leave off their vices out of mere weariness, rather than undergo the toil and hazard, and perhaps the expense, of practising them perpetually in private. And I believe it is often with religion as it is with love ; which, by much dissembling, at last grows real.

All other projects to this great end have proved hitherto ineffectual. Laws against immorality have not been executed, and proclamations occasionally issued out to enforce them are wholly unregarded, as things of form. Religious societies, though begun with excellent intentions, and by persons of true piety, are said, I know not whether truly or not, to have dwindled into factious clubs, and grown a trade to enrich little knavish informers of the meanest rank, such as common constables and broken shopkeepers.

And that some effectual attempt should be made toward such a reformation, is perhaps more necessary than people commonly apprehend ; because the ruin of a state is generally preceded by a universal degeneracy of manners and contempt of religion; which is entirely our case at present.

Diis te minorem, quod geris, imperas.[1]—HORACE.

Neither is this a matter to be deferred till a more convenient time of peace and leisure; because a reformation in men's faith and morals is the best natural as well as religious means to bring the war to a good conclusion. For if men in trust performed their duty for conscience sake, affairs would not suffer through fraud, falsehood, and neglect, as they now perpetually do. And if they believed a God and his providence, and acted accordingly, they might reasonably hope for his divine assistance in so just a cause as ours.

Nor could the majesty of the English crown appear, upon any occasion, in a greater lustre, either to foreigners or subjects, than by an administration which, producing such great effects, would discover so much power. And power being the natural appetite of princes, a limited monarch cannot so well gratify it in anything as in a strict execution of the laws.

Besides, all parties would be obliged to close with so good a work as this, for their own reputation: neither is any expedient more likely to unite them. For the most violent party men I have ever observed are such as, in the conduct of their lives, have dis-

---

[1] ' That you the power Divine obey,
Boundless on earth extend your sway.'—FRANCIS.

covered least sense of religion or morality ; and when all such are laid aside, at least those among them who shall be found incorrigible, it will be a matter perhaps of no great difficulty to reconcile the rest.

The many corruptions at present in every branch of business are almost inconceivable. I have heard it computed by skilful persons, that of £6,000,000 raised every year for the service of the public, one third at least is sunk and intercepted through the several classes and subordinations of artful men in office, before the remainder is applied to the proper uses. This is an accidental ill effect of our freedom. And while such men are in trust, who have no check from within, nor any views but toward their interest, there is no other fence against them but the certainty of being hanged upon the first discovery, by the arbitrary will of an unlimited monarch or his vizier. Among us, the only danger to be apprehended is the loss of an employment ; and that danger is to be eluded a thousand ways. Besides, when fraud is great, it furnishes weapons to defend itself : and at worst, if the crimes be so flagrant that a man is laid aside out of perfect shame (which rarely happens), he retires loaded with the spoils of the nation ; *et fruitur diis iratis.* I could name a commission where several persons, out of a salary of £500, without other visible revenues, have always lived at the rate of £2,000, and laid out £40,000 or £50,000 upon purchases of lands or annuities. A hundred other instances of the same kind might easily be produced. What remedy, therefore, can be found against such grievances in a constitution like ours, but to bring religion into countenance, and encourage those who, from the hope of future reward and dread of future punishment, will be moved to act with justice and integrity?

This is not to be accomplished any other way than by introducing religion as much as possible to be the turn and fashion of the age, which only lies in the power of the administration; the prince with utmost strictness regulating the court, the ministry, and other persons in great employment; and these, by their example and authority, reforming all who have dependence on them.

It is certain that a reformation, successfully carried on in this great town, would in time spread itself over the whole kingdom; since most of the considerable youth pass here that season of their lives wherein the strongest impressions are made, in order to improve their education or advance their fortunes, and those among them who return into their several counties are sure to be followed and imitated as the greatest patterns of wit and good breeding.

And if things were once in this train, that is, if virtue and religion were established as the necessary titles to reputation and preferment; and if vice and infidelity were not only laden with infamy, but made the infallible ruin of all men's pretensions; our duty, by becoming our interest, would take root in our natures, and mix with the very genius of our people, so that it would not be easy for the example of one wicked prince to bring us back to our former corruptions.

I have confined myself (as it is before observed) to those methods for the advancement of piety which are in the power of a prince limited, like ours, by a strict execution of the laws already in force. And this is enough for a project that comes without any name or recommendation ; I doubt, a great deal more than will suddenly be reduced into practice. Though, if any disposition should appear toward so good a work, it is certain that the assistance of the legislative power would be necessary to make it more complete. I will instance only a few particulars :

In order to reform the vices of this town, which, as we have said, has so mighty an influence on the whole kingdom, it would be very instrumental to have a law made that all taverns and alehouses should be obliged to dismiss their company by twelve at night, and shut up their doors ; and that no woman should be suffered to enter any tavern or alehouse upon any pretence whatsoever. It is easy to conceive what a number of ill consequences such a law would prevent ; the mischiefs of quarrels, and lewdness, and thefts, and midnight brawls, the diseases of intemperance and venery, and a thousand other evils needless to mention. Nor would it be amiss if the masters of those public houses were obliged, upon the severest penalties, to give only a proportioned quantity of drink to every company; and, when he found his guests disordered with excess, to refuse them any more.

I believe there is hardly a nation in Christendom where all kind of fraud is practised in so unmeasurable a degree as with us. The lawyer, the tradesman, the mechanic, have found so many arts to deceive in their several callings, that they far outgrow the common prudence of mankind, which is in no sort able to fence against them. Neither could the legislature in anything more consult the public good, than by providing some effectual remedy against this evil, which, in several cases, deserves greater punishment than many crimes that are capital among us. The vintner who, by mixing poison with his wines, destroys more lives than any one disease in the bill of mortality; the lawyer who persuades you to a purchase which he knows is mortgaged for more than the worth, to the ruin of you and your family; the goldsmith or scrivener who takes all your fortune to dispose of, when he has beforehand resolved to break the following day; do surely deserve the gallows much better than the wretch who is carried thither for stealing a horse.

It cannot easily be answered to God or man why a law is not made for limiting the press; at least so far as to prevent the publishing of such pernicious books as, under pretence of freethinking, endeavour to overthrow those tenets in religion which have been held inviolable, almost in all ages, by every sect that

pretend to be Christian ; and cannot therefore with
any colour of reason be called points in controversy,
or matters of speculation, as some would pretend.
The doctrine of the Trinity, the divinity of Christ,
the immortality of the soul, and even the truth of all
revelation, are daily exploded and denied in books
openly printed ; though it is to be supposed neither
party will avow such principles, or own the supporting
of them to be any way necessary to their service.

It would be endless to set down every corruption
or defect which requires a remedy from the legislative
power. Senates are likely to have little regard for any
proposals that come from without doors ; though,
under a due sense of my own inabilities, I am fully
convinced that the unbiassed thoughts of an honest
and wise man, employed on the good of his country,
may be better digested than the results of a multitude,
where faction and interest too often prevail ; as a
single guide may direct the way better than five
hundred who have contrary views, or look asquint, or
shut their eyes.

I shall therefore mention but one more particular,
which I think the parliament ought to take under
consideration ; whether it be not a shame to our
country, and a scandal to Christianity, that in many
towns, where there is a prodigious increase in the
number of houses and inhabitants, so little care should
be taken for the building of churches, that five parts
in six of the people are absolutely hindered from
hearing divine service ? Particularly here in London,

where a single minister, with one or two sorry curates, has the care sometimes of above twenty thousand souls incumbent on him ; a neglect of religion so ignominious, in my opinion, that it can hardly be equalled in any civilised age or country.

But, to leave these airy imaginations of introducing new laws for the amendment of mankind, what I principally insist on is a due execution of the old ; which lies wholly in the crown, and in the authority thence derived. I return, therefore, to my former assertion, that if stations of power, trust, profit, and honour, were constantly made the rewards of virtue and piety, such an administration must needs have a mighty influence on the faith and morals of the whole kingdom : and men of great abilities would then endeavour to excel in the duties of a religious life, in order to qualify themselves for public service. I may possibly be wrong in some of the means I prescribe towards this end ; but that is no material objection against the design itself. Let those who are at the helm contrive it better, which, perhaps, they may easily do. Everybody will agree that the disease is manifest, as well as dangerous ; that some remedy is necessary, and that none yet applied has been effectual ; which is a sufficient excuse for any man who wishes well to his country to offer his thoughts, when he can have no other end in view but the public good. The present queen is a princess of as many and great virtues as ever filled a throne : how would it brighten her character to the present

and after ages, if she would exert her utmost authority
to instil some share of those virtues into her people,
which they are too degenerate to learn only from her
example ! and, be it spoke with all the veneration
possible for so excellent a sovereign, her best endeavours in this weighty affair are a most important part
of her duty, as well as of her interest and her honour.

But it must be confessed that, as things are now,
every man thinks he has laid in a sufficient stock of
merit, and may pretend to any employment, provided
he has been loud and frequent in declaring himself
hearty for the government. It is true, he is a man of
pleasure and a free-thinker ; that is, in other words,
he is profligate in his morals and a despiser of
religion ; but, in point of party, he is one to be
confided in ; he is an assertor of liberty and property ;
he rattles it out against Popery and arbitrary power,
and priestcraft and High Church. It is enough : he
is a person fully qualified for any employment, in
the court or the navy, the law or the revenue ; where
he will be sure to leave no arts untried, of bribery,
fraud, injustice, oppression, that he can practise with
any hope of impunity. No wonder such men are
true to a government where liberty runs high, where
property, however attained, is so well secured, and
where the administration is at least so gentle : it is
impossible they could choose any other constitution
without changing to their loss.

Fidelity to a present establishment is indeed the
principal means to defend it from a foreign enemy,

but, without other qualifications, will not prevent corruptions from within ; and states are more often ruined by these than the other.

To conclude : whether the proposals I have offered towards a reformation be such as are most prudent and convenient, may probably be a question, but it is none at all whether some reformation be absolutely necessary ; because the nature of things is such that, if abuses be not remedied, they will certainly increase, nor ever stop till they end in the subversion of a commonwealth. As there must always of necessity be some corruptions, so, in a well instituted state, the executive power will be always contending against them, by reducing things (as Machiavel speaks) to their first principles, never letting abuses grow inveterate, or multiply so far that it will be hard to find remedies, and perhaps impossible to apply them. As he that would keep his house in repair must attend every little breach or flaw, and supply it immediately, else time alone will bring all to ruin,— how much more the common accidents of storms and rain ? He must live in perpetual danger of his house falling about his ears, and find it cheaper to throw it quite down and build it again from the ground, perhaps upon a new foundation, or at least in a new form which may neither be so safe nor so convenient as the old.

On Temptation

JOHN WESLEY

✝

There hath no temptation taken you but such as is common to man : And God is faithful, who will not suffer you to be tempted above that ye are able ; but will with the temptation also make a way to escape, that ye may be able to bear it.—1 COR. x. 13.

ON TEMPTATION

JOHN WESLEY

IN the foregoing part of the chapter, the Apostle
has been reciting, on the one hand, the unparalleled
mercies of God to the Israelites ; and, on the other,
the unparalleled ingratitude of that disobedient and
gainsaying people. And all these things, as the
Apostle observes, ' were written for our ensample ' ;
that we might take warning from them, so as to
avoid their grievous sins, and escape their terrible
punishment. He then adds that solemn and important caution, ' Let him that thinketh he standeth,
take heed lest he fall.'

But if we observe these words attentively, will there
not appear a considerable difficulty in them ? ' Let
him that thinketh he standeth take heed lest he fall.'
If a man only *thinks he stands*, he is in no danger of
falling. It is not possible that any one should fall,
if he only *thinks he stands*. The same difficulty occurs,
according to our translation, in those well-known
words of our Lord (the importance of which we may
easily learn from their being repeated in the Gospel
no less than eight times), ' To him that hath shall

be given ; but from him that hath not, shall be taken away even what he seemeth to have.' ' That which he *seemeth to have !* ' Nay, if he only *seems to have it*, it is impossible it should be taken away. None can take away from another what he only *seems to have*. What a man only seems to have, he cannot possibly lose. This difficulty may, at first, appear impossible to be surmounted. It is really so : It cannot be surmounted, if the common translation be allowed. But if we observe the proper meaning of the original word, the difficulty vanishes away. It may be allowed that the word δοκεῖ does (sometimes at least, in some authors) mean no more than *to seem*. But I much doubt whether it ever bears that meaning in any part of the inspired writings. By a careful consideration of every text in the New Testament wherein this word occurs, I am fully convinced, that it nowhere lessens, but everywhere strengthens, the sense of the word to which it is annexed. Accordingly ὃ δοκεῖ ἔχειν, does not mean, *what he seems to have*, but, on the contrary, *what he assuredly hath*. And so ὁ δοκῶν ἑστάναι, not *he that seemeth to stand*, or he that *thinketh he standeth*, but *he that assuredly standeth* ; he who standeth so fast, that he does not appear to be in any danger of falling ; he that saith, like David, ' I shall never be moved : Thou, Lord, hast made my hill so strong.' Yet at that very time, thus saith the Lord, ' Be not high-minded, but fear. Else shalt thou be cut off ' : Else shalt thou also be moved from thy steadfastness. The strength which thou assuredly hast, shall be taken away. As firmly as thou didst really stand, thou wilt fall into sin, if not into hell.

But lest any should be discouraged by the consideration of those who once ran well, and were afterwards overcome by temptation ; lest the fearful of heart should be utterly cast down, supposing it impossible for them to stand ; the Apostle subjoins to that serious exhortation, these comfortable words : ' There hath no temptation taken you but such as is common to man : But God is faithful, who will not suffer you to be tempted above that ye are able ; but will with the temptation also make a way to escape, that ye may be able to bear it.'

Let us begin with the observation which ushers in this comfortable promise : ' There hath no temptation taken you but such as is common to man.' Our translators seem to have been sensible that this expression, *common to man*, does by no means reach the force of the original word. Hence they substitute another in the margin, *moderate*. But this seems to be less significant than the other, and farther from the meaning of it. Indeed it is not easy to find any word in the English tongue, which answers the word ἀνθρώπινος. I believe the sense of it can only be expressed by some such circumlocution as this : ' Such as is suited to the nature and circumstances of man ; such as every man may reasonably expect, if he considers the nature of his body and his soul, and his situation in the present world.' If we duly consider these, we shall not be surprised at any temptation that hath befallen us ; seeing it is no other than such a creature, in such a situation, has all reason to expect.

Consider, First, the nature of that body with which your soul is connected. How many are the evils which it is every day, every hour, liable to ! Weakness, sickness, and disorders of a thousand kinds are its natural attendants. Consider the inconceivably minute fibres, threads, abundantly finer than hair (called from thence capillary vessels), whereof every part of it is composed ; consider the innumerable multitude of equally fine pipes and strainers, all filled with circulating juice ! And will not the breach of a few of these fibres, or the obstruction of a few of these tubes, particularly in the brain, or heart, or lungs, destroy our ease, health, strength, if not life itself ? Now, if we observe that all pain implies temptation, how numberless must the temptations be which will beset every man, more or less, sooner or later, while he dwells in this corruptible body !

Consider, Secondly, the present state of the soul, as long as it inhabits the house of clay. I do not mean in its unregenerate state ; while it lies in darkness and the shadow of death ; under the dominion of the prince of darkness, without hope, and without God in the world : No ; look upon men who are raised above that deplorable state. See those who have tasted that the Lord is gracious. Yet still how weak is their understanding ! How limited its extent ! How confused, how inaccurate, are our apprehensions of even the things that are round about us. How liable are the wisest of men to mistake ! to form false judgments ;—to take falsehood for truth, and truth for falsehood ; evil for good, and good for evil ! What starts, what wanderings of imagination, are we continually subject to ! And how many are the temptations which we have to expect even from these innocent infirmities !

Consider, Thirdly, what is the present situation of even those that fear God. They dwell in the ruins of a disordered world, among men that know not God, that care not for him, and whose heart is fully set in them to do evil. How many are forced to cry out, ' Woe is me, that I am constrained to dwell with Mesech ; to have my habitations among the tents of Kedar ! ' among the enemies of God and man. How immensely out-numbered are those that would do well, by them that neither fear God nor regard man ! And how striking is Cowley's observation : ' If a man that was armed cap-à-pie was closed in by a thousand naked Indians, their number would give them such advantage over him that it would be scarce possible for him to escape. What hope then would there be for a naked, unarmed man to escape, who was surrounded by a thousand armed men ? ' Now, this is the case of every good man. He is not armed either with force or fraud, and is turned out, naked as he is, among thousands that are armed with the whole armour of Satan, and provided with all the weapons which the prince of this world can supply out of the armory of hell. If then he is not destroyed, yet how must a good man be tempted in the midst of this evil world !

But is it only from wicked men that temptations arise to them that fear God ? It is very natural to imagine this ; and almost every one thinks so. Hence how many of us have said in our hearts, ' O if my lot were but cast among good men, among those that loved or even feared God, I should be free from all these temptations ! ' Perhaps you would : Probably you would not find the same sort of temptations which you have now to encounter. But you would surely meet with temptations of some other kind, which you would find equally hard to bear. For even good men, in general, though sin has not dominion over them, yet are not freed from the remains of it. They have still the remains of an evil heart, ever prone to ' depart from the living God.' They have the seeds of pride, of anger, of foolish desire ; indeed, of every unholy temper. And any of these, if they do not continually watch and pray, may, and naturally will, spring up, and trouble, not themselves only, but all that are round about them. We must not therefore depend upon finding no temptation from those that fear, yea, in a measure love, God. Much less must we be surprised, if some of those who once loved God in sincerity, should lay greater temptations in our way than many of those that never knew him.

'But can we expect to find any temptation from those that are *perfected in love* ?' This is an important question, and deserves a particular consideration. I answer, First, You may find every kind of temptation from those who *suppose* they are perfected when indeed they are not : And so you may, Secondly, from those who once really were so, but are now moved from their steadfastness. And if you are not aware of this, if you think they are still what they were once, the temptation will be harder to bear. Nay, Thirdly, even those who ' stand fast in the liberty wherewith Christ has made them free,' who are now really perfect in love, may still be an occasion of temptation to *you* ; for they are still encompassed with infirmities. They may be dull of apprehension ; they may have a natural heedlessness, or a treacherous memory ; they may have too lively an imagination : And any of these may cause little improprieties, either in speech or behaviour, which, though not sinful in themselves, may try all the grace you have : Especially if you impute to perverseness of will (as it is very natural to do) what is really owing to defect of memory, or weakness of understanding ;—if these appear to you to be voluntary mistakes, which are really involuntary. So proper was the answer which a saint of God (now in Abraham's bosom) gave me some years ago, when I said, ' Jenny, surely now your mistress and you can neither of you be a trial to the other, as God has saved you both from sin !' 'O, Sir,' said she, ' if we are saved from sin, we still have infirmities enough to try all the grace that God has given us ! '

But besides evil men, do not evil spirits also continually surround us on every side ? Do not Satan and his angels continually go about seeking whom they may devour ? Who is out of the reach of their malice and subtlety ? Not the wisest or the best of the children of men. ' The servant is not above his Master.' If then they tempted him, will they not tempt us also ? Yea, it may be, should God see good to permit, more or less, to the end of our lives. ' No temptation,' therefore, ' hath taken us,' which we had not reason to expect, either from our body or soul ; either from evil spirits or evil men ; yea, or even from good men, till our spirits return to God that gave them.

Meantime, what a comfort it is to know, with the utmost certainty, that ' God is faithful, who will not suffer us to be tempted above that we are able.' He knoweth what our ability is, and cannot be mistaken. ' He knoweth ' precisely ' whereof we are made : He remembereth that we are but dust.' And he will suffer no temptation to befal us but such as is proportioned to our strength. Not only his justice requires this, which could not punish us for not resisting any temptation if it were so disproportioned to our strength that it was impossible for us to resist it ; not only his mercy—that tender mercy which is over us, as well as over all his works—but, above all, his faithfulness : Seeing all his words are faithful and true ; and the whole tenor of his promises altogether agrees with that declaration, ' As thy days, so thy strength shall be.'

In that execrable slaughter-house, the Romish Inquisition (most unfortunately called, The House of Mercy !), it is the custom of those holy butchers, while they are tearing a man's sinews upon the rack, to have the physician of the house standing by. His business is, from time to time, to observe the eyes, the pulse, and other circumstances of the sufferer, and to give notice when the torture has continued so long as it can without putting an end to his life ; that it may be preserved long enough for him to undergo the residue of their tortures. But notwithstanding all the physician's care, he is sometimes mistaken ; and death puts a period to the sufferings of the patient before his tormentors are aware. We may observe something like this in our own case. In whatever sufferings or temptations we are, our great Physician never departs from us. He is about our bed, and about our path. He observes every symptom of our distress, that it may not rise above our strength. And he cannot be mistaken concerning us. He knows the souls and bodies which he has given us. He sees exactly how much we can endure with our present degree of strength. And if this is not sufficient, he can increase it to whatever degree it pleases him. Nothing, therefore, is more certain, than that, in consequence of his wisdom, as well as his justice, mercy, and faithfulness, he never will, he never can, suffer us to be tempted above that we are able : Above the strength which he either hath given already, or will give as soon as we need it.

' He will with the temptation also ' (this is the Third point we are to consider) ' make a way to escape, that we may be able to bear it.'

The word ἔκστασιν, which we render *a way to escape*, is extremely significant. The meaning of it is nearly expressed by the English word *out-let* ; but more exact by the old word *out-gate*, still frequently used by the Scottish writers. It literally means *a way out*. And this God will either find or make ; which He that hath all wisdom, as well as all power in heaven and earth, can never be at a loss how to do.

Either he *makes a way to escape* out of the temptation, by removing the occasion of it, or *in the temptation* ; that is, the occasion remaining as it was, it is a temptation no longer. First, He makes a way to escape out of the temptation, by removing the occasion of it. The histories of mankind, of the Church in particular, afford us numberless instances of this. And many have occurred in our own memory, and within the little circle of our acquaintance. One of many I think it worth while to relate, as a memorable instance of the faithfulness of God, in making a way to escape out of temptation :— Elizabeth Chadsey, then living in London (whose daughter is living at this day, and is no dishonour to her parent), was advised to administer to her husband, who was supposed to leave much substance behind him. But when a full inquiry into his circumstances was made, it appeared that this supposition was utterly destitute of foundation; and that he not only left nothing at all behind him, but also was very considerably in debt. It was not long after his burial, that a person came to her house, and said, ' Mrs. Chadsey, you are much indebted to your landlord, and he has sent me to demand the rent that is due to him.' She answered, ' Sir, I have not so much money in the world : Indeed I have none at all ! ' ' But,' said he, ' have you nothing that will fetch money ? ' She replied, ' Sir, you see all that I have. I have nothing in the house but these six little children.' ' Then,' said he, ' I must execute my writ, and carry you to Newgate. But it is a hard case. I will leave you here till to-morrow, and will go and try if I cannot persuade your landlord to give you time.' He returned the next morning, and said, ' I have done all I can, I have used all the arguments I could think of, but your landlord is not to be moved. He vows, if I do not carry you to prison without delay, I shall go thither myself.' She answered, ' You have done *your* part. The will of the Lord be done ! ' He said, ' I will venture to make one trial more, and will come again in the morning.' He came in the morning, and said, ' Mrs. Chadsey, God has undertaken your cause. None can give you any trouble now; for your landlord died last night. But he has left no will; and no one knows who is heir to the estate.'

Thus God is able to deliver out of temptations, by removing the occasion of them. But are there not temptations, the occasions of which cannot be taken away? Is it not a striking instance of this kind, which we have in a late publication? 'I was walking,' says the writer of the letter, 'over Dover cliffs, in a calm, pleasant evening, with a person whom I tenderly loved, and to whom I was to be married in a few days. While we were engaged in earnest conversation, her foot slipped, she fell down, and I saw her dashed in pieces on the beach. I lifted up my hands, and cried out, " This evil admits of no remedy. I must now go mourning all my days ! My wound is incurable. It is impossible I should ever find such another woman ! one so every way fitted for me." I added in an agony, " This is such an affliction as even God himself cannot redress ! " And just as I uttered the words, I awoke : For it was a dream ! '—Just so can God remove any possible temptation ; making it like a dream when one waketh !

Thus is God able to deliver out of temptation, by taking away the very ground of it. And he is equally able to deliver in the temptation ; which, perhaps, is the greatest deliverance of all. I mean, suffering the occasion to remain as it was, he will take away the bitterness of it ; so that it shall not be a temptation at all, but only an occasion of thanksgiving. How many proofs of this have the children of God, even in their daily experience ! How frequently are

they encompassed with trouble, or visited with pain
or sickness ! And when they cry unto the Lord, at
some times he takes away the cup from them : He
removes the trouble, or sickness, or pain ; and it is
as though it never had been : At other times he does
not make any outward change ; outward trouble, or
pain, or sickness continues ; but the consolations of
the Holy One so increase, as to over-balance them all ;
and they can boldly declare,

> Labour is rest, and pain is sweet,
> When thou, my God, art near.

An eminent instance of this kind of deliverance is
that which occurs in the Life of that excellent man,
the Marquis de Renty. When he was in a violent
fit of the rheumatism, a friend asked him, ' Sir, are
you in much pain ? ' He answered, ' My pains are
extreme : But through the mercy of God, I give
myself up, not to them, but to him.' It was in the
same spirit that my own father answered, though
exhausted with a severe illness (an ulcer in the bowels,
which had given him little rest day or night, for
upwards of seven months), when I asked, ' Sir, are
you in pain now ? ' He answered, with a strong and
loud voice, ' God does indeed chasten me with pain ;
yea, all my bones with strong pain. But I thank
him for all ; I bless him for all ; I love him for all.'
  We may observe one more instance of a somewhat
similar kind, in the Life of the Marquis de Renty.

When his wife, whom he very tenderly loved, was exceeding ill, and supposed to be near death, a friend took the liberty to inquire how he felt himself on the occasion. He replied, ' I cannot but say, that this trial affects me in the most tender part. I am exquisitely sensible of my loss. I feel more than it is possible to express. And yet I am so satisfied, that the will of God is done, and not the will of a vile sinner, that, were it not for fear of giving offence to others, I could dance and sing ! ' Thus the merciful, the just, the faithful God, will, in one way or other, ' in every temptation make a way to escape, that we may be able to bear it.'

This whole passage is fruitful of instruction. Some of the lessons which we may learn from it are :

First. ' Let him that most assuredly standeth, take heed lest he fall ' into *murmuring* ; lest he say in his heart, ' Surely no one's case is like mine ; no one was ever tried like *me*.' Yea, ten thousand. ' There has no temptation taken you,' but such as is ' common to man ' ; such as you might reasonably expect, if you considered *what you are* ; a sinner born to die ; a sinful inhabitant of a mortal body, liable to number-less inward and outward sufferings ;—and *where you are* ; in a shattered, disordered world, surrounded by evil men, and evil spirits. Consider this, and you will not repine at the common lot, the general condition of humanity.

Secondly. ' Let him that standeth, take heed lest he fall ' ; lest he *tempt* God, by thinking or saying,

'This is insupportable; this is too hard; I can never get through it; my burden is heavier than I can bear.' Not so; unless something is too hard for God. He will not suffer you to be 'tempted above that ye are able.' He proportions the burden to your strength. If you want more strength, 'ask, and it shall be given you.'

Thirdly. 'Let him that standeth, take heed lest he fall'; lest he tempt God by *unbelief*; by distrusting his faithfulness. Hath he said, 'in every temptation he will make a way to escape'? And shall he not do it? Yea, verily;

> And far above thy thought
> His counsel shall appear,
> When fully he the work hath wrought
> That caused thy needless fear.

Let us then receive every trial with calm resignation, and with humble confidence that He who hath all power, all wisdom, all mercy, and all faithfulness, will first support us in every temptation, and then deliver us out of all: So that in the end all things shall work together for good, and we shall happily experience, that all these things were for our profit, that we 'might be partakers of his holiness.'

Upon the Government
of the Tongue

JOSEPH BUTLER

✝

If any man among you seem to be religious, and bridleth not his tongue, but deceiveth his own heart, this man's religion is vain.—JAMES i. 26.

UPON THE GOVERNMENT
OF THE TONGUE

JOSEPH BUTLER

THE translation of this text would be more determinate by being more literal, thus : *If any man among you seemeth to be religious, not bridling his tongue, but deceiving his own heart, this man's religion is vain.* This determines that the words, *but deceiveth his own heart,* are not put in opposition to, *seemeth to be religious,* but to, *bridleth not his tongue.* The certain determinate meaning of the text then being, that he who seemeth to be religious, and bridleth not his tongue, but in that particular deceiveth his own heart, this man's religion is vain ; we may observe somewhat very forcible and expressive in these words of St. James. As if the apostle had said, No man surely can make any pretences to religion, who does not at least believe that he bridleth his tongue : if he puts on any appearance or face of religion, and yet does not govern his tongue, he must surely deceive himself in that particular, and think he does : and whoever is so unhappy as to deceive himself in this, to imagine he keeps that unruly faculty in due subjection, when indeed he does not, whatever the other part of his life be, his religion is vain ; the government of the tongue being a most material restraint which virtue lays us under : without it no man can be truly religious.

In treating upon this subject, I will consider—

First, What is the general vice or fault here referred to : or what disposition in men is supposed in moral reflections and precepts concerning *bridling the tongue*.

Secondly, When it may be said of any one, that he has a due government over himself in this respect.

I. Now the fault referred to, and the disposition supposed, in precepts and reflections concerning the government of the tongue, is not evil-speaking from malice, nor lying or bearing false witness from indirect [1] selfish designs. The disposition to these, and the actual vices themselves, all come under other subjects. The tongue may be employed about and made to serve all the purposes of vice, in tempting and deceiving, in perjury and injustice. But the thing here supposed and referred to, is talkativeness : a disposition to be talking, abstracted from the consideration of what is to be said ; with very little or no regard to, or thought of doing, either good or harm. And let not any imagine this to be a slight matter, and that it deserves not to have so great weight laid upon it ; till he has considered, what evil is implied in it, and the bad effects which follow from it. It is perhaps true, that they who are addicted

[1] *i.e.* not straightforward.

to this folly would choose to confine themselves to trifles and indifferent subjects, and so intend only to be guilty of being impertinent : but as they cannot go on for ever talking of nothing, as common matters will not afford a sufficient fund for perpetual continued discourse : when subjects of this kind are exhausted, they will go on to defamation, scandal, divulging of secrets, their own secrets as well as those of others, anything rather than be silent. They are plainly hurried on in the heat of their talk to say quite different things from what they first intended, and which they afterwards wish unsaid ; or improper things, which they had no other end in saying, but only to afford employment to their tongue. And if these people expect to be heard and regarded, for there are some content merely with talking, they will invent to engage your attention : and, when they have heard the least imperfect hint of an affair, they will out of their own head add the circumstances of time and place, and other matters to make out their story, and give the appearance of probability to it : not that they have any concern about being believed, otherwise than as a means of being heard. The thing is, to engage your attention ; to take you up wholly for the present time : what reflections will be made afterwards, is in truth the least of their thoughts. And further ; when persons, who indulge themselves in these liberties of the tongue, are in any degree offended with another, as little disgusts and misunderstandings will be, they allow themselves to

defame and revile such an one without any moderation
or bounds ; though the offence is so very slight, that
they themselves would not do, nor perhaps wish him
an injury in any other way. And in this case the
scandal and revilings are chiefly owing to talkativeness,
and not bridling their tongue ; and so come under
our present subject. The least occasion in the world
will make the humour break out in this particular
way, or in another. It is like a torrent, which must
and will flow ; but the least thing imaginable will
first of all give it either this or another direction, turn
it into this or that channel : or like a fire, the nature
of which, when in a heap of combustible matter, is to
spread and lay waste all around ; but any one of a
thousand little accidents will occasion it to break out
first either in this or another particular part.

The subject then before us, though it does run up
into, and can scarce be treated as entirely distinct
from all others ; yet it needs not to be so much
mixed and blended with them as it often is. Every
faculty and power may be used as the instrument of
premeditated vice and wickedness, merely as the most
proper and effectual means of executing such designs.
But if a man, from deep malice and desire of revenge,
should meditate a falsehood with a settled design to
ruin his neighbour's reputation, and should with
great coolness and deliberation spread it ; nobody
would choose to say of such an one, that he had no
government of his tongue. A man may use the
faculty of speech as an instrument of false witness,

who yet has so entire a command over that faculty, as never to speak but from forethought and cool design. Here the crime is injustice and perjury: and, strictly speaking, no more belongs to the present subject, than perjury and injustice in any other way. But there is such a thing as a disposition to be talking for its own sake; from which persons often say anything, good or bad, of others, merely as a subject of discourse, according to the particular temper they themselves happen to be in, and to pass away the present time. There is likewise to be observed in persons such a strong and eager desire of engaging attention to what they say, that they will speak good or evil, truth or otherwise, merely as one or the other seems to be most hearkened to: and this, though it is sometimes joined, is not the same with the desire of being thought important and men of consequence. There is in some such a disposition to be talking, that an offence of the slightest kind, and such as would not raise any other resentment, yet raises, if I may so speak, the resentment of the tongue, puts it into a flame, into the most ungovernable motions. This outrage, when the person it respects is present, we distinguish in the lower rank of people by a peculiar term: and let it be observed, that though the decencies of behaviour are a little kept; the same outrage and virulence, indulged when he is absent, is an offence of the same kind. But not to distinguish any farther in this manner: men run into faults and follies, which cannot so properly be referred to any one general head at this, that they have not a due government over their tongue.

And this unrestrained volubility and wantonness of speech is the occasion of numberless evils and vexations in life. It begets resentment in him who is the subject of it ; sows the seed of strife and dissension amongst others ; and inflames little disgusts and offences, which if let alone would wear away of themselves : it is often of as bad effect upon the good name of others, as deep envy or malice : and, to say the least of it in this respect, it destroys and perverts a certain equity of the utmost importance to society to be observed ; namely, that praise and dispraise, a good or bad character, should always be bestowed according to desert. The tongue used in such a licentious manner is like a sword in the hand of a madman ; it is employed at random, it can scarce possibly do any good, and for the most part does a world of mischief ; and implies not only great folly and a trifling spirit, but great viciousness of mind, great indifference to truth and falsity, and to the reputation, welfare and good of others. So much reason is there for what St. James says of the tongue.[1] *It is a fire, a world of iniquity, it defileth the whole body, setteth on fire the course of nature, and is itself set on fire of hell.* This is the faculty or disposition which we are required to keep a guard upon : these are the vices and follies it runs into, when not kept under due restraint.

[1] Chap. iii. 6.

II. Wherein the due government of the tongue consists, or when it may be said of any one in a moral and religious sense that he *bridleth his tongue*, I come now to consider.

The due and proper use of any natural faculty or power, is to be judged of by the end and design for which it was given us. The chief purpose, for which the faculty of speech was given to man, is plainly that we might communicate our thoughts to each other, in order to carry on the affairs of the world ; for business, and for our improvement in knowledge and learning. But the good Author of our nature designed us not only necessaries, but likewise enjoyment and satisfaction, in that being he hath graciously given, and in that condition of life he hath placed us in. There are secondary uses of our faculties : they administer to delight, as well as to necessity : and as they are equally adapted to both, there is no doubt but he intended them for our gratification, as well as for the support and continuance of our being. The secondary use of speech is to please and be entertaining to each other in conversation. This is in every respect allowable and right : it unites men closer in alliances and friendships ; gives us a fellow feeling of the prosperity and unhappiness of each other ; and is in several respects serviceable to virtue, and to promote good behaviour in the world. And provided there be not too much time spent in it, if it were considered only in the way of gratification and delight, men must have strange notions of God and of religion, to think that he can be offended with it, or that it is any way inconsistent with the strictest virtue. But the truth is, such sort of conversation, though it has no particular good tendency, yet it has a general good one : it is social and friendly ; and tends to promote humanity, good nature and civility.

As the end and use, so likewise the abuse of speech, relates to the one or other of these ; either to business, or to conversation. As to the former ; deceit in the management of business and affairs does not properly belong to the subject now before us : though one may just mention that multitude, that endless number of words, with which business is perplexed ; when a much fewer would, as it should seem, better serve the purpose : but this must be left to those who understand the matter. The government of the tongue, considered as a subject of itself, relates chiefly to conversation ; to that kind of discourse which usually fills up the time spent in friendly meetings, and visits of civility. And the danger is, lest persons entertain themselves and others at the expense of their wisdom and their virtue, and to the injury or offence of their neighbour. If they will observe and keep clear of these, they may be as free, and easy, and unreserved, as they can desire.

The cautions to be given for avoiding these dangers, and to render conversation innocent and agreeable, fall under the following particulars : silence ; talking of indifferent things ; and, which makes up too great

243

a part of conversation, giving of characters, speaking well or evil of others.

The Wise Man observes, that *there is a time to speak and a time to keep silence*.[1] One meets with people in the world, who seem never to have made the last of these observations. And yet these great talkers do not at all speak from their having anything to say, as every sentence shows, but only from their inclination to be talking. Their conversation is merely an exercise of the tongue : no other human faculty has any share in it. It is strange these persons can help reflecting, that unless they have in truth a superior capacity, and are in an extraordinary manner furnished for conversation ; if they are entertaining, it is at their own expense. Is it possible, that it should never come into people's thoughts to suspect, whether or no it be to their advantage to show so very much of themselves ? *Oh that you would altogether hold your peace, and it should be your wisdom*.[2] Remember likewise there are persons who love fewer words, an inoffensive sort of people, and who deserve some regard, though of too still and composed tempers for you. Of this number was the son of *Sirach* : for he plainly speaks from experience, when he says, *As hills of sand are to the steps of the aged, so is one of many words to a quiet man*.[3] But one would think it should be obvious to every one, that when they are in company with their superiors of any kind, in years, knowledge and experience ; when proper and useful

---

[1] [Eccles. iii. 7.]   [2] Job xiii. 5.   [3] [Ecclus. xxv. 20.]

subjects are discoursed of, which they cannot bear a part in ; that these are times for silence : when they should learn to hear, and be attentive ; at least in their turn. It is indeed a very unhappy way these people are in : they in a manner cut themselves out from all advantage of conversation, except that of being entertained with their own talk : their business in coming into company not being at all to be informed, to hear, to learn ; but to display themselves ; or rather to exert their faculty, and talk without any design at all. And if we consider conversation as an entertainment, as somewhat to unbend the mind ; as a diversion from the cares, the business and the sorrows of life ; it is of the very nature of it, that the discourse be mutual. This I say, is implied in the very notion of what we distinguish by conversation, or being in company. Attention to the continued discourse of one alone grows more painful often than the cares and business we come to be diverted from. He therefore who imposes this upon us is guilty of a double offence ; arbitrarily enjoining silence upon all the rest, and likewise obliging them to this painful attention.

I am sensible these things are apt to be passed over, as too little to come into a serious discourse : but in reality men are obliged, even in point of morality and virtue, to observe all the decencies of behaviour. The greatest evils in life have had their rise from somewhat, which was thought of too little importance to be attended to. And as to the matter we are now upon, it is absolutely necessary to be considered. For if people will not maintain a due government over themselves, in regarding proper times and seasons for silence, but *will* be talking ; they certainly, whether they design it or not at first, will go on to scandal and evil-speaking, and divulging secrets.

If it were needful to say anything further, to persuade men to learn this lesson of silence ; one might put them in mind, how insignificant they render themselves by this excessive talkativeness : insomuch that, if they do chance to say anything which deserves to be attended to and regarded, it is lost in the variety and abundance which they utter of another sort.

The occasions of silence then are obvious, and one would think should be easily distinguished by everybody : namely, when a man has nothing to say ; or nothing, but what is better unsaid : better, either in regard to the particular person he is present with ; or from its being an interruption to conversation itself ; or to conversation of a more agreeable kind ; or better, lastly, with regard to himself. I will end this particular with two reflections of the Wise Man ; one of which, in the strongest manner, exposes the ridiculous part of this licentiousness of the tongue ; and the other, the great danger and viciousness of it. *When he that is a fool walketh by the way side, his wisdom faileth him, and he saith to every one that he is a fool.*[1]

[1] Eccles. x. 3.

The other is, *In the multitude of words there wanteth not sin.*[1]

As to the government of the tongue in respect to talking upon indifferent subjects : after what has been said concerning the due government of it in respect to the occasions and times for silence, there is little more necessary, than only to caution men to be fully satisfied, that the subjects are indeed of an indifferent nature ; and not to spend too much time in conversation of this kind. But persons must be sure to take heed, that the subject of their discourse be at least of an indifferent nature : that it be no way offensive to virtue, religion, or good manners ; that it be not of a licentious dissolute sort, this leaving always ill impressions upon the mind ; that it be no way injurious or vexatious to others ; and that too much time be not spent this way, to the neglect of those duties and offices of life which belong to their station and condition in the world. However, though there is not any necessity that men should aim at being important and weighty in every sentence they speak : yet since useful subjects, at least of some kinds, are as entertaining as others ; a wise man, even when he desires to unbend his mind from business, would choose that the conversation might turn upon somewhat instructive.

The last thing is, the government of the tongue as relating to discourse of the affairs of others, and giving of characters. These are in a manner the same : and

[1] Prov. x. 19.

247

one can scarce call it an indifferent subject, because discourse upon it almost perpetually runs into somewhat criminal.

And first of all, it were very much to be wished that this did not take up so great a part of conversation; because it is indeed a subject of a dangerous nature. Let any one consider the various interests, competitions, and little misunderstandings which arise amongst men; and he will soon see, that he is not unprejudiced and impartial; that he is not, as I may speak, neutral enough, to trust himself with talking of the character and concerns of his neighbour, in a free, careless and unreserved manner. There is perpetually, and often it is not attended to, a rivalship amongst people of one kind or another, in respect to wit, beauty, learning, fortune; and that one thing will insensibly influence them to speak to the disadvantage of others, even where there is no formed malice or ill design. Since therefore it is so hard to enter into this subject without offending, the first thing to be observed is, that people should learn to decline it; to get over that strong inclination most have to be talking of the concerns and behaviour of their neighbour.

But since it is impossible that this subject should be wholly excluded conversation, and since it is necessary that the characters of men should be known: the next thing is, that it is a matter of importance what is said; and therefore, that we should be religiously scrupulous and exact to say nothing, either

248

good or bad, but what is true. I put it thus, because it is in reality of as great importance to the good of society, that the characters of bad men should be known, as that the characters of good men should. People, who are given to scandal and detraction, may indeed make an ill use of this observation : but truths, which are of service towards regulating our conduct, are not to be disowned, or even concealed, because a bad use may be made of them. This however would be effectually prevented, if these two things were attended to. *First*, That, though it is equally of bad consequence to society, that men should have either good or ill characters which they do not deserve ; yet, when you say somewhat good of a man which he does not deserve, there is no wrong done him in particular ; whereas, when you say evil of a man which he does not deserve, here is a direct formal injury, a real piece of injustice, done him. This therefore makes a wide difference ; and gives us, in point of virtue, much greater latitude in speaking well than ill of others. *Secondly*, A good man is friendly to his fellow-creatures, and a lover of mankind ; and so will, upon every occasion, and often without any, say all the good he can of everybody : but, so far as he is a good man, will never be disposed to speak evil of any, unless there be some other reason for it, besides barely that it is true. If he be charged with having given an ill character, he will scarce think it a sufficient justification of himself to say it was a true one ; unless he can also give

some further account how he came to do so : a just
indignation against particular instances of villainy,
where they are great and scandalous ; or to prevent
an innocent man from being deceived and betrayed,
when he has great trust and confidence in one who
does not deserve it. Justice must be done to every
part of a subject when we are considering it. If
there be a man, who bears a fair character in the
world, whom yet we know to be without faith or
honesty, to be really an ill man ; it must be allowed
in general, that we shall do a piece of service to
society by letting such an one's true character be
known. This is no more than what we have an
instance of in our Saviour himself ; though he was
mild and gentle beyond example.[1] However, no
words can express too strongly the caution which
should be used in such a case as this.

Upon the whole matter : If people would observe
the obvious occasions of silence ; if they would
subdue the inclination to tale-bearing ; and that
eager desire to engage attention, which is an original
disease in some minds ; they would be in little
danger of offending with their tongue ; and would,
in a moral and religious sense, have due government
over it.

I will conclude with some precepts and reflections
of the son of *Sirach* upon this subject. *Be swift
to hear : and, if thou hast understanding, answer thy
neighbour ; if not, lay thy hand upon thy mouth. Honour*

[1] Mark xii. 38, 40.

and shame is in talk. A man of an ill tongue is dangerous in his city, and he that is rash in his talk shall be hated. A wise man will hold his tongue, till he see opportunity; but a babbler and a fool will regard no time. He that useth many words shall be abhorred; and he that taketh to himself authority therein shall be hated. A backbiting tongue hath disquieted many; strong cities hath it pulled down, and overthrown the houses of great men. The tongue of a man is his fall; but if thou love to hear, thou shalt receive understanding.[1]

[1] [Ecclus. v. 11–13, ix. 18, xx. 7, 8, xxviii. 14, v. 13, vi. 33.]

The Invisible World

JOHN HENRY NEWMAN

✦

While we look not at the things which are seen, but at the things which are not seen : for the things which are seen are temporal ; but the things which are not seen are eternal.—2 COR. iv. 18.

THE INVISIBLE WORLD

JOHN HENRY NEWMAN

THERE are two worlds, 'the visible and the invisible,' as the Creed speaks,—the world we see, and the world we do not see; and the world which we do not see as really exists as the world we do see. It really exists though we see it not. The world that we see we know to exist, because we see it. We have but to lift up our eyes and look around us, and we have proof of it: our eyes tell us. We see the sun, moon and stars, earth and sky, hills and valleys, woods and plains, seas and rivers. And again, we see men, and the works of men. We see cities, and stately buildings, and their inhabitants; men running to and fro, and busying themselves to provide for themselves and their families, or to accomplish great designs, or for the very business' sake. All that meets our eyes forms one world. It is an immense world; it reaches to the stars. Thousands on thousands of years might we speed up the sky, and though we were swifter than the light itself, we should not reach them all. They are at distances from us greater than any that is assignable.

So high, so wide, so deep is the world ; and yet it also comes near and close to us. It is everywhere ; and it seems to leave no room for any other world.

And yet in spite of this universal world which we see, there is another world, quite as far-spreading, quite as close to us, and more wonderful ; another world all around us, though we see it not, and more wonderful than the world we see, for this reason if for no other, that we do not see it. All around us are numberless objects, coming and going, watching, working or waiting, which we see not : this is that other world, which the eyes reach not unto, but faith only.

Let us dwell upon this thought. We are born into a world of sense ; that is, of the real things which lie round about us, one great department comes to us, accosts us, through our bodily organs, our eyes, ears, and fingers. We feel, hear, and see them ; and we know they exist, because we do thus perceive them. Things innumerable lie about us, animate and inanimate ; but one particular class of these innumerable things is thus brought home to us through our senses. And moreover, while they act upon us, they make their presence known. We are sensible of them at the time, we are conscious that we perceive them. We not only see, but know that we see them ; we not only hold intercourse, but know that we do. We are among men, and we know that we are. We feel cold and hunger ; we know what sensible things remove them. We eat, drink,

clothe ourselves, dwell in houses, converse and act
with others, and perform the duties of social life ;
and we feel vividly that we are doing so, while we
do so. Such is our relation towards one part of the
innumerable beings which lie around us. They act
upon us, and we know it ; and we act upon them in
turn, and know we do.

But all this does not interfere with the existence
of that other world which I speak of, acting upon
us, yet not impressing us with the consciousness that
it does so. It may as really be present and exert an
influence as that which reveals itself to us. And
that such a world there is, Scripture tells us. Do
you ask what it is, and what it contains ? I will not
say that all that belongs to it is vastly more important
than what we see, for among things visible are our
fellow-men, and nothing created is more precious and
noble than a son of man. But still, taking the things
which we see altogether, and the things we do not
see altogether, the world we do not see is on the
whole a much higher world than that which we do
see. For, first of all, he is there who is above all
beings, who has created all, before whom they all
are as nothing, and with whom nothing can be
compared. Almighty God, we know, exists more
really and absolutely than any of those fellow-men
whose existence is conveyed to us through the senses ;
yet we see him not, hear him not, we do but ' feel
after him,' yet without finding him. It appears,
then, that the things which are seen are but a part,

and but a secondary part of the beings about us, were it only on this ground, that Almighty God, the Being of beings, is not in their number, but among 'the things which are not seen.' Once, and once only, for thirty-three years, has he condescended to become one of the beings which are seen, when he, the second Person of the Ever-blessed Trinity, was, by an unspeakable mercy, born of the Virgin Mary into this sensible world. And then he was seen, heard, handled; he ate, he drank, he slept, he conversed, he went about, he acted as other men: but excepting this brief period, his presence has never been perceptible; he has never made us conscious of his existence by means of our senses. He came, and he retired beyond the veil: and to us individually, it is as if he had never shown himself; we have as little sensible experience of his presence. Yet 'He liveth evermore.'

And in that other world are the souls also of the dead. They too, when they depart hence, do not cease to exist, but they retire from this visible scene of things; or, in other words, they cease to act towards us and before us through our senses. They live as they lived before; but that outward frame, through which they were able to hold communion with other men, is in some way, we know not how, separated from them, and dries away and shrivels up as leaves may drop off a tree. They remain, but without the usual means of approach towards us, and correspondence with us. As when a man loses his voice or hand, he still exists as before, but cannot any longer talk or write, or otherwise hold intercourse with us ; so when he loses not voice and hand only, but his whole frame, or is said to die, there is nothing to show that he is gone, but we have lost our means of apprehending him.

Again : Angels also are inhabitants of the world invisible, and concerning them much more is told us than concerning the souls of the faithful departed, because the latter ' rest from their labours ' ; but the Angels are actively employed among us in the Church. They are said to be ' ministering spirits, sent forth to minister for them who shall be heirs of salvation.' No Christian is so humble but he has Angels to attend on him, if he lives by faith and love. Though they are so great, so glorious, so pure, so wonderful, that the very sight of them (if we were allowed to see them) would strike us to the earth, as it did the prophet Daniel, holy and righteous as he was ; yet they are our ' fellow-servants ' and our fellow-workers, and they carefully watch over and defend even the humblest of us, if we be Christ's. That they form a part of our unseen world, appears from the vision seen by the patriarch Jacob. We are told that when he fled from his brother Esau, ' he lighted upon a certain place, and tarried there all night, because the sun had set ; and he took of the stones of that place, and put them for his pillows, and lay down in that place to sleep.' How little did he think that there was anything very wonderful

in this spot ! It looked like any other spot. It was
a lone, uncomfortable place : there was no house
there : night was coming on ; and he had to sleep
upon the bare rock. Yet how different was the
truth ! He saw but the world that is seen ; he saw
not the world that is not seen ; yet the world that
is not seen was there. It was there, though it did not
at once make known its presence, but needed to be
supernaturally displayed to him. He saw it in his
sleep. 'He dreamed, and behold, a ladder set up
on the earth, and the top of it reached up to heaven ;
and behold, the Angels of God ascending and descending on it. And behold, the Lord stood above it.'
This was the other world. Now, let this be observed.
Persons commonly speak as if the other world did
not exist now, but would after death. No : it exists
now, though we see it not. It is among us and around
us. Jacob was shown this in his dream. Angels were
all about him, though he knew it not. And what
Jacob saw in his sleep, that Elisha's servant saw as if
with his eyes ; and the shepherds at the time of the
Nativity, not only saw, but heard. They heard the
voices of those blessed spirits who praise God day
and night, and whom we, in our lower state of being,
are allowed to copy and assist.

We are then in a world of spirits, as well as in a
world of sense, and we hold communion with it,
and take part in it, though we are not conscious of
doing so. If this seems strange to any one, let him
reflect that we are undeniably taking part in a third

world, which we do indeed see, but about which we
do not know more than about the Angelic hosts,—the
world of brute animals. Can anything be more
marvellous or startling, unless we were used to it,
than that we should have a race of beings about us
whom we do see, and as little know their state, or
can describe their interests, or their destiny, as we
can tell of the inhabitants of the sun and moon? It
is indeed a very overpowering thought, when we
get to fix our minds on it, that we familiarly use, I
may say hold intercourse with, creatures who are as
much strangers to us, as mysterious, as if they were
the fabulous, unearthly beings, more powerful than
man, and yet his slaves, which Eastern superstitions
have invented. We have more real knowledge about
the Angels than about the brutes. They have apparently passions, habits, and a certain accountableness,
but all is mystery about them. We do not know
whether they can sin or not, whether they are under
punishment, whether they are to live after this life.
We inflict very great sufferings on a portion of them,
and they in turn, every now and then, seem to
retaliate upon us, as if by a wonderful law. We
depend upon them in various important ways; we
use their labour, we eat their flesh. This however
relates to such of them as come near us: cast your
thoughts abroad on the whole number of them, large
and small, in vast forests, or in the water, or in the
air; and then say whether the presence of such
countless multitudes, so various in their natures, so

strange and wild in their shapes, living on the earth without ascertainable object, is not as mysterious as anything which Scripture says about the Angels? Is it not plain to our senses that there is a world inferior to us in the scale of beings, with which we are connected without understanding what it is? and is it difficult to faith to admit the word of Scripture concerning our connexion with a world superior to us?

When, indeed, persons feel it so difficult to conceive the existence among us of the world of spirits, because they are not aware of it, they should recollect how many worlds all at once are in fact contained in human society itself. We speak of the political world, the scientific, the learned, the literary, the religious world; and suitably: for men are so closely united with some men, and so divided from others, they have such distinct objects of pursuit one from another, and such distinct principles and engagements in consequence, that in one and the same place there exist together a number of circles or (as they may be called) worlds, made up of visible men, but themselves invisible, unknown, nay, unintelligible to each other. Men move about in the common paths of life, and look the same; but there is little community of feeling between them; each knows little about what goes on in any other sphere than his own; and a stranger coming into any neighbourhood would, according to his own pursuits or acquaintances, go away with an utterly distinct or a reverse impression of it, viewed as a whole. Or again, leave for a while the political and commercial excitement of some large city, and take refuge in a secluded village ; and there, in the absence of news of the day, consider the mode of life and habits of mind, the employments and views of its inhabitants ; and say whether the world, when regarded in its separate portions, is not more unlike itself than it is unlike the world of Angels which Scripture places in the midst of it.

The world of spirits then, though unseen, is present ; present, not future, not distant. It is not above the sky, it is not beyond the grave ; it is now and here ; the kingdom of God is among us. Of this the text speaks ;—' We look,' says St. Paul, ' not at the things which are seen, but at the things which are not seen ; for the things which are seen are temporal, but the things which are not seen are eternal.' You see he regarded it as a practical truth, which was to influence our conduct. Not only does he speak of the world invisible, but of the duty of ' looking at ' it ; not only does he contrast the things of time with it, but says that their belonging to time is a reason, not for looking at, but for looking off them. Eternity was not distant because it reached to the future ; nor the unseen state without its influence on us, because it was impalpable. In like manner, he says in another Epistle, ' Our conversation is in heaven.' And again, ' God hath raised us up together, and made us sit together in heavenly places in Christ Jesus.' And again, ' Your life is hid with Christ in

God.' And to the same purport are St. Peter's words, ' Whom having not seen, ye love ; in whom, though now ye see him not, yet believing, ye rejoice with joy unspeakable and full of glory.' And again, St. Paul speaking of the Apostles, ' We are made a spectacle unto the world, and to Angels, and to men.' And again in words already quoted, he speaks of the Angels as ' ministering spirits sent forth to minister for them who shall be heirs of salvation.'

Such is the hidden kingdom of God ; and, as it is now hidden, so in due season it shall be revealed. Men think that they are lords of the world, and may do as they will. They think this earth their property, and its movements in their power ; whereas it has other lords besides them, and is the scene of a higher conflict than they are capable of conceiving. It contains Christ's little ones whom they despise, and his Angels whom they disbelieve ; and these at length shall take possession of it and be manifested. At present, ' all things,' to appearance, ' continue as they were from the beginning of the creation ' ; and scoffers ask, ' Where is the promise of his coming ? ' but at the appointed time there will be a ' manifesta- tion of the sons of God,' and the hidden saints ' shall shine out as the sun in the kingdom of their Father.' When the Angels appeared to the shepherds it was a sudden appearance,—' *Suddenly* there was with the Angel a multitude of the heavenly host.' How wonderful a sight ! The night had before that seemed just like any other night ; as the evening on which

Jacob saw the vision seemed like any other evening. They were keeping watch over their sheep ; they were watching the night as it passed. The stars moved on,—it was midnight. They had no idea of such a thing when the Angel appeared. Such are the power and virtue hidden in things which are seen, and at God's will they are manifested. They were manifested for a moment to Jacob, for a moment to Elisha's servant, for a moment to the shepherds. They will be manifested for ever when Christ comes at the last Day ' in the glory of his Father with the holy Angels.' Then this world will fade away and the other world will shine forth.

Let these be your thoughts, my brethren, especially in the spring season, when the whole face of nature is so rich and beautiful. Once only in the year, yet once, does the world which we see show forth its hidden powers, and in a manner manifest itself. Then the leaves come out, and the blossoms on the fruit trees and flowers ; and the grass and corn spring up. There is a sudden rush and burst outwardly of that hidden life which God has lodged in the material world. Well, that shows you, as by a sample, what it can do at God's command, when he gives the word. This earth, which now buds forth in leaves and blossoms, will one day burst forth into a new world of light and glory, in which we shall see Saints and Angels dwelling. Who would think, except from his experience of former springs all through his life, who could conceive two or three months before, that it was possible that the face of nature, which then seemed so lifeless, should become so splendid and varied ? How different is a tree, how different is a prospect, when leaves are on it and off it ! How unlikely it would seem, before the event, that the dry and naked branches should suddenly be clothed with what is so bright and so refreshing ! Yet in God's good time leaves come on the trees. The season may delay, but come it will at last. So it is with the coming of that Eternal Spring, for which all Christians are waiting. Come it will, though it delay ; yet though it tarry, let us wait for it, ' because it will surely come, it will not tarry.' Therefore we say day by day, ' Thy kingdom come ' ; which means,—O Lord, show thyself ; manifest thyself ; thou that sittest between the Cherubim, show thyself ; stir up thy strength and come and help us. The earth that we see does not satisfy us ; it is but a beginning ; it is but a promise of something beyond it ; even when it is gayest, with all its blossoms on, and shows most touchingly what lies hid in it, yet it is not enough. We know much more lies hid in it than we see. A world of Saints and Angels, a glorious world, the palace of God, the mountain of the Lord of Hosts, the heavenly Jerusalem, the throne of God and Christ, all these wonders, everlasting, all-precious, mysterious, and incomprehensible, lie hid in what we see. What we see is the outward shell of an eternal kingdom ; and on that kingdom we fix the eyes of our faith. Shine forth, O Lord, as when on thy Nativity thine Angels visited the shepherds ; let thy glory blossom forth as bloom and foliage on the trees ; change with thy mighty power this visible world into that diviner world, which as yet we see not ; destroy what we see, that it may pass and be transformed into what we believe. Bright as is the sun, and the sky, and the clouds ; green as are the leaves and the fields ; sweet as is the singing of the birds ; we know that they are not all, and we will not take up with a part for the whole. They proceed from a centre of love and goodness, which is God himself ; but they are not his fulness ; they speak of heaven, but they are not heaven ; they are but as stray beams and dim reflections of his Image ; they are but crumbs from the table. We are looking for the coming of the day of God, when all this outward world, fair though it be, shall perish ; when the heavens shall be burnt, and the earth melt away. We can bear the loss, for we know it will be but the removing of a veil. We know that to remove the world which is seen, will be the manifestation of the world which is not seen. We know that what we see is as a screen hiding from us God and Christ, and his Saints and Angels. And we earnestly desire and pray for the dissolution of all that we see, from our longing after that which we do not see.

O blessed they indeed, who are destined for the sight of those wonders in which they now stand, at which they now look, but which they do not recognize ! Blessed they who shall at length behold what as yet mortal eye hath not seen and faith only enjoys ! Those wonderful things of the new world are even now as they shall be then. They are immortal and eternal ; and the souls who shall then be made conscious of them, will see them in their calmness and their majesty where they ever have been. But who can express the surprise and rapture which will come upon those, who then at last apprehend them for the first time, and to whose perceptions they are new ! Who can imagine by a stretch of fancy the feelings of those who having died in faith, wake up to enjoyment ! The life then begun, we know, will last for ever; yet surely if memory be to us then what it is now, that will be a day much to be observed unto the Lord through all the ages of eternity. We may increase indeed for ever in knowledge and in love, still that first waking from the dead, the day at once of our birth and our espousals, will ever be endeared and hallowed in our thoughts. When we find outselves after long rest gifted with fresh powers, vigorous with the seed of eternal life within us, able to love God as we wish, conscious that all trouble, sorrow, pain, anxiety, bereavement, is over for ever, blessed in the full affection of those earthly friends whom we loved so poorly, and could protect so feebly, while they were with us in the flesh, and above all, visited by the immediate visible ineffable Presence of God Almighty, with his Only-begotten Son our Lord Jesus Christ, and his Co-equal Co-eternal Spirit, that great sight in which is the fulness of joy and pleasure for evermore,—what deep, incommunicable, unimaginable thoughts will be then upon us ! what depths will be stirred up within us ! what secret harmonies awaked, of which human nature seemed incapable ! Earthly words are indeed all worthless to minister to such high anticipations. Let us close our eyes and keep silence.

' All flesh is grass, and all the goodliness thereof is as the flower of the field. The grass withereth, the flower fadeth, because the Spirit of the Lord bloweth upon it : surely the people is grass. The grass withereth, the flower fadeth ; but the Word of our God shall stand for ever.'

The Law of Christian Conscience

FREDERICK W. ROBERTSON

✛

Howbeit there is not in every man that knowledge : for some, with conscience of the idol, unto this hour, eat it as a thing offered unto an idol ; and their conscience being weak is defiled. But meat commendeth us not to God : for neither if we eat are we the better ; neither if we eat not are we the worse. But take heed lest by any means this liberty of yours become a stumbling-block to them that are weak. For if any man see thee, which hast knowledge, sit at meat in the idol's temple, shall not the conscience of him which is weak be emboldened to eat those things which are offered to idols ; and through thy knowledge shall the weak brother perish for whom Christ died ? But when ye sin so against the brethren and wound their weak conscience ye sin against Christ. Wherefore if meat make my brother to offend I will eat no flesh while the world standeth, lest I make my brother to offend.—1 COR. viii. 7–13.

THE LAW OF CHRISTIAN CONSCIENCE

FREDERICK W. ROBERTSON

WE have already divided this chapter into two branches—the former portion of it containing the difference between Christian knowledge and secular knowledge, and the second portion containing the apostolic exposition of the law of Christian conscience. The first of these we endeavoured to expound last Sunday, but it may be well briefly to recapitulate the principles of that discourse in a somewhat different form. Corinth, as we all know and remember, was a city built on the sea coast, having a large and free communication with all foreign nations; and there was also within it, and going on amongst its inhabitants, a free interchange of thought, and a vivid power of communicating the philosophy and truths of those days to each other. Now it is plain that to a society in such a state, and to minds so educated, the gospel of Christ must have presented a peculiar attraction, presenting itself to them as it did, as a law of Christian liberty. And so in Corinth the gospel had 'free course and was glorified,' and was received with great joy by almost all men, and

by minds of all classes and all sects ; and a large
number of these attached themselves to the teaching
of the Apostle Paul as the most accredited expounder
of Christianity—the ' royal law of liberty.' But it
seems, from what we read in this epistle, that a
large number of these men receive Christianity as a
thing intellectual, and that alone—and not as a thing
which touched the conscience, and swayed and purified
the affections. And so, this liberty became to them
almost *all*—they ran into sin or went to extravagance
—they rejoiced in their freedom from the superstitions, the ignorances, and the scruples which bound
their weaker brethren ; but had no charity—none of
that intense charity which characterized the Apostle
Paul—for those still struggling in the delusions and
darkness from which they themselves were free.
More than that, they demanded their right, their
Christian liberty of expressing their opinions in the
church, merely for the sake of *exhibiting* the Christian
graces and spiritual gifts which had been showered
upon them so largely ; until by degrees those very
assemblies became a lamentable exhibition of their
own depravity, and led to numerous irregularities
which we find severely rebuked by the Apostle Paul.
Their women, rejoicing in the emancipation which
had been given to the Christian community, laid
aside the old habits of attire which had been consecrated so long by Grecian and Jewish custom, and
appeared with their heads uncovered in the Christian
community. Still further than that, the Lord's

Supper exhibited an absence of all solemnity, and seemed more a meeting for licentious gratification, where ' one was hungry, and another was drunken '—a place in which earthly drunkenness, the mere enjoyment of the appetites, had taken the place of Christian charity towards each other. And the same feeling— this love of mere liberty—liberty in itself—manifested itself in many other directions. Holding by this freedom, their philosophy taught that the body, that is the flesh, was the only cause of sin ; that the soul was holy and pure ; and that, therefore, to be free from the body would be entire, perfect, Christian emancipation. And so came in that strange, wrong doctrine, exhibited in Corinth, where immortality was taught separate from, and in opposition to, the doctrine of the resurrection. And afterwards they went on with their conclusions about liberty to maintain that the body, justified by the sacrifice of Christ, was no longer capable of sin ; and that in the evil which was done by the body, the soul had taken no part. And therefore sin was to them but as a name, from which a Christian conscience was to be freed altogether. So that when one of their number had fallen into grievous sin, and had committed fornication, ' such as was not so much as named among the Gentiles,' so far from being humbled by it, they were ' puffed up,' as if they were exhibiting to the world an enlightened, true, perfect Christianity—separate from all prejudices. To such a society, and to such a state of mind, the

Apostle Paul preached in all its length, breadth, and fulness, the humbling doctrines of the Cross of Christ. He taught that knowledge was one thing—that charity was *another* thing ; that ' knowledge puffeth up, but charity buildeth up.' He reminded them that love was the perfection of knowledge, that, ' if any man loved God, the same was known of Him.' In other words, his teaching came to this : there are two kinds of knowledge ; the one the knowledge of the intellect, the other the knowledge of the heart. Intellectually, God never can be known. He must be known by Love—for, ' if any man love God the same is known of Him.' Here, then, we have arrived in another way at precisely the same conclusion at which we arrived last Sunday. Here are two kinds of knowledge, secular knowledge and Christian knowledge ; and Christian knowledge is this—to know by Love.

Let us now consider the remainder of the chapter, which treats of the law of Christian conscience. You will observe that it divides itself into two branches— the first containing an exposition of the law itself, and the second the Christian applications which flow out of this exposition.

I. The way in which the apostle expounds the law of Christian conscience is this :—Guilt is contracted by the soul, in so far as it sins against and transgresses the law of God, by doing that which it believes to be wrong : not so much what *is* wrong as what *appears* to *it* to be wrong. This is the doctrine

distinctly laid down in the seventh and eighth verses.
The apostle tells the Corinthians—these strong-
minded Corinthians—that the superstitions of their
weaker brethren were unquestionably wrong. ' Meat,'
he says, ' commendeth us not to God ; for neither
if we eat are we the better ; neither if we eat not
are we the worse.' He then tells them further,
that ' there is not in every man that knowledge ;
for some, with conscience of the idol, eat it as a thing
offered unto an idol.' Here, then, is an ignorant,
mistaken, ill-informed conscience ; and yet he goes
on to tell them that this conscience, so ill-informed,
yet binds the possessor of it : ' and their conscience,
being weak, is defiled.' For example ; there could
be no harm in eating the flesh of an animal that had
been offered to an idol or false god ; for a false god
is nothing, and it is impossible for it to have contracted positive defilement by being offered to that
which is a positive and absolute negation. And yet
if any man thought it wrong to eat such flesh, to
him it *was* wrong ; for in that act there would be a
deliberate act of transgression—a deliberate preference
of that which was mere enjoyment, to that which was
apparently, though it may be only apparently,
sanctioned by the law of God. And so it would
carry with it all the disobedience, all the guilt, and
all the misery which belongs to the doing of an act
altogether wrong ; or, as St. Paul expresses it, the
conscience would become defiled.

Here, then, we arrive at the first distinction—the

distinction between absolute and relative right and wrong. Absolute right and absolute wrong, like absolute truth, can each be but *one* and unalterable in the sight of God. The one absolute *right*—the charity of God and the sacrifice of Christ—this, from eternity to eternity must be the sole measure of eternal right. But human right or human wrong, that is, the merit or demerit of any action done by any particular man, must be measured, not by that absolute standard, but as a matter relative to his particular circumstances, the state of the age in which he lives, and his own knowledge of right and wrong. For we come into this world with a moral sense ; or, to speak more Christianly, with a conscience. And yet that will tell us but very little distinctly. It tells us broadly that which is right and that which is wrong, so that every child can understand this. That charity and self-denial are right—this we see recognized in almost every nation. But the boundaries of these two—when and how far self-denial is right—what are the bounds of charity—this it is for different circumstances yet to bring out and determine. And so, it will be found that there is a different standard among different nations and in different ages. That, for example, which was the standard among the Israelites in the earlier ages, and before their settlement in Canaan, was very different from the higher and truer standard of right and wrong recognized by the later prophets. And the standard in the third and fourth centuries after Christ was truly and unquestionably an entirely different one from that recognized in the nineteenth century among ourselves. Let me not be mistaken. I do not say that right and wrong are merely conventional, or merely chronological or geographical, or that they vary with latitude and longitude. I do not say that there ever was or ever can be a nation so utterly blinded and perverted in its moral sense as to acknowledge that which is wrong—seen and known to be wrong—as right ; or, on the other hand, to profess that which is seen and understood as right, to be wrong. But what I do say is this : that the form and aspect in which different deeds appear, so vary, that there will be for ever a change and alteration in men's opinions, and that which is really most generous may seem most base, and that which is really most base may appear most generous. So, for example, as I have already said, there are two things universally recognized—recognized as right by every man whose conscience is not absolutely perverted—charity and self-denial. The charity of God, the sacrifice of Christ—these are the two grand, leading principles of the Gospel ; and in some form or other you will find these lying at the roots of every profession and state of feeling in almost every age. But the form in which these appear, will vary with all the gradations which are to be found between the lowest savage state and the highest and most enlightened Christianity.

For example : in ancient Israel the law of love

was expounded thus :—' Thou shalt love thy neighbour, and hate thine enemy.' Among the American Indians and at the Cape, the only homage perchance given to self-denial, was the strange admiration given to that prisoner of war who bore with unflinching fortitude the torture of his country's enemies. In ancient India the same principle was exhibited, but in a more strange and perverted manner. The homage there given to self-denial, self-sacrifice, was this—that the highest form of religion was considered to be that exhibited by the devotee who sat in a tree until the birds had built their nests in his hair—until his nails, like those of the King of Babylon, had grown like birds' talons—until they had grown into his hands—and he became absorbed into the Divinity. We will take another instance, and one better known. In ancient Sparta it was the custom to teach children to steal. And here there would seem to be a contradiction to our proposition—here it would seem as if right and wrong were matters merely conventional ; for surely stealing can never be anything but wrong. But if we look deeper we shall see that there is no contradiction here. It was not stealing which was admired ; the child was punished if the theft was discovered ; but it was the dexterity which was admired, and that because it was a warlike virtue, necessary it may be to a people in continual rivalry with their neighbours. It was not that honesty was despised and dishonesty esteemed, but that honesty and dishonesty were made subordinate to that which appeared to them of higher importance, namely, the duty of concealment. And so we come back to the principle which we laid down at first. In every age, among all nations, the same broad principle remains ; but the application of it varies. The conscience may be ill-informed, and in this sense only are right and wrong conventional— varying with latitude and longitude, depending upon chronology and geography.

The principle laid down by the Apostle Paul is this :—A man will be judged, not by the abstract law of God, not by the rule of absolute right, but much rather by the relative law of conscience. This he states most distinctly—looking at the question on both sides. That which seems to a man to be right is, in a certain sense, right to him ; and that which seems to a man to be wrong, in a certain sense *is* wrong to him. For example : he says in his Epistle to the Romans (v. 14) that ' sin is not imputed when there is no law,' in other words, if a man does not really know a thing to be wrong there is a sense in which, if not right to him, it ceases to be so wrong as it would otherwise be. With respect to the other of these sides, however, the case is still more distinct and plain. Here, in the judgment which the apostle delivers in the parallel chapter of the Epistle to the Romans (the 14th), he says, ' I know, and am persuaded of the Lord Jesus, that there is nothing unclean of itself : but to him that esteemeth anything to be unclean, to him it is unclean.' In other words,

whatever may be the abstract merits of the question—
however in God's jurisprudence any particular act
may stand—to you, thinking it to be wrong, it
manifestly *is* wrong, and your conscience will gather
round it a stain of guilt if you do it. In order to
understand this more fully, let us take a few instances.
There is a difference between *truth* and *veracity*.
Veracity—mere veracity—is a small, poor thing.
Truth is something greater and higher. Veracity is
merely the correspondence between some particular
statement and facts—truth is the correspondence
between a man's whole soul and reality. It is
possible for a man to say that which, unknown to
him, is false ; and yet he may be true : because
if deprived of truth he is deprived of it unwillingly.
It is possible, on the other hand, for a man to utter
veracities, and yet at the very time that he is uttering
those veracities to be false to himself, to his brother,
and to his God. One of the most signal instances
of this is to be seen in the Book of Job. Most of
what Job's friends said to him were veracious state-
ments. Much of what Job said for himself was
unveracious and mistaken. And yet those veracities
of theirs were so torn from all connection with fact
and truth, that they became falsehoods ; and they
were, as has been said, nothing more than ' orthodox
liars ' in the sight of God. On the other hand, Job,
blundering perpetually, and falling into false doctrine,
was yet a true man—searching for and striving after
the truth ; and if deprived of it for a time, deprived

of it with all his heart and soul unwillingly. And therefore it was that at last the Lord appeared out of the whirlwind, to confound the men of mere veracity, and to stand by and support the honour of the heartily true.

Let us apply the principle further. It is a matter of less importance that a man should state true views, than that he should state views truly. We will put this in its strongest form. Unitarianism is false—Trinitarianism is true. But yet, in the sight of God, and with respect to a man's eternal destinies hereafter, it would surely be better for him earnestly, honestly, truly, to hold the doctrines of Unitarianism, than in a cowardly or indifferent spirit, or influenced by authority, or from considerations of interest, or for the sake of lucre, to hold the doctrines of Trinitarianism. For instance :—Not many years ago the Church of Scotland was severed into two great divisions, and gave to this age a marvellous proof that there is still amongst us the power of living faith—when five hundred ministers gave up all that earth holds dear—position in the church they had loved ; friendships and affections formed, and consecrated by long fellowship, in its communion ; and almost their hopes of gaining a livelihood—rather than assert a principle which seemed to them to be a false one. Now, my brethren, surely the question in such a case for us to consider is not this, merely—whether of the two sections held the abstract *right*—held the principle in its integrity—but surely far rather, this : who on either side was true to the light within, true to God, true to the truth as God had revealed it to his soul.

Now it is precisely upon this principle that we are enabled to indulge a Christian hope that many of those who in ancient times were persecutors, for example, may yet be justified at the bar of Christ. Nothing can make persecution right—it is wrong, essentially, eternally wrong in the sight of God. And yet, if a man sincerely and assuredly thinks that Christ has laid upon him a command to persecute with fire and sword, it is surely better that he should, in spite of all feelings of tenderness and compassion, cast aside the dearest affections at the command of his Redeemer, than that he should, in mere laxity and tenderness, turn aside from what seemed to him to be his duty. At least, this appears to be the opinion of the Apostle Paul. He tells us that he was ' a blasphemer and a persecutor and injurious,' that ' he did many things contrary to the name of Jesus of Nazareth,' that ' being exceedingly mad against the disciples, he persecuted them even unto strange cities.' But he tells us further that, ' for this cause he obtained mercy, because he did it ignorantly in unbelief.' Now take a case precisely opposite. In ancient times the Jews did that by which it appeared to them that they would contract defilement and guilt—they spared the lives of the enemies which they had taken in battle. Brethren, the eternal law is, that charity is right, and that law is eternally

281

right which says, 'Thou shalt love thine enemy.' And had the Jews acted upon this principle they would have done well to spare their enemies : but they did it thinking it to be wrong, transgressing that law which commanded them to slay their idolatrous enemies—not from generosity, but in cupidity—not from charity, but from lax zeal. And so doing, the act was altogether wrong.

II. Such is the apostle's exposition of the law of Christian conscience. Let us now, in the second place, consider the applications both of a personal and of a public nature, which arise out of it.

1. The first application is a personal one. It is This :—Do what *seems* to *you* to be right : it is only so that you will at last learn by the grace of God to see clearly what *is* right. A man thinks within himself that it is God's law and God's will that he should act thus and thus. There is nothing possible for us to say—there is no advice for us to give, but this—' You *must* so act.' He is responsible for the opinions he holds, and still more for the way in which he arrived at them—whether in a slothful and selfish, or in an honest and truth-seeking manner ; but being now his soul's convictions, you can give no other law than this—' You must obey your conscience.' For no man's conscience gets so seared by doing what is wrong unknowingly, as by doing that which appears to be wrong to his conscience. The Jews' consciences did not get seared by their slaying the Canaanites, but they did become seared

by their failing to do what appeared to them to be right. Therefore, woe to you if you do what others think right, instead of obeying the dictates of your own conscience ; woe to you if you allow authority, or prescription, or fashion, or influence, or any other human thing, to interfere with that awful and sacred thing—responsibility. ' Every man,' said the apostle, ' must give an account of himself to God.'

2. The second application of this principle has reference to others. No doubt to the large, free, enlightened mind of the Apostle Paul, all these scruples and superstitions must have seemed mean, trivial, and small indeed. It was a matter to him of far less importance that truth should be *established* than that it should be arrived at truly—a matter of far less importance, even, that right should be done, than that right should be done rightly. Conscience was far more sacred to him than even liberty—it was to him a prerogative far more precious to assert the rights of Christian conscience, than to magnify the privileges of Christian liberty. The scruple may be small and foolish, but it may be impossible to uproot the scruple without tearing up the feeling of the sanctity of conscience, and of reverence to the law of God, associated with this scruple. And therefore the Apostle Paul counsels these men to abridge their Christian liberty, and not to eat of those things which had been sacrificed to idols, but to have compassion upon the scruples of their weaker brethren. And this, for two reasons. The first of these is a mere

reason of Christian feeling. It might cause exquisite pain to sensitive minds to see those things which appeared to them to be wrong, done by Christian brethren. Now, you may take a parallel case. It may be, if you will, mere superstition to bow at the name of Jesus. It may be, and no doubt is, founded upon a mistaken interpretation of that passage in the Epistle to the Philippians (ii. 10), which says that ' at the name of Jesus every knee shall bow.' But there are many congregations in which this has been the long-established rule, and there are many Christians who would feel pained to see such a practice discontinued—as if it implied a declension from the reverence due to ' that name which is above every name.' Now, what in this case is the Christian duty ? Is it this—to stand upon our Christian liberty ? Or is it not rather this—to comply with a prejudice which is manifestly a harmless one, rather than give pain to a Christian brother ? Take another case. It may be a mistaken scruple ; but there is no doubt that it causes much pain to many Christians to see a carriage used on the Lord's day. But you, with higher views of the spirit of Christianity, who know that ' the Sabbath was made for man, and not man for the Sabbath '—who can enter more deeply into the truth taught by our blessed Lord, that every day is to be dedicated to Him and con- secrated to His service—upon the high principle of Christian liberty you can use your carriage—you can exercise your liberty. But if there are Christian brethren to whom this would give pain—then I humbly ask you, but most earnestly—What is the duty here? Is it not this—to abridge your Christian liberty—and to go through rain, and mud, and snow, rather than give pain to one Christian conscience? To give one more instance. The words, and garb, and customs of that sect of Christians called Quakers may be formal enough; founded, no doubt, as in the former case, upon a mistaken interpretation of a passage in the Bible. But they are at least harmless; and have long been associated with the simplicity, and benevolence, and Christian humbleness of this body of Christians—the followers of one who, three hundred years ago, set out upon the glorious enterprise of making all men friends. Now, would it be Christian, or would it not rather be something more than unchristian—would it not be gross rudeness and coarse unfeelingness to treat such words, and habits, and customs, with anything but respect and reverence?

Further: the apostle enjoined this duty upon the Corinthian converts, of abridging their Christian liberty, not merely because it might give pain to indulge it, but also because it might even lead their brethren into sin. For, if any man should eat of the flesh offered to an idol, feeling himself justified by his conscience, it were well: but if any man, overborne by authority or interest, were to do this, not according to conscience, but against it, there would be a distinct and direct act of disobedience—a conflict between his sense of right and the gratification of his appetites, or the power of influence ; and then his compliance would as much damage his conscience and moral sense as if the act had been wrong in itself.

Now, in the personal application of these remarks, there are three things which we have to say. The first is this :—Distinguish, I pray you, between this tenderness for a brother's conscience and mere time-serving. This same apostle whom we here see so gracefully giving way upon the ground of expediency when Christian principles were left entire, was the same who stood firm and strong as a rock when any-thing was demanded which trenched upon Christian principle. When some required, as a matter of necessity for salvation, that these converts should be circumcised, the apostle says—' To whom we gave place by subjection, no, not for an hour ! ' It was not indifference—it was not cowardice—it was not the mere love of peace, purchased by the sacrifice of principle, that prompted this counsel—but it was Christian love—that delicate and Christian love which dreads to tamper with the sanctities of a brother's conscience.

2. The second thing we have to say is this—that this abridgement of their liberty is a duty more especially incumbent upon all who are possessed of influence. There are some men, happily for themselves we may say, who are so insignificant that they can take their course quietly in the valleys of life, and who can exercise the fullest Christian liberty without giving pain to others. But it is the price which all

who are possessed of influence must pay—that their acts must be measured, not in themselves, but according to their influence on others. So, my Christian brethren, to bring this matter home to every-day experience and common life, if the landlord uses his authority and influence to induce his tenant to vote against his conscience, it may be he has secured one voice to the principle which is right, or, at all events, to that which seemed to him to be right : but he has gained that single voice at the sacrifice and expense of a brother's soul. Or, again— if for the sake of ensuring personal politeness and attention, the rich man puts a gratuity into the hand of a servant of some company which has forbidden him to receive it, he gains the attention, he ensures the politeness, but he gains it at the sacrifice and expense of a man and a Christian brother.

3. The last remark which we have to make is this : —How possible it is to mix together the vigour of a masculine and manly intellect with the tenderness and charity which is taught by the gospel of Christ ! No man ever breathed so freely when on earth the air and atmosphere of heaven as the Apostle Paul—no man ever soared so high above all prejudices, narrowness, littlenesses, scruples, as he : and yet no man ever bound himself as Paul bound himself to the ignorance, the scruples, the prejudices of his brethren. So that what in other cases was infirmity, imbecility, and superstition, gathered round it in his case the pure high spirit of Christian charity and Christian

delicacy. And now, out of the writings, and sayings, and deeds of those who loudly proclaim the 'rights of man' and the 'rights of liberty,' match us if you can with one sentence so sublime, so noble, one that will so stand at the bar of God hereafter, as this single, glorious sentence of his, in which he asserts the rights of Christian conscience above the claims of Christian liberty—' Wherefore, if meat make my brother to offend, I will eat no flesh while the world standeth, lest I make my brother to offend.'

The Immutability of God

CHARLES HADDON SPURGEON

✝

*I am the Lord, I change not ; therefore ye sons of Jacob
are not consumed.*—MAL. iii. 6.

THE IMMUTABILITY OF GOD

CHARLES HADDON SPURGEON

IT has been said by some one that 'the proper study of mankind is man.' I will not oppose the idea, but I believe it is equally true that the proper study of God's elect is God; the proper study of a Christian is the Godhead. The highest science, the loftiest speculation, the mightiest philosophy, which can ever engage the attention of a child of God, is the name, the nature, the person, the work, the doings, and the existence of the great God whom he calls his Father. There is something exceedingly improving to the mind in a contemplation of the Divinity. It is a subject so vast, that all our thoughts are lost in its immensity; so deep, that our pride is drowned in its infinity. Other subjects we can compass and grapple with; in them we feel a kind of self-content, and go our way with the thought, 'Behold, I am wise.' But when we come to this master-science, finding that our plumb-line cannot sound its depth, and that our eagle eye cannot see its height, we turn away with the thought, that vain man would be wise, but he is like a wild ass's colt; and with the solemn exclamation, ' I am but of yesterday, and know nothing.' No subject of contemplation will tend more to humble the mind, than thoughts of God. We shall be obliged to feel

> ' Great God, how infinite art thou,
> What worthless worms are we ! '

But while the subject *humbles* the mind it also *expands* it. He who often thinks of God, will have a larger mind than the man who simply plods around this narrow globe. He may be a naturalist, boasting of his ability to dissect a beetle, anatomize a fly, or arrange insects and animals in classes with well-nigh unutterable names; he may be a geologist, able to discourse of the megatherium and the plesiosaurus, and all kinds of extinct animals; he may imagine that his science, whatever it is, ennobles and enlarges his mind. I dare say it does, but after all, the most excellent study for expanding the soul is the science of Christ, and him crucified, and the knowledge of the Godhead in the glorious Trinity. Nothing will so enlarge the intellect, nothing so magnify the whole soul of man, as a devout, earnest, continued investigation of the great subject of the Deity. And, whilst humbling and expanding, this subject is eminently *consolatory*. Oh, there is, in contemplating Christ, a balm for every wound; in musing on the Father, there is a quietus for every grief; and in the influence of the Holy Ghost, there is a balsam for every sore. Would you lose your sorrows? Would you drown your cares? Then go, plunge yourself in the Godhead's deepest sea; be lost in his immensity; and you shall come forth as from a couch of rest, refreshed and invigorated. I know nothing which can so comfort the soul; so calm the swelling billows of grief and sorrow; so speak peace to the winds of trial, as a devout musing upon the subject of the Godhead. It is to that subject that I invite you this morning. We shall present you with one view of it—that is *the immutability of the glorious Jehovah*. ' I am,' says my text, ' Jehovah ' (for so it should be translated)—' I am Jehovah, I change not; therefore ye sons of Jacob are not consumed.'

There are three things this morning. First of all, *an unchanging God*; secondly, *the persons who derive benefit from this glorious attribute*, ' the sons of Jacob '; and thirdly, *the benefit they so derive*, they ' are not consumed.' We address ourselves to these points.

I. First of all, we have set before us the doctrine of THE IMMUTABILITY OF GOD. ' I am God, I change not.' Here I shall attempt to expound, or rather to enlarge the thought, and then afterwards to bring a few arguments to prove its truth.

1. I shall offer some exposition of my text, by first saying, that God is Jehovah, and he changes not *in his essence*. We cannot tell you what Godhead is. We do not know what substance that is which we call God. It is an existence, it is a being; but what that is, we know not. However, whatever it

is, we call it his essence, and that essence never changes. The substance of mortal things is ever changing. The mountains, with their snow-white crowns, doff their old diadems in summer, in rivers trickling down their sides, while the storm cloud gives them another coronation ; the ocean, with its mighty floods, loses its water when the sunbeams kiss the waves, and snatch them in mists to heaven ; even the sun himself requires fresh fuel from the hand of the Infinite Almighty, to replenish his ever-burning furnace. All creatures change. Man, especially as to his body, is always undergoing revolution. Very probably there is not a single particle in my body which was in it a few years ago. This frame has been worn away by activity, its atoms have been removed by friction, fresh particles of matter have in the meantime constantly accrued to my body, and so it has been replenished ; but its substance is altered. The fabric of which this world is made is ever passing away ; like a stream of water, drops are running away and others are following after, keeping the river still full, but always changing in its elements. But God is perpetually the same. He is not composed of any substance or material, but is spirit—pure, essential, and ethereal spirit— and therefore he is immutable. He remains ever-lastingly the same. There are no furrows on his eternal brow. No age hath palsied him ; no years have marked him with the mementoes of their flight ; he sees ages pass, but with him it is ever *now*. He is

the great I AM—the Great Unchangeable. Mark
you, his essence did not undergo a change when it
became united with the manhood. When Christ in
past years did gird himself with mortal clay, the
essence of his divinity was not changed ; flesh did
not become God, nor did God become flesh by a
real actual change of nature ; the two were united
in hypostatical union, but the Godhead was still the
same. It was the same when he was a babe in the
manger, as it was when he stretched the curtains of
heaven ; it was the same God that hung upon the
cross, and whose blood flowed down in a purple
river, the self-same God that holds the world upon
his everlasting shoulders, and bears in his hands the
keys of death and hell. He never has been changed
in his essence, not even by his incarnation ; he
remains everlastingly, eternally, the one unchanging
God, the Father of lights, with whom there is no
variableness, neither the shadow of a change.

2. He changes not *in his attributes*. Whatever the
attributes of God were of old, that they are now ;
and of each of them we may sing, ' As it was in the
beginning, is now, and ever shall be, world without
end, Amen.' Was he *powerful* ? Was he the mighty
God when he spake the world out of the womb of
non-existence ? Was he the Omnipotent when he
piled the mountains and scooped out the hollow
places for the rolling deep ? Yes, he was powerful
then, and his arm is unpalsied now ; he is the same
giant in his might ; the sap of his nourishment is

undried, and the strength of his soul stands the same for ever. Was he wise when he constituted this mighty globe, when he laid the foundations of the universe ? Had he *wisdom* when he planned the way of our salvation, and when from all eternity he marked out his awful plans ? Yes, and he is wise now ; he is not less skilful, he has not less knowledge ; his eye which seeth all things is undimmed ; his ear, which heareth all the cries, sighs, sobs, and groans of his people, is not rendered heavy by the years which he hath heard their prayers. He is unchanged in his wisdom ; he knows as much now as ever, neither more nor less ; he has the same consummate skill, and the same infinite forecastings. He is unchanged, blessed be his name, in his *justice*. Just and holy was he in the past ; just and holy is he now. He is unchanged in his *truth* ; he has promised, and he brings it to pass ; he hath said it, and it shall be done. He varies not in the *goodness*, and generosity and benevolence of his nature. He is not become an Almighty tyrant, whereas he was once an Almighty Father ; but his strong love stands like a granite rock, unmoved by the hurricanes of our iniquity. And blessed be his dear name, he is unchanged in his *love*. When he first wrote the covenant, how full his heart was with affection to his people. He knew that his Son must die to ratify the articles of that agreement. He knew right well that he must rend his best beloved from his bowels, and send him down to earth to bleed and die. He did not hesitate to sign that mighty covenant ; nor did he shun its fulfilment. He loves as much now as he did then ; and when suns shall cease to shine, and moons to show their feeble light, he still shall love on for ever and for ever. Take any one attribute of God, and I will write *semper idem* on it (always the same). Take any one thing you can say of God now, and it may be said not only in the dark past, but in the bright future it shall always remain the same : 'I am Jehovah, I change not.'

3. Then again, God changes not in his *plans*. That man began to build, but was not able to finish, and therefore he changed his plan, as every wise man would do in such a case ; he built upon a smaller foundation and commenced again. But has it ever been said that God began to build but was not able to finish ? Nay. When he hath boundless stores at his command, and when his own right hand would create worlds as numerous as drops of morning dew, shall he ever stay because he has not power ? and reverse, or alter, or disarrange his plan, because he cannot carry it out ? 'But,' say some, 'perhaps God never had a plan.' Do you think God is more foolish than yourself then, sir ? Do you go to work without a plan ? 'No,' say you. 'I have always a scheme.' So has God. Every man has his plan, and God has a plan too. God is a master-mind ; he arranged everything in his gigantic intellect long before he did it ; and once having settled it, mark you, he never alters it. 'This shall be done,' saith

he, and the iron hand of destiny marks it down, and it is brought to pass. 'This is my purpose,' and it stands, nor can earth or hell alter it. 'This is my decree,' saith he, promulgate it, angels; rend it down from the gate of heaven, ye devils; but ye cannot alter the decree; it shall be done. God altereth not his plans; why should he? He is Almighty, and therefore can perform his pleasure. Why should he? He is the All-wise, and therefore cannot have planned wrongly. Why should he? He is the everlasting God, and therefore cannot die before his plan is accomplished. Why should he change? Ye worthless atoms of existence, ephemera of the day! ye creeping insects upon this bay-leaf of existence! ye may change *your* plans, but he shall never, never change *his*. Then has he told me that his plan is to save me? If so, I am safe.

> ' My name from the palms of his hands
>   Eternity will not erase ;
>   Impress'd on his heart it remains,
>   In marks of indelible grace.'

4. Yet again, God is unchanging in his *promises*. Ah! we love to speak about the sweet promises of God; but if we could ever suppose that one of them could be changed, we would not talk anything more about them. If I thought that the notes of the Bank of England could not be cashed next week, I should decline to take them; and if I thought that God's promises would never be fulfilled—if I thought

that God would see it right to alter some word in
his promises—farewell Scriptures ! I want immutable
things ; and I find that I have immutable promises
when I turn to the Bible : for, ' by two immutable
things in which it is impossible for God to lie,' he
hath signed, confirmed, and sealed every promise of
his. The gospel is not ' yea and nay,' it is not
promising to-day, and denying to-morrow ; but the
gospel is ' yea, yea,' to the glory of God. Believer !
there was a delightful promise which you had
yesterday ; and this morning when you turned to
the Bible the promise was not sweet. Do you know
why ? Do you think the promise had changed ? Ah,
no ! *You* changed ; that is where the matter lies.
You had been eating some of the grapes of Sodom,
and your mouth was thereby put out of taste, and
you could not detect the sweetness. But there was
the same honey there, depend upon it, the same
preciousness. ' Oh ! ' says one child of God, ' I had
built my house firmly once upon some stable
promises ; there came a wind, and I said, O Lord,
I am cast down and I shall be lost.' Oh ! the
promises were not cast down ; the foundations were
not removed ; it was your little ' wood, hay, stubble '
hut, that you had been building. It was that which
fell down. *You* have been shaken *on* the rock, not
the rock *under* you. But let me tell you what is the
best way of living in the world. I have heard that a
gentleman said to a negro, ' I can't think how it is
you are always so happy in the Lord, and I am often

downcast.' ' Why, Massa,' said he, ' I throw myself flat down on the promise—there I lie ; you stand on your promise—you have a little to do with it, and down you go when the wind comes, and then you cry, ' Oh ! I am down ' ; whereas I go flat on the promise at once, and that is why I fear no fall.' Then let us always say, ' Lord, there is the promise ; it is thy business to fulfil it.' Down I go on the promise flat ! no standing up for me. That is where you should go—prostrate on the promise ; and remember, every promise is a rock, an unchanging thing. There-fore, at his feet cast yourself, and rest there for ever.

5. But now comes one jarring note to spoil the theme. To some of you God is unchanging in his *threatenings.* If every promise stands fast and every oath of the covenant is fulfilled, hark thee, sinner ! —mark the word—hear the death-knell of thy carnal hopes ; see the funeral of thy fleshly trustings. Every threatening of God, as well as every promise, shall be fulfilled. Talk of decrees ! I will tell you of a decree : ' He that believeth not shall be damned.' That is a decree, and a statute that can never change. Be as good as you please, be as moral as you can, be as honest as you will, walk as uprightly as you may,— there stands the unchangeable threatening : ' He that believeth not shall be damned.' What sayest thou to that, moralist ? Oh, thou wishest thou couldst alter it, and say, ' He that does not live a holy life shall be damned.' That will be true ; but it does not say so. It says, ' He that believeth not.' Here

is the stone of stumbling, and the rock of offence ; but you cannot alter it. You must believe or be damned, saith the Bible ; and mark, that threat of God is as unchangeable as God himself. And when a thousand years of hell's torments shall have passed away, you shall look on high, and see written in burning letters of fire, ' He that believeth not *shall* be damned.' ' But, Lord, I *am* damned.' Nevertheless it says ' *shall be* ' still. And when a million ages have rolled away, and you are exhausted by your pains and agonies, you shall turn up your eye and still read ' SHALL BE DAMNED,' unchanged, unaltered. And when you shall have thought that eternity must have spun out its last thread—that every particle of that which we call eternity must have run out, you shall still see it written up there, ' SHALL BE DAMNED.' O terrific thought ! How dare I utter it ? But I must. Ye must be warned, sirs, ' lest ye also come into this place of torment.' Ye must be told rough things ; for if God's gospel is not a rough thing, the law is a rough thing ; Mount Sinai is a rough thing. Woe unto the watchman that warns not the ungodly ! God is unchanging in his threatenings. Beware, O sinner, for ' it is a fearful thing to fall into the hands of the living God.'

6. We must just hint at one thought before we pass away, and that is—God is unchanging in the *objects of his love*—not only in his love, but in the *objects* of it.

> ' If ever it should come to pass,
>   That sheep of Christ might fall away,
> My fickle, feeble soul, alas,
>   Would fall a thousand times a day.'

If one dear saint of God had perished, so might all ;
if one of the covenant ones be lost, so may all be ;
and then there is no gospel promise true, but the
Bible is a lie, and there is nothing in it worth my
acceptance. I will be an infidel at once, when I can
believe that a saint of God can ever fall finally. If
God hath loved me once, then he will love me for
ever.

> ' Did Jesus once upon me shine,
>   Then Jesus is for ever mine.'

The objects of everlasting love never change. Those
whom God hath called, he will justify ; whom he
has justified, he will sanctify ; and whom he sanctifies,
he will glorify.

1. Having thus taken a great deal too much time,
perhaps, in simply expanding the thought of an
unchanging God, I will now try to prove that *he is*
unchangeable. I am not much of an argumentative
preacher, but one argument that I will mention is
this : *the very existence and being of a God seem to me to
imply immutability.* Let me think a moment. There
is a God ; this God rules and governs all things ;
this God fashioned the world ; he upholds and
maintains it. What kind of being must he be ? It
does strike me that you cannot think of a changeable

301

God. I conceive that the thought is so repugnant to common sense, that if you for one moment think of a changing God, the words seem to clash, and you are obliged to say, ' Then he must be a kind of man,' and get a Mormonite idea of God. I imagine it is impossible to conceive of a changing God ; it is so to me. Others may be capable of such an idea, but I could not entertain it. I could no more think of a changing God, than I could of a round square, or any other absurdity. The thing seems so contrary, that I am obliged, when once I say God, to include the idea of an unchanging being.

2. Well, I think that one argument will be enough, but another good argument may be found in the fact of *God's perfection*. I believe God to be a perfect being. Now, if he is a perfect being, he cannot change. Do you not see this ? Suppose I am perfect to-day, if it were possible for me to change, should I be perfect to-morrow after the alteration ? If I changed, I must either change from a good state to a better—and then if I could get better, I could not be perfect *now*—or else from a better state to a worse—and if I were worse, I should not be perfect *then*. If I am perfect, I cannot be altered without being imperfect. If I am perfect to-day, I must keep the same to-morrow if I am to be perfect then. So, if God is perfect, he must be the same ; for change would imply imperfection now, or imperfection then.

3. Again, there is the fact of *God's infinity*, which

puts change out of the question. God is an infinite being. What do you mean by that? There is no man who can tell you what he means by an infinite being. But there cannot be two infinities. If one thing is infinite, there is no room for anything else; for infinite means all. It means not bounded, not finite, having no end. Well, there cannot be two infinities. If God is infinite to-day, and then should change and be infinite to-morrow, there would be two infinities. But that cannot be. Suppose he is infinite and then changes, he must become finite, and could not be God; either he is finite to-day and finite to-morrow, or infinite to-day and finite to-morrow, or finite to-day and infinite to-morrow— all of which suppositions are equally absurd. The fact of his being an infinite being at once quashes the thought of his being a changeable being. Infinity has written on its very brow the word ' immutability.'

4. But then, dear friends, let us look at *the past* : and there we shall gather some proofs of God's immutable nature. ' Hath he spoken, and hath he not done it? Hath he sworn, and hath it not come to pass?' Can it not be said of Jehovah, ' He hath done all his will, and he hath accomplished all his purpose?' Turn ye to Philistia; ask where she is. God said, ' Howl, Ashdod, and ye gates of Gaza, for ye shall fall'; and where are they? Where is Edom? Ask Petra and its ruined walls. Will they not echo back the truth that God hath said, ' Edom shall be a prey, and shall be destroyed?' Where

is Babel, and where Nineveh? Where Moab and
where Ammon? Where are the nations God hath
said he would destroy? Hath he not uprooted them
and cast out the remembrance of them from the
earth? And hath God cast off his people? Hath
he once been unmindful of his promise? Hath he
once broken his oath and covenant, or once departed
from his plan? Ah! no. Point to one instance in
history where God has changed! Ye cannot, sirs;
for throughout all history there stands the fact, that
God has been immutable in his purposes. Methinks
I hear some one say, 'I can remember one passage
in Scripture where God changed!' And so did I
think once. The case I mean, is that of the death
of Hezekiah. Isaiah came in and said, 'Hezekiah,
you must die, your disease is incurable, set your
house in order.' He turned his face to the wall and
began to pray; and before Isaiah was in the outer
court, he was told to go back and say, 'Thou shalt
live fifteen years more.' You may think that proves
that God changes; but really I cannot see in it the
slightest proof in the world. How do you know
that God did not know that? Oh! but God did
know it; he knew that Hezekiah would live. Then
he did not change, for if he knew that, how could
he change? That is what I want to know. But do
you know one little thing?—that Hezekiah's son,
Manasseh, was not born at that time, and that had
Hezekiah died, there would have been no Manasseh,
and no Josiah, and no Christ, because Christ came

from that very line. You will find that Manasseh was twelve years old when his father died ; so that he must have been born three years after this. And do you not believe that God decreed the birth of Manasseh, and foreknew it ? Certainly. Then he decreed that Isaiah should go and tell Hezekiah that his disease was incurable, and then say also in the same breath, ' But I will cure it, and thou shalt live.' He said that to stir up Hezekiah to prayer. He spoke, in the first place, as a man. ' According to all human probability your disease is incurable, and you must die.' Then he waited till Hezekiah prayed ; then came a little ' but ' at the end of the sentence. Isaiah had not finished the sentence. He said, ' You must put your house in order, for there is no human cure ; but ' (and then he walked out. Hezekiah prayed a little, and then he came in again, and said) ' *But* I will heal thee.' Where is there any contradiction there, except in the brain of those who fight against the Lord, and wish to make him a changeable being ?

II. Now secondly, let me say a word on THE PERSONS TO WHOM THIS UNCHANGEABLE GOD IS A BENEFIT. ' I am God, I change not ; therefore ye sons of Jacob are not consumed.' Now, who are ' the sons of Jacob,' who can rejoice in an immutable God ?

1. First, they are the *sons of God's election* ; for it is written, ' Jacob have I loved, and Esau have I hated, the children being not yet born, neither having

done good nor evil.' It was written, ' The elder
shall serve the younger.' ' The sons of Jacob.'

> ' Are the sons of God's election,
>> Who through sovereign grace believe ;
> By eternal destination
>> Grace and glory they receive.'

God's elect are here meant by ' the sons of Jacob,'—
those whom he foreknew and fore-ordained to
everlasting salvation.

2. By ' the sons of Jacob ' are meant, in the second
place, *persons who enjoy peculiar rights and titles.* Jacob,
you know, had no rights by birth ; but he soon
acquired them. He changed a mess of pottage with
his brother Esau, and thus gained the birthright. I
do not justify the means ; but he did also obtain the
blessing, and so acquired peculiar rights. By ' the
sons of Jacob ' here are meant persons who have
peculiar rights and titles. Unto them that believe,
he hath given the right and power to become sons of
God. They have an interest in the blood of Christ ;
they have a right to ' enter in through the gates into
the city ' ; they have a title to eternal honours ; they
have a promise to everlasting glory ; they have a
right to call themselves sons of God. Oh ! there
are peculiar rights and privileges belonging to the
' sons of Jacob.'

3. But, then next, these ' sons of Jacob ' were
men of peculiar manifestations. Jacob had had peculiar

manifestations from his God, and thus he was highly honoured. Once at night-time he lay down and slept; he had the hedges for his curtains, the sky for his canopy, a stone for his pillow, and the earth for his bed. Oh! then he had a peculiar manifestation. There was a ladder, and he saw the angels of God ascending and descending. He thus had a manifestation of Christ Jesus, as the ladder which reaches from earth to heaven, up and down which angels came to bring us mercies. Then what a manifestation there was at Mahanaim, when the angels of God met him; and again at Peniel, when he wrestled with God, and saw him face to face. Those were peculiar manifestations; and this passage refers to those who, like Jacob, have had peculiar manifestations.

Now, then, how many of you have had personal manifestations? 'Oh!' you say 'that is enthusiasm; that is fanaticism.' Well, it is a blessed enthusiasm, too, for the sons of Jacob have had peculiar manifestations. They have talked with God as a man talketh with his friend; they have whispered in the ear of Jehovah; Christ hath been with them to sup with them, and they with Christ; and the Holy Spirit hath shone into their souls with such a mighty radiance, that they could not doubt about special manifestations. The 'sons of Jacob' are the men who enjoy these manifestations.

4. Then again, they are *men of peculiar trials*. Ah! poor Jacob! I should not choose Jacob's lot if I

had not the prospect of Jacob's blessing ; for a hard lot his was. He had to run away from his father's house to Laban's ; and then that surly old Laban cheated him all the years he was there—cheated him of his wife, cheated him in his wages, cheated him in his flocks, and cheated him all through the story. By-and-by he had to run away from Laban, who pursued and overtook him. Next came Esau with four hundred men to cut him up root and branch. Then there was a season of prayer, and afterwards he wrestled, and had to go all his life with his thigh out of joint. But a little further on, Rachel, his dear beloved, died. Then his daughter Dinah is led astray, and the sons murder the Shechemites. Anon there is dear Joseph sold into Egypt, and a famine comes. Then Reuben goes up to his couch and pollutes it ; Judah commits incest with his own daughter-in-law ; and all his sons become a plague to him. At last Benjamin is taken away, and the old man, almost broken-hearted, cries, ' Joseph is not, and Simeon is not, and ye will take Benjamin away.' Never was man more tried than Jacob all through the one sin of cheating his brother. All through his life God chastised him. But I believe there are many who can sympathize with dear old Jacob. They have had to pass through trials very much like his. Well, cross-bearers ! God says, ' I change not ; therefore ye sons of Jacob are not consumed.' Poor tried souls ! ye are not consumed because of the unchanging nature of your God. Now do not get fretting, and say, with the self-conceit of misery, 'I am the man who hath seen affliction.' Why, 'the Man of Sorrows' was afflicted more than you; Jesus was indeed a mourner. You only see the skirts of the garments of affliction. You never have trials like his. You do not understand what troubles mean; you have hardly sipped the cup of trouble; you have only had a drop or two, but Jesus drunk the dregs. Fear not, saith God, 'I am the Lord, I change not; therefore ye sons of Jacob,' men of peculiar trials, 'are not consumed.'

5. Then one more thought about who are the 'sons of Jacob,' for I should like you to find out whether you are 'sons of Jacob,' yourselves. They are *men of peculiar character*; for though there were some things about Jacob's character which we cannot commend, there are one or two things which God commends. There was Jacob's faith, by which Jacob had his name written amongst the mighty worthies who obtained not the promises on earth, but shall obtain them in heaven. Are you men of faith, beloved? Do you know what it is to walk by faith, to live by faith, to get your temporary food by faith, to live on spiritual manna—all by faith? Is faith the rule of your life? if so, you are the 'sons of Jacob.'

Then Jacob was a man of prayer—a man who wrestled, and groaned, and prayed. There is a man up yonder who never prayed this morning, before coming up to the house of God. Ah! you poor heathen, don't you pray? No! he says, 'I never thought of such a thing; for years I have not prayed.' Well, I hope you may before you die. Live and die without prayer, and you will pray long enough when you get to hell. There is a woman: she did not pray this morning; she was so busy sending her children to the Sunday-school, she had no time to pray. No time to pray? Had you time to dress? There is a time for every purpose under heaven, and if you had purposed to pray, you would have prayed. Sons of God cannot live without prayer. They are wrestling Jacobs. They are men in whom the Holy Ghost so works, that they can no more live without prayer than I can live without breathing. They must pray. Sirs, mark you, if you are living without prayer, you are living without Christ; and dying like that, your portion will be in the lake which burneth with fire. God redeem you, God rescue you from such a lot! But you who are 'the sons of Jacob,' take comfort, for God is immutable.

III. Thirdly, I can only say a word about the other point—THE BENEFIT WHICH THESE 'SONS OF JACOB' RECEIVE FROM AN UNCHANGING GOD. 'Therefore ye sons of Jacob are not consumed.' 'Consumed?' How? how can man be consumed? Why, there are two ways. We might have been consumed in hell. If God had been a changing God, the 'sons of Jacob' here this morning might have been consumed in hell; but for God's unchanging love I should have been a

faggot in the fire. But there is a way of being consumed in this world; there is such a thing as being
condemned before you die—'condemned already';
there is such a thing as being alive, and yet being
absolutely dead. We might have been left to our
own devices; and then where should we have been
now? Revelling with the drunkard, blaspheming
Almighty God. Oh! had he left you, dearly beloved,
had he been a changing God, ye had been amongst
the filthiest of the filthy, and the vilest of the vile.
Cannot you remember in your life, seasons similar to
those I have felt? I have gone right to the edge of
sin; some strong temptation has taken hold of both
my arms, so that I could not wrestle with it. I have
been pulled along, dragged as by an awful satanic
power to the very edge of some horrid precipice. I
have looked down, down, down, and seen my portion;
I quivered on the brink of ruin. I have been horrified,
as, with my hair upright, I have thought of the sin
I was about to commit, the horrible pit into which
I was about to fall. A strong arm hath saved me.
I have started back and cried, O God! could I have
gone so near sin, and yet come back again? Could I
have walked right up to the furnace and not fallen
down, like Nebuchadnezzar's strong men, devoured
by the very heat? Oh! is it possible I should be
here this morning, when I think of the sins I have
committed, and the crimes which have crossed my
wicked imagination? Yes, I am here, unconsumed,
because the Lord changes not. Oh! if he had

changed, we should have been consumed in a dozen ways ; if the Lord had changed, you and I should have been consumed by ourselves ; for after all, Mr. Self is the worst enemy a Christian has. We should have proved suicides to our own souls ; we should have mixed the cup of poison for our own spirits, if the Lord had not been an unchanging God, and dashed the cup out of our hands when we were about to drink it. Then we should have been consumed by God himself if he had not been a changeless God. We call God a Father ; but there is not a father in this world who would not have killed all his children long ago, so provoked would he have been with them, if he had been half as much troubled as God has been with his family. He has the most troublesome family in the whole world—unbelieving, ungrateful, disobedient, forgetful, rebellious, wandering, murmuring, and stiff-necked. Well it is that he is longsuffering, or else he would have taken not only the rod, but the sword to some of us long ago. But there was nothing in us to love at first, so there cannot be less now. John Newton used to tell a whimsical story, and laugh at it too, of a good woman who said in order to prove the doctrine of Election, ' Ah ! sir, the Lord must have loved me before I was born, or else he would not have seen anything in me to love afterwards.' I am sure it is true in my case, and true in respect to most of God's people ; for there is little to love in them after they are born, that if he had not loved them before then, he would have seen no reason to choose them after ; but since he loved them without works, he loves them without works still ; since their good works did not win his affection, bad works cannot sever that affection ; since their righteousness did not bind his love to them, so their wickedness cannot snap the golden links. He loved them out of pure sovereign grace, and he will love them still. But we should have been consumed by the devil, and by our enemies—consumed by the world, consumed by our sins, by our trials, and in a hundred other ways, if God had ever changed.

Well, now, time fails us, and I can say but little. I have only just cursorily touched on the text. I now hand it to you. May the Lord help you ' sons of Jacob ' to take home this portion of meat ; digest it well, and feed upon it. May the Holy Ghost sweetly apply the glorious things that are written ! And may you have ' a feast of fat things, of wines on the lees well refined ! ' Remember God is the same, whatever is removed. Your friends may be dis-affected, your ministers may be taken away, everything may change ; but God does not. Your brethren may change and cast out your name as vile ; but God will love you still. Let your station in life change, and your property be gone ; let your whole life be shaken, and you become weak and sickly ; let every-thing flee away—there is one place where change cannot put his finger ; there is one name on which mutability can never be written ; there is one heart which can never alter; that heart is God's—that name Love.

> ' Trust him, he will ne'er deceive you,
>   Though you hardly of him deem ;
> He will never, never leave you,
>   Nor will let you quite leave him.'

The Ethics of Forgiveness

WILLIAM CONNOR MAGEE

✝

Forgive us our debts, as we forgive our debtors.
—MATT. vi. 12.

THE ETHICS OF FORGIVENESS

WILLIAM CONNOR MAGEE

He who taught us these words of prayer is more than a Teacher. He is more to us even than a Divinely inspired Teacher. We regard him—in common with the whole Catholic Church throughout the world—as our Divine Redeemer and Mediator. We believe that he has come amongst us not only to tell us that we may approach the Father, but to make that approach possible. We believe that he has come not only to reveal to us the way to God, but to be himself that way. ' I am the way, the truth, and the life : no man cometh unto the Father but by me ' ; and, ' Whatsoever ye shall ask the Father in my name, he will give it you,' is the teaching of our Lord, and has ever been the teaching of his Church. She has ever placed him where he has claimed to place himself—between the human soul and God. The doctrines of atonement and of intercession are inseparably connected in all her teaching with the great central doctrine of her creeds, the incarnation of our Lord Jesus Christ. Christianity does not call upon us to believe in the stupendous mystery of

THE ETHICS OF FORGIVENESS

God becoming man without an adequate reason for it. The publication of a new religion would be no such adequate reason—that might need an inspired teacher, not an incarnate one ; it might need a Moses, but it could not need a Christ. The Church, therefore, when she proclaims her belief in the incarnate Christ, expresses her belief in the doctrine that God is in Christ reconciling the world unto himself, and not imputing their trespasses unto men. She declares that it was ' for us men, and for our salvation,' that ' the very God of very God ' came down from heaven, ' and was incarnate, by the Holy Ghost, of the Virgin Mary.' Incarnation and Atonement. Inseparably these two ideas are linked together. Take away one, and the other will not long remain. Take away the belief in the divine and eternal Christ, and we lose the true ground of the Atonement. Take away the idea of the Atonement, and we lose the only sufficient reason for the Incarnation. The time would then come, and come very soon too—as many of our modern seers are anticipating—when men would no more care to discuss the nature of Christ, than they care now to discuss the nature of Socrates ; and in truth it would concern them very little more to do so.

Closely related, however, as these two great Christian dogmas are, they are rejected by modern thought on very different grounds. One of them, the Incarnation, is rejected as impossible ; the other, the Atonement, as immoral. Incarnation is a miracle, and modern science, we are told, pronounces miracles to be impossibilities. Of course for those who so think there is an end of the question. It would be absurd to expect them to discuss the moral bearings of an event which, they believe, not only never happened—but never could possibly have happened. Not so, however, as regards the doctrine of the Atonement ; that is impugned not on scientific but on moral grounds. It rests, we are told, upon a low and unworthy conception of the moral nature of God. To say to him, that he requires, as the condition of his forgiving our offences against him, the sufferings and the mediation of Christ, is to represent him, it is urged, as less merciful and forgiving than we expect an ordinarily good man to be. A good man is, before all things, merciful and compassionate ; he forgives fully and freely those who offend against him, and the more fully and freely he does so, the better and the nobler man we hold him to be. How then can we suppose the perfectly good God to be less placable than we feel that we ourselves ought to be ? Why should we go out of our way to mar the grand and noble conception of a Loving Father of all men freely forgiving the sins of his penitent children, by adding to it the barbarous and superfluous idea of an apparatus of sacrifice and intercession, which are somehow to induce him to be merciful ? What is this doctrine of atonement and mediation but a survival of the old pagan conception of angry deities, whose grudges against offending mortals could only be satisfied by suffering, or bribed away by gifts? Why, we are asked, if you cannot advance with modern thought, will you not at least go back to the older and better teachings contained in your own Bibles? Why cannot you rise to the sublime ideas of the Hebrew prophets and psalmists, who, in their protest against the sanguinary ritual of their day, could take their place beside altars smoking with the blood of innocent victims, and proclaim a God who ' desired not sacrifice,' else would they give it him—a God who could not ' eat the flesh of bulls, or drink the blood of goats '—a ' merciful and compassionate ' Lord, who only bids the wicked ' forsake his way and the unrighteous man his thoughts ' in order that he may ' abundantly pardon him ' ? If Christianity had only caught the true spirit of such teaching as this, it could never, we are told, have retained in its creed the pagan old-world notions of sacrifice and atonement that now disfigure it.

Now such an objection as this, resting as it does on moral grounds, is a far more formidable one than any of those that rest on merely scientific grounds.

These, even if now unanswered, need not be regarded as unanswerable. Science has not yet spoken her last word. It is quite conceivable, at least, that some new scientific discovery might place science on the side of miracles. Not so with the decisions of the conscience ; these are final and unanswerable, and the grounds for them lie fully within the ken of all

men. Once prove that the God of the Christian is
not a perfectly moral being and he ceases for ever to
be our God, our supreme good. Most carefully
therefore does it behove us to weigh any objection
against our creed which appeals, as this does, to the
moral sense of mankind.

And in dealing with this objection let us above all
things do so honestly. Let us attempt no theological
evasion of the difficulty ; let us not lie for God ; let
us not say, for instance, that we cannot argue from
the analogy of human forgiveness to the Divine
forgiveness, because God's ways are not as our ways,
nor his thoughts as our thoughts. That may be true
in some respects, but it is not true as regards this.
It never can be true when God uses the same word to
describe his ways and our ways ; for if, in that case,
our ways are not like his, then the words which he
uses are not so much misleading as utterly unmeaning.
They are merely arbitrary and unintelligible symbols.
If the words forgiveness, mercy, compassion, do not
mean, when they are used respecting God, at least as
much as they mean when we use them respecting
men, they have for us no meaning whatever. Let us
be sure then that—when we are told that God loves,
that God forgives—we are to understand by those
words just what we understand by the words man
loves and man forgives. Other and deeper meanings
they may have, but at least they have this. Let us
then, as I have said, deal honestly with this difficulty ;
let us see whether, taking it for granted, as we are

bound to do, that there is a real analogy between Divine and human forgiveness, we may not find in that very fact good reasons for our belief in the doctrines of Atonement and Mediation. Let us see, in one word, what is the true idea of human forgiveness, by what difficulties, if any, it is beset, and what are the laws which really govern it amongst us men as we try to forgive our debtors, and then let us proceed to see how these laws apply to God's forgiveness of our debts to him.

I. In the first place, then, let us see what is our Lord's teaching concerning the forgiveness of sin, in the words ' Forgive us our debts.' What does our Lord here teach us respecting sin ? He teaches us that it is something that needs forgiveness. That is to say, that it is not merely a disease to be healed, nor an imperfection to be remedied, but an offence, and an offence entailing a penalty, which cleaves to the offender as a debt, until it is paid or remitted, cleaves to the debtor. And he further teaches us that for this debt there is a possibility of remission— the forgiveness of sin being analogous to the remitting of a debt. That is to say, our Lord gives us this as the popular, ordinary, human idea of forgiveness ; namely that it is the letting off to a man of the debt he owes ; it is the putting of him by the creditor, as far as he can do so, in the position he would have occupied, if he had never contracted that debt. Briefly then our Lord's statement is this : first, in all

sin there is guilt ; secondly, a debt of penalty for
that guilt ; thirdly, the possibility of the remission
of that debt ; and fourthly, a close analogy between
the remission of that debt by God to us and our
remission of debt to one another. The question then
at once arises for us, How far and under what conditions is it possible for us to forgive our human
debtors, those who have offended against us ? Let
us study this question first in its simplest form. Let
us suppose an offence committed between two equals,
who have no other relation between them than that
of their common humanity. Let us suppose that
any one of us has been so unfortunate as to have
committed some wrong against a fellow man. The
instant you do so that man becomes, in spite of you
and of himself, your creditor. You are his debtor
for two great debts—the debt of penitence, and the
debt of reparation. You feel that you ought to be
sorry for what you have done and that you ought to
make amends for it ; and you owe this twofold debt
by virtue of a law which either he or you may set in
motion, but which neither he nor you can restrain—
the law of your own conscience. There is that within
you which, when you have injured another, claims
from you at once the double penalty of repentance
and restitution. There is within your own breast
an advocate of the man you have wronged. There is
a voice within you crying against you to the throne
of God, the judge of all, and if you cannot agree with
this your adversary, it gives you over to the tormentors,

remorse and shame, that abide in your own heart and will not depart from it, until you have paid the uttermost farthing of such debt. Such is the nature of the case as it arises instantly and necessarily between your human creditor and you, his debtor. Now it is quite true that your creditor may remit this debt to you and you hold it to be the noblest charity if he does. He forgives you then, we will suppose, fully, freely, unconditionally, lovingly, nobly if you will— what then ? Is all the penalty remitted ? Have you escaped all the punishment of your act ? He has forgiven you ; but have you for that reason forgiven yourself ? Nay, is it not the very fullness and freeness of his forgiveness that is heaping coals of fire upon your head, kindled and fanned into a flame by the very breath of his compassion ? We know that it is so, and that in all finer and better natures it is ever most keenly so. Already, then, we have discovered this—that there is, even between equals, no complete remission of penalty for sins possible. Behind the figure of the creditor—even of the forgiving creditor— there already begins to rise up and to project itself upon our path the shadow of law—which, because it is law, is pitiless, unforgiving and inevitable. Even in this simplest and most rudimentary case of forgiveness, there is therefore no absolute remission.

Now let us take one step further—let us pass on to the case of social forgiveness. Let us suppose the wrong-doing has had spectators. Let us imagine ourselves spectators of some cruel martyrdom and that we hear the martyr, with his dying breath, breathing out his forgiveness and blessing on his murderers. They are fully forgiven by him. Would any one of us feel disposed to take up that legacy of forgiveness and to repeat the blessings we had just heard the martyr pronounce upon his tormentors? Should we not rather feel our hearts stirred with the deepest and most righteous indignation, calling, in a very passion of justice, for vengeance upon his murderers? Should we not feel that the forgiveness he pronounced, though in him it were the highest expression of charity, were in us the lowest and most exquisite baseness? Should we not feel that we could never know rest nor peace until we had avenged him of his cruel wrong and that this would not, after all, be revenge, but righteous judgment? But why is it that we could not forgive such a wrong upon another? Just for this reason: It is his wrong and not ours. We are not, and cannot be, merely spectators of this crime; we are, by the very fact of our being members of a society to which he and we belong, its judges, and we feel that, as such, we have no right to remit its just and righteous penalty.

But there is another reason why we cannot forgive this offence. The instinct of self-preservation is strong in our hearts, as it is strong in the heart of society. Society cannot afford to suffer martyrdom; still less to court or submit to martyrdom. The myriad interests that are entrusted to its guardianship would be sacrificed if it were to allow of crime with impunity. A society founded upon the basis of pure benevolence and universal forgiveness of offences, could not hold together for a single day. Society dare not, cannot, forgive its debtors. You see, we have now advanced a step further ; we have still the debtor to be paid, and we have still the law and the person or persons who are to enforce it ; but you observe to what small dimensions the personal element in this equation has already shrunk. You see how large already looms the idea of law ; you see that the debtor and creditor are already becoming, both together, debtors to a great, inexorable law which binds the creditor to punish and the debtor to suffer. In this aspect then we begin to see that human forgiveness is not such an easy thing. The criminal may have little to fear from the anger of his judge who is enforcing the law, but for that very reason he has nothing to hope from his compassion ; for law because it is passionless must also be pitiless.

And now let us take one step, and only one step further. Let us suppose the offender to have paid the penalty for his offence ; such penalty at least as he can pay and yet live. He has given, we will suppose, in the way of reparation, all that society claimed from him ; but is he thereupon freed from all further penalty ? Does society that forgives him give him back what it was compelled to take from him ? Can it give him back the happy promise of his now wasted life ? Can it bring him back the

opportunities, the vanished hopes and joys, of the
past? Can it restore to him the honour, love,
obedience, that once were his? Can it compel men
who shrink from his contact as they would from that
of a leper,—to give him the honoured place, as a guest
at life's banquet, which he might once have been
entitled to? Can it cut off the consequences of his
sin, as it continues to injure others by its example or
its consequences, and so goes on multiplying and
replenishing the earth with its evil progeny, while
the birth of every fresh sin that springs from its
parentage multiplies guilt against him? Can it do
this? Never. And thus we see how, by the very
condition of things in which we exist, we reach at
last a point at which the personal elements of pity,
compassion, justice even, seem to vanish altogether,
and man is face to face with a stern, impersonal,
mechanical, universal law, certain as death, merciless
as the grave, which proclaims that for sin in such a
constitution of things there is no possibility of remission. So, then, human forgiveness is not quite so
simple; the idea of human remission of all penalty for
an offence is not quite so natural and easily intelligible
as it appears to us when we first hear these words,
'Forgive us our debts, as we forgive our debtors.'

II. Let us proceed, in the next place, to apply these
analogies to the doctrine of Divine forgiveness of
sin—to the case of the Divine Creditor and the
human debtor. God will forgive us, we assume, as

easily as we forgive our fellow-men. But we have seen that the idea of the complete forgiveness of a fellow-man is only conceivable on one condition— namely, that we completely isolate the debtor and the creditor from all other relations and regard them only as equals, one of whom has done the other wrong ; and yet is it not clear that that is just the very position in which God can never stand towards any one of us ? If there be one thing more certain than another, it is that by no ill deed of ours can we wrong or injure God. Our ' goodness extendeth not unto him ' ; how then can our wrong-doing hurt him ? Can he be supposed to cherish against us a passion of revenge which needs to be appeased ? Can he keep a debtor and creditor account of vengeance with us the creatures of his breath ? It is impossible. The one relation in which we cannot stand towards him is that of an equal dealing with an equal for offence and wrong-doing. But as regards our other relations, what is he to us ? He is the ruler of all the complex system of society in which wrong produces endless debt. He is the judge of that vast multitude of human beings whom he has created, every one of whom has a claim at his judgment-seat against his fellow who has wronged him. There has been no drop of blood that has ever been shed on this earth, since the blood of righteous Abel, that has not cried for justice to the Lord God of Sabaoth. There has been no groan of suffering, there has been no complaint of wrong, there has been no cry from wounded and agonized hearts, smarting under the wrongful dealing of fellow-men, that has not echoed in the ears of our righteous Ruler ; and if the earthly judges he appoints bear not the sword in vain, how can we suppose that this eternal appeal to him of suffering humanity for justice shall be in vain ? Is it alleged however that God forgives, not of mere compassion, but on condition of penitence, and that he who truly repents has thereby satisfied his requirements and may therefore claim to be forgiven, while he who remains impenitent does so of his own act and choice and therefore deserves his fate ? Surely the answer to this is obvious. The refusal of the impenitent to repent is either a sin or a defect : either he will not or he cannot repent. If it is a sin, why not forgive it like any other sin ? If it is only an imperfection, why punish it at all ? Is it not clear moreover that if God forgives only the penitent he is less compassionate than he bids us to be when he tells us to forgive all our debtors whether penitent or impenitent ? And if, on the other hand, penitence is a necessarily antecedent condition of forgiveness, arising out of the nature and constitution of things, then equally so, for aught we can tell, may atonement and mediation be such conditions too. Then there is this further difficulty. God is the author of that very constitution of things, of those inexorable and unalterable laws, under which, as we have seen, forgiveness is scarcely conceivable. Are we to suppose, then, that he will deflect these laws at our bidding ?

328

Are we to suppose that those mills of God, which grind so slowly, and yet so surely that nothing escapes them, will cease to revolve at our prayer, after he has once set them in motion ? Can we suppose that the great red presses of the vintage of the wrath of God, that are ever crushing out the lees of sin and judgment, will be stayed because some trembling penitent asks that they may be stayed ? Where is there room then in the moral constitution of the universe, ruled by a Moral Ruler, for forgiveness of sin ? Where then can we find place for the idea of the easily-forgiving God, whom at first we pictured to ourselves ? Do you not see that all this magniloquent and windy talk about a merciful and compassionate God, so facile and easy in his forgiveness, is a mere conception of modern Theism ; that it is, after all, the poorest and lowest idea we can form of God ; that it does not rise above the low thought of the savage, which pictures him merely as an angry and offended man ? Rise but one degree above that, rise up in your thought to the idea of him as the Judge of all the earth ; rise one degree higher to the idea of him as the Author and Controller of the moral universe, and all this talk about easy, good-natured forgiveness vanishes in your nobler but more awful conception of God, as the cloud-wreath vanishes at the rising of the sun.

III. And now let us see what hope there remains, on the gospel theory, as to the possibility of forgiveness. What does our reason tell us as we contemplate the moral constitution of the world? Does it not tell us that unless the moral laws which surround us can be suspended, or turned aside by some power or other, there is no hope of forgiveness? And what do we call the act that suspends and turns aside some natural law by the introduction of a supernatural law? We call it a miracle; and miracle is a word which modern science forbids religion to speak. But a miracle, nevertheless, is needed in order to the possibility of forgiveness. It needs as much a moral miracle on the part of God to save the sinner from the consequence of his sin, when he transgresses the moral laws of the universe, as it would need a physical miracle to snatch him from a storm or an earthquake. The one is as necessary as the other, and the one is as easy or as difficult to imagine as the other. We thank God then for the fact which Revelation assures us of, that, to accomplish our forgiveness, a miracle has been wrought. What is it that Revelation teaches us concerning the atonement and mediation of Christ but this, that taken together with his incarnation they make the divinest and mightiest of all miracles; that the God who has framed this inexorable moral constitution of things has entered this natural world, where men sin and suffer by the operation of its terrible laws, has taken unto himself their sinful and suffering humanity and made it, in the person of his Son, a new and perfect humanity? Does it not tell us how that Son has

died and risen supernaturally to heaven, and that, in
so doing, he has miraculously created for every one
who dies and rises with him, a supernatural kingdom
in which they who enter it are no longer under the
law of sin and its natural penalty, death, but are
under the supernatural law of forgiveness and of
everlasting life ? Yes, that is what Revelation reveals
to us. It reveals to us the miracle of a new world,
even the kingdom of the Lord Jesus Christ, into
which we may flee and be delivered from the operation of those terrible laws of natural justice and
punishment from which otherwise there is no escape.
And is this, then, to be regarded as a barbarous
addition to the idea of forgiveness ? Is this thought
of the mediation and atonement of Christ a different
system of forgiveness from that described in the
story of the Prodigal Son, for instance ; or is it not
rather the eternal basis and ground which makes that
story, with its eternal promise of free forgiveness,
possible and true ? Picture to yourselves, for one
moment, the Hebrew prophet standing, as we supposed him to stand, by the altar of sacrifice and
declaring his conviction that sacrifice was worthless
and that God would accept the offering of his contrite
heart instead—imagine that on the heart of that
prophet, thus glowing with love and hope, there had
descended some pitiless demonstration of the intellect
which had clearly proved to him that there is logically
no possibility of his contrite heart being thus accepted
of God. Imagine—as this conclusion fell coldly and

chillingly upon his heart, quenching all its hopeful
aspirations as some driving storm of rain might have
quenched the brands upon the altar of his sacrifice
—imagine that to such a heart, chilled with terror
by the proof that for sin there is no remission, there
had come the revelation which Christ has given to
us in himself and in his gospel ; that there had
come the assurance that the forgiveness, which his
intellect so clearly demonstrated to him could not
be had without miracle, was to be had by miracle ;
that there had come to him this revelation of marvel
and of mystery, ' God so loved the world, that he
gave his only begotten Son, that whosoever believeth
in him should not perish, but have everlasting life ' ;
can we suppose that such a revelation would have
been an obstacle and a hindrance, instead of an
encouragement and a help to him, in drawing nearer
to his Father ? True, there might still, there would
still have remained for his intellect the question as
to the how and the why of this great miracle of
forgiveness ; but such intellectual difficulties would
no more have hindered his approach, and need no
more hinder our approach, to the mercy-seat of the
Father, than the unfathomed depths of the waters
that rose right and left for the passage of the
ransomed people of God could have hindered their
march between their dark walls on to the safe shore
beyond.

And now let us gather up the lessons which this
great word of our Lord's concerning God's and man's

forgiveness has brought before us. We gather them up finally thus :

To the contemplation of the idea of man's forgiveness there come three different parts of his nature—the conscience, which tells him of a certain and just penalty for sin ; the understanding, which tells him either that there is no such thing as sin at all, or that for sin there can be no forgiveness ; and the heart that cries, as the human heart will ever cry, ' O God, be merciful to me, a sinner.' And there is one doctrine and one only—there is one revelation and one only that meets and answers and justifies itself as it meets and answers these three utterances from the troubled nature of man. To the conscience which speaks of penalty Revelation answers, ' There is a penalty,' and deepens the voice of conscience by telling us that this penalty is due for an offence against the Father of our spirits and that it consists in our being cast out of the supernatural kingdom of forgiveness into the natural kingdom of justice and punishment. To the reason which demands a miracle as the essential condition of forgiveness, it speaks of the greatest of miracles, the Incarnation and the Atonement. And then to the heart, the trembling, anxious, yearning human heart, which still refuses to believe that man is a mere victim of necessity, and persists, in spite of all demonstration to the contrary, in believing that there is a compassionate heart in him who has fashioned us after his image—it gives the answer—' Verily there is forgiveness with him.

Rise up and go to your Father that he may forgive ! '
And so we clasp our gospel to our heart ; so we kneel
before the Divine presence of the Son of God and
Son of Man, in whom we see incarnated the miraculous
might of Divine love and Divine forgiveness ; so,
spite of all intellectual hindrances that would bar us
from our Father's presence, spite of the remorsefulness
of our memory, spite of the terrible accusations of
our conscience, we can still say—' I WILL arise and
go to my Father, and I WILL say to him, Father, I
have sinned against heaven and before thee.' Such
is our gospel ! a gospel of hope and of joy ; and we
hold it to be not only more hopeful, but more truly
scientific—more in accordance with the facts of man's
nature and of his place in God's world—than is that
other gospel of fate and of despair that is offered in
its stead.

Criticism and the Resurrection
HENRY SCOTT HOLLAND

✠

If Christ be not raised, your faith is vain.—1 COR. xv. 17.

CRITICISM AND THE RESURRECTION

HENRY SCOTT HOLLAND

THE voice that speaks gives no uncertain sound.
It is firm and vigorous enough. Here, certainly,
is no shadowy outline, no vague emotion, no loose
and unsteady outbreak of mystic rapture. The issue
is stated in most sharp and decisive directness. No
disguises, no veiling modifications, slip between. We
still feel the shock of the startling frankness, of the
unhesitating decision with which the voice rings out
its terrible alternative : ' If Christ be not raised,
your faith is vain ; ye are yet in your sins.'

Yet it is the earliest voice with which we find
Christianity speaking.

Let us remember where we are as we listen. We
are back behind the written Gospels ; earlier by
some interval than the first three ; earlier by thirty
or forty years than the date at which tradition
supposes the fourth to have been written. We are
listening to the first voice with which historic
Christianity speaks through recorded documents. As
soon as we find it at all, it is speaking in these
decisive tones.

Nor are those tones, when you hear them, new. St. Paul is appealing to a familiar truth, long held, long known to his hearers ; appealing to it as the established fact on the strength of which they had been converted ; appealing to it as to solid and undeniable ground, beyond all dispute or denial, on which he or they can take their stand in the new argument that has sprung up as to their own bodily resurrection. For already men were hotly discussing whether their own resurrection would be an actual, concrete, physical act in time, or an ideal, spiritual truth ; so early, so rapidly were disputes at work which forced them to consider the value of facts. And it is in order to bring into the discussion some point of indisputable, unwavering certainty, wherewith to dispel the mists of a shifty, idealistic treatment, to touch solid ground, to have grip on something that could not fail, or totter, or crumble, or dissolve, that St. Paul takes his hearers back to the very ground of all belief, to the first premise of all discussion, to the core and heart of the Creed, ' the Resurrection of Christ.' Here, at any rate, he argues, is no idea, but a fact ; no spiritual ideal, but an actual event. And just by the force of this, its concrete, solid, matter-of-fact actuality, it determined the question of their own resurrection in a sense directly contrary to that of the idealists.

' If Christ be not raised, your faith is vain.' That earliest voice of the faith rings still in our ears, with its loud challenge to face, and measure, without flinching, the great issue that is ever before us. How sharply it pierces our souls, as we stand puzzled and distressed by all the sore anxieties which beset the discussions which have busied themselves with the origin of the Christian religion !

We have been flooded with new knowledge of the old days in which St. Paul uttered this bold cry—new knowledge of the ways, and habits, and conditions of those earliest believers—ways and manners so strangely different from our own. We have gained knowledge, too, of a multitude of other religions, with their strange parallels to our own, yet with dissimilarities at least as strange. And, moreover, we have been given, too, not new knowledge only, but new methods of knowledge—methods, before unused, of comparison, of insight, of discovery, of judgment. And all these we cannot but bring to bear upon the matter of our belief ; for we carry them with us, as we read the old books with minds already trained to appreciate the new materials and exercise the new methods.

Now, this being our case, it is of vital importance that we should make absolutely clear to ourselves what is the exact problem which the origin of the Christian religion offers to our critical examination. What is its distinctive characteristic ?

It has, no doubt, many resemblances to the rise and movement of other religions ; and these resemblances will permit of comparisons, and of speculative reconstructions, and of suggestive probabilities, by which we may pass across from the critical study of these other faiths to throw light on dark places in our Christian record.

But these cannot ever carry us, of course, to the heart of the problem ; for that must always lie, not in the resemblances, but in the differences.

The crucial task of all criticism is to fix on, to signalize, to detach, to notify, to examine that particular and unique point in a religious creed which marks it off from all other facts of the same general kind.

And this it will accomplish by searching for its main, and central, and peculiar thought. What, it will ask, is the idea which originates and animates this or that religion ? What is the formation and conception at its root ? What is it which accounts for its existence, and justifies its ardour, and prompts its primary activity, and moulds its growth, and directs its work, and distributes its limits and parts into their due place and proportion ? What is that without which the religion under review is a mere medley of those spiritual elements which are the common matter of all religion ? What is that by recognition of which all these common elements cease to be a chaos of possibilities, and come together into a distinct and forcible reality, rationally coherent, emphatically and vividly distinguishable from all other spiritual phenomena ? On that point in each religion, whatever it be, criticism must relentlessly fasten ; round and about that point it must loyally circle.

Now, there can be no doubt at all where the central, and originative, and distinctive point is to be discovered in the Christian religion. St. Paul has signalized it for us, once for all, in words that can never lose their tingling force of truth : ' If Christ be not raised, your faith is vain ; ye are yet in your sins.'

Belief in the Resurrection is the root of Christianity. Everything runs back to it ; everything flows from it.

For if there is any matter about which the Christian documents give authentic and unqualified evidence, it is to the absolute insufficiency of our Lord's earthly Life and Mission to give the momentum which originates a new religion. Nothing had been done at all, antecedent to the bitter end on Calvary, which can the least account for the after-consequences. Nothing stable had been rooted and established ; nothing had taken more than the most tentative shape. There was no decisive and intelligible idea planted in the hearts of men with effective precision. Much had been dimly hinted ; much seemed about to be happening. There was great talk of a kingdom that should come, of a Church that should be built. But nothing did come ; nothing had happened ; the kingdom did not appear ; the Church was not built. Now and again the hopes of the crowd rose, and they cried aloud on some happy day, ' Surely it has come ! Is not this Messias ? Was it ever seen in this fashion ? We will make Him a king.' And then He Himself deserted their hopes, defeated their longings, broke up their zeal. He fled ; He hid ; He scattered them. He set Himself to bewilder, to baffle, to disappoint them. Nothing came of it all, but a sense of splendid promise that yet never took shape or substance. No wonder that John the Baptist himself wondered at the fruitless postponement, and sent to inquire from the prison whether the kingdom was ever going to show itself.

And the few, the very few who clung in dumb loyalty to the Person Whose sublimity held them in thrall, they could not tell what it was that they had been called to receive, what thrones they were to occupy. They were lost in the enigmas offered them. Now they seemed to have got the thread of the Master's teaching ; now it was lost. Whenever they thought that they understood, they found themselves the more perplexed. If they tried to make assertions of their own, they only blundered. Always, to the very last, they remained below the level of understanding demanded of them ; without any fixed or intelligible creed to proclaim ; possessed of nothing, that did not shatter into hopeless fragments under the shock of the naked Cross.

What a brief moment, after all, it had been ! The broken bits of a couple of years were all that they had to look back upon ; only a dozen or eighteen months of closer intercourse with the Master ; and these months had been months not of gathering success or of steadying assurance, but months of failure, months of confusion, months of ever-darkening disaster,—months of flight or of desertion, of dreary pause, of disheartening suspense, of blind mis-understanding, of impenetrable mystery.

Once, and once only, had there looked like a gleam of daylight. Once, and once only, had there begun to be a moment at which the Master seemed to be preparing to act. Once, and once only, did He set Himself to own the Messiahship in a way that was comprehensible, and the dawn of the kingdom, so long deferred, seemed at last to draw near. It was that day for which He had prepared so carefully and so long, when He bade them bring the ass, and lay their garments upon it, and He rode as the prophetic King into Zion, and beneath Him were the strewn robes for royal feet, and about Him the waving palms of triumph, and before Him and behind Him the multitudes who shouted the Messianic greeting, ' Hosanna in the highest.' At last it was to begin ; at last He would act. Ah ! the despair ! He takes but the first step, and, lo ! it is His last. He makes but one challenge, and, lo ! all is over. Down breaks the storm that had hung so long in black menace above Him. Down it sweeps—the roaring storm of hate, of cruelty, of rage. Down it sweeps, in one overpowering rush, and He is gone—gone ! without a struggle, without an effort ; gone ! broken, defeated, crushed ; not a shred remains of that fair promise ; not a wreck is left behind of that shattered vision of hope and joy. All have forsaken and fled. No power breaks forth to shield Him ; no refuge opens to Him a door of escape ! His enemies have Him, hold Him, work their will on Him ; they taunt Him for His impotence, without fear, without rebuke. Ah ! well indeed if a horrible dread can be shut off from those stricken souls—a dread lest it is not only the work of man, but even the very curse of God Himself, that has fallen upon Him who was hung on a tree !

Surely, in our love for the sweet memory of our Lord on earth, a Man among us so tender and so strong, we forget how it would have looked if nothing had ever followed ; how terribly short and swift its passage ; how miserably small and unstable its actual achievement ! Nothing in that brief Life, taken by itself, can account for Christian belief in the Lord, or for the creation of the Church. It is the Resurrection which alone gave constructive force to the Life that lay behind it. A vision of unutterable beauty, indeed, that Life would ever have been ; but a vision that came and passed and vanished before men's bewildered eyes had had time to secure it, or their hearts to apprehend what was there, for a fleeting moment, in their midst. A few deep, incomparable words would have lingered about their memories ; a few marvellous hours would never be forgotten, in which the sick had known the touch of power, and the sorrow and sighing had all fled away. Some dozen men and a knot of women would have nursed a sick and fading secret, low buried in their silent souls—the secret of what once they had believed, as, in the tranced mystery of one historic evening, they had heard a quiet voice in their ears, which said, ' Take, eat ; this is My Body. Do this in memory of Me.'

But the very memory of this high promise, of this passing vision, far from driving them forth on a victorious mission, could but break their hearts with despair, as they recalled the utter and absolute ruin in which it had been so swiftly engulfed !

In the Resurrection, it was not the Lord only who was raised from the dead. His Life on earth rose with Him ; it was lifted up into its real light. That which had been but a suggestion, but a fragment, but a disappointment, but a failure, won, for the first time, out of the Resurrection a force that gave it significance and cohesion. The Spirit had come upon it ; and that which had been all partial and piecemeal now first cohered together and showed itself substantial, and became a living thing. Now, first, the promises gained reality, the vision became concrete, the symbolic acts obtained solid footing, the deep words lost their shadowy, intangible remoteness. A light flashed back from Easter morning, and poured daylight on what had been so dark. The events that had seemed so tangled and confusing now strung themselves together on a clear and comprehensible method. The cue was given, and all was intelligible.

We feel this in every word and motion of the

Apostles. Every one knows, every one is astonished at, the entire change that has passed over them, between the Gospels and the earliest records stored for us in the Acts. The naturalness and yet the strangeness of this change is one of our most convincing evidences of the reliability of those primitive documents. The simplicity with which the transformation is told is overpoweringly persuasive. The men who, in the Gospels, never can win possession of the Lord's mind, never are level with His meaning, never can follow His transitions, never can ask a question without blundering, never can get sure of themselves, never can help misunderstanding His teaching, never can get out of themselves, never can understand to what the Master is leading them, not though He take them aside and prepare them, and shut Himself up with them to school them, and reiterates again and again the deliberate purpose with which He goes to Jerusalem ; the men who were still, after all the miracles, without understanding— having ears, heard not ; the men who understood none of those things, but the ' saying was hid from them, and they perceived not the things that were said ' ; the men who could despair, as Thomas, or could forsake, as all did, or could deny, as Peter ;— these very men are found, in the first chapter of the Acts, in complete and secure possession of the Lord's secret. Yet they are the same men, with the same characters. Who can mistake them ? John, with the same impressive silence ; Cephas, with the same

impetuous speech. Not that they are not still liable
to painful complexities and struggles in the working
out of the details ; but of one thing they can never
doubt again—they can never doubt what the significance was of the days during which they had walked
and talked with Jesus during His sojourn on earth.
That, from beginning to end—from the baptism of
John until the day of His taking up—has become a
consistent, coherent, intelligible act, complete and
whole in all its parts. All the words that ever fell
from the Master's lips—words which then baffled,
startled, upset, distressed them—are now to them
clear and limpid as the day. Every syllable carries
its meaning with it. And His mind is laid open to
them, and they apprehend it with easy freedom ; and
their faith in Him is no longer a blind, personal
fascination—' Lord, to whom shall we go ? ' it is
rational, articulate, and secure. It knows its grounds ;
it puts out its reasons ; it handles its premises ; it is
in possession of itself ; it is beyond the possibility
of mistrust or of bewilderment. They speak with
emphasis, these men who once babbled like children ;
they act with decision, these who once were so
incapable of initiation.

It is the Resurrection that has made the change.
The Resurrection is the core of truth, in which and
to which all adheres. It is to them the animating,
formative fact, which interprets, which justifies,
which supports, which quickens the fabric of faith
and life. They have got fast hold of the key ;

therefore every lock once closed flies open. They stand in the light, and therefore stumble no longer. The path is clear, the gate is open ; they know the road they have to travel. ' Lord,' they had once cried in blank bewilderment, ' we know not whither Thou goest, and how can we know the way ? ' Now they understand whither He has gone ; and therefore He Who is the Resurrection is at once made to them also the Way, the Truth, and the Life.

What, then, are we to say of a school of criticism, with which we are all familiar, which finds a parallel to our Gospel in the stories of those heroes whose lives were so momentous and so masterful, that when they died no one could believe them to have passed away ? So long and so deeply had they occupied the world's drama, that the stage seemed empty without their name to fill it ; so that still men's eyes looked for some mysterious return of the vanished presence, and still their ears listened for some rallying cry from the voice that could not, surely, be lost for ever.

Such dim hopes, faintly lingering round the grave of some King Arthur, or some Frederic Barbarossa, or even round the close of some hideous nightmare, like the tyranny of Nero, embody and symbolize nothing else but the profound impression which their actual lives had built up and established, until it had become a part of the common material of general human existence. The violence of its swift removal leaves behind a vague pain, a hunger, a

347

wonder; and these may relieve themselves in mythical expectations, in mysterious rumours, in haunting hopes, which gather like clouds at evening round a setting sun, and glow with ravishing splendour for some rare moments, before they pale and scatter under the chill wind of that night which is ever creeping up, ashen and relentless. So a 'cloud of myth' may hang loose about the hero's vanishing; but the myth is meaningless and unintelligible, except as a reflex of the impressiveness and solidity and importance of the real life lived. It witnesses to that and to nothing else. Strip it away and the life remains, real, comprehensible, valid.

But what fragment of parallel is there here to the Gospel? With our Lord, it is not the *life* which makes the supernatural myth intelligible, but it is the supernatural act which alone makes the life intelligible. Here is no faint supernatural vapour, embosoming a solid core of impressive natural incidents. Nay! It is the human career which is so fragmentary, so slight, so rapid, so fleeting, until it is endowed with a solid core of substance and force by the marvel of the Resurrection. On that it stands; it is compacted by that; out from the Resurrection flows the energy which carries the entire story. It is by believing in His Resurrection that His followers first lay hold of the real significance of His Life on earth, and first acquire that vital faith in Him which constitutes them missionaries of a new religion.

This is the cardinal fact that has got to be accounted for ; and any criticism, therefore—let us be sure of this—which fails to find the primary and original and formative germ of Christianity in the belief in a risen Lord ; any criticism which supposes that this belief can be treated as surplusage, as a merely decorative accident, as the mythical expression of enthusiasm, as comparable to the apotheosis of a great heroic figure ; any criticism which begins by omitting all this supernaturalism from its calculation, and sets itself to extract from the human story which preceded the death the motive impulse which explains the faith ;—any such criticism as this, whatever form it take, has missed the point which it undertakes to explain. It has slipped off the scientific track ; it has ruled itself out of court. Far from offering us a solution, it simply fails to meet the issue, for it omits the one essential and characteristic and vital element in the problem to be solved.

Beloved, we may discard such criticism from discussion, yet it remains that there are anxious and serious questions which beset and oppress us. Yes, indeed ; and, before attempting to answer them, let us remember the one condition under which they can be met and solved. We shall only obtain certainty and conviction when the Resurrection has become to our own little human story on earth that which, in its unique degree, it was to the earthly Life of the Lord. It must become, I mean, the key which makes our own story intelligible, the cypher by which all its strange hieroglyphics can be read off and interpreted.

We who so sorely pine for certainty of intellectual conviction have to ask ourselves, first of all, whether we are living a life which demands our resurrection in Christ as its only adequate solution—a life which is built on that sure hope, formed after that pattern, sustained by that underlying motive ; a life which schools itself after the discipline which such a hope imposes, curbing and bending the motives and the desires of the flesh so that they seek not here, in this fair but unstable earth, their home and their promise, but are ever forcing themselves into the strong current of the victorious will, which sets from within our deepest selves towards that far land of purity and peace to which He calls us, Who is the Living One, and was dead, and, behold, He is alive for evermore ! Unless this be, in some measure, true, we could not know the certainty of Christ's Resurrection.

Let us ask ourselves, Would your ways and mine be incomprehensible if there were no Resurrection ? Have we any motives, real and animating, on which we act, which would be meaningless if we were not to rise again ? Have we made any moral venture on the strength of this assurance ? Is there anything on earth that we could rightly have and hold, and yet which we deny ourselves, and treat as worthless, in face of the far more glorious hope set before us ? Are we so living that we should be of all men most miserable, most silly, most befooled, if Christ be not raised?

Ah! surely, it is not only intellectually that the Resurrection is apt to seem to us but a piece of poetical supernaturalism, a decorative incident which satisfies the dramatic feelings, a relief to our artistic judgment, a beautiful picture at the end of an heroic life, an imaginative and visionary ideal. It too often is no more than this to our faith, as well as to our reason. It hangs loosely outside our own spiritual story. It lays no direct or forcible pressure upon our moral life. Yet, so long as this is so, we have not touched the core of the Christian verity. We have not reached its central secret, its heart of grace. Believe me, our faith is still vain if the Resurrection of Christ be not the fount and spring of all our living, the support on which we buttress ourselves, round which the very fibres of the practical will wind and bind themselves. Our faith is vain if the risen Christ be not the rock on which we rest, the refuge which we hide, the fortress out of which we descend to walk the lower ways of earth. Our faith is vain if the risen Christ be not the formative or energetic reality which dominates our mind, and regulates our practice, and shapes our thought, and controls our passions, and organizes our motives, and builds our character, and lays hands upon our entire self, to rule, possess, transform it. That is the 'Christian life'; that is 'walking in Christ.' St. Paul can acknowledge nothing short of that.

Alas! it is because this resurrection life is so little true of us that our faith is so empty and vain. Alas! it is because this walking in the risen Christ is so strange to us, so unattempted, that we find ourselves lightly discussing the possibility of omitting the Resurrection from our Creed, and yet remaining as good Christians as we were before. God grant us grace, in fear and humiliation, to measure, by our readiness to imagine this possibility, the terrible interval which separates our practical daily religion from the faith of that Apostle who cried aloud to his trembling converts, 'If Christ be not raised, your faith is vain ; ye are yet in your sins.'

The Psalm of the Two Ways

G. CAMPBELL MORGAN

✦

Jehovah knoweth the way of the righteous ; but the way of the ungodly shall perish.—Ps. i. 6.

THE PSALM OF THE TWO WAYS

G. CAMPBELL MORGAN

Dr. THIRTLE has called this 'The Psalm of the Two Ways,' and the aptness of that designation is patent. This final verse summarizes all the teaching of the psalm. The first movement, verses one to three, describes one way, the way of the righteous. The second movement, verses four and five, describes another way, the way of the wicked. The last verse makes a declaration concerning these two ways.

The general idea of this psalm is common in Biblical literature. The Old Testament teaches it in the Law, enforces it in the Prophets, interprets it in poetry; and illustrates it in history. That idea may thus be briefly stated: righteousness pays, and wickedness does not; and therefore righteousness is the secret of happiness, and wickedness is the cause of misery.

That is an extremely old-fashioned idea, and it is certainly out of date to-day. Yet that conception of life was accepted generally by people born and brought up in the light of the Biblical Revelation.

It was so accepted until the closing years of the nineteenth century ; and then it began to go out of fashion. That general idea ran through all Shakespeare's plays ; and was interpreted in all fiction until the closing years of the nineteenth century. Shakespeare's plays all have a moral drift. Macbeth never escapes ; Shylock must come to judgment. Always righteousness pays, wickedness does not. It is the fashion to-day to laugh at the old fiction in which people went through all sorts of processes, and married, and were happy ever after. That is not popular now. In the fiction I read in my youth, the villain always got his deserts before the book was done. He seemed to be very successful for a while, but he got run to earth at last. All that is out of fashion. Modern plays ignore it, and the general drift of modern fiction laughs at the idea that righteousness pays and wickedness does not ; that righteousness is the secret of happiness, and that wickedness is the cause of misery.

Well, it may at least be well to remind ourselves that old-fashioned ideas are not necessarily untrue, and that newness is not a guarantee of truth. It is good occasionally to make a commonplace remark like that, to help us in our thinking. It is the fashion now if you want to dismiss anything to call it Victorian. If a thing is Victorian, it is considered as something out of date. That does not prove it wrong. There may have been some very futile things in the Victorian age. I lived and was born and brought up in it, thank God ; and all its influence is with me, and will be to the end ; and I know that there were in it some foolish things, some of them almost as foolish as some of the things mastering the thinking of men to-day.

But because a thing is old, it is not necessarily wrong, and because it is new it is not necessarily right ; and I am going to submit to you that in this matter the old is certainly the true, and all the new which contradicts it in philosophy and fiction, or in any other realm, is untrue to the facts of life.

This old singer in the Hebrew economy looked out on life, and he saw two ways of living which he has described for us, and described them with singular accuracy pictorially and definitively ; and he sums the whole thing up at last by saying : *Jehovah knoweth the way of the righteous, but the way of the wicked shall perish.* Or literally as to the Hebrew word, ' The way of the wicked shall run out,' the picture suggested being that of the track trodden by the cattle, that presently is lost in the prairie ; it runs out ; ultimately it is not a way at all ; it perishes. The way of the righteous is known to Jehovah. The way of the wicked runs out, leads nowhere, arrives nowhere. That is the summary of the singer.

Now let us first consider these two ways as they are here described ; and then let us bring the description of the psalm to the test of experience.

We will first take the way of the wicked. As to description, it comes last in the psalm, and yet it is referred to in the opening verses, ' the counsel of the wicked,' ' the way of sinners,' ' the seat of scoffers.' Let us examine these carefully chosen words. He speaks of the counsel of the wicked, *counsel* ; the way of sinners, *way* ; the seat of the scoffers, *seat*.

' The *counsel* of the wicked. This word ' counsel ' means advice, deliberation, finding, and so philosophy. The counsel is the philosophy of the wicked ; that is, that which condones, justifies, or excuses wickedness.

Much of the literature which is being poured out upon us in this day is literature either justifying, or condoning, or defending, or ignoring what our fathers called wickedness. That is the philosophy of the non-moral, or more accurately of the immoral. Every form of thinking and writing, whether in philosophic treatise, or fictional representation, or religious literature which minimizes sin, is the counsel of wickedness, the philosophy of wickedness.

' The *way* of sinners.' That is, the road, the course of life, the activity, which harmonizes with the counsel ; the way of sinners. All conduct is the outcome of conception. Man does nothing save as the outcome of his thinking. ' As a man thinketh in his heart, so is he.'

' The *seat* of scoffers.' The word ' seat ' here means a session. The session of the scoffers, that is, their settled agreement, their unanimous position ; the mental attitude of those holding the philosophy of the wicked, is that of scoffing at goodness.

That is one way of life. Its philosophy, the denial

357

of morality ; its way, conduct that harmonizes with the denial ; its seat, its session, its unanimity, scoffing at goodness.

That is a remarkably accurate diagnosis of the atmosphere of the hour in which we are living to-day. First of all, the philosophy of the age is condoning or justifying or ignoring sin ; so that if a brilliant man writes the biography of Heine, he will so do it as to suggest that all the rotten corruption of the man was merely artistic expression. That way lies hell ! This philosophy, the counsel of the non-moral, is producing the way of to-day, which is the way of sinners, and of rampant wrong-doing. And at last there is general unanimity, and we hear those so influenced, and so acting, with unanimity laughing at goodness. In much brilliant journalism, and clever literature, and vulgar comic papers, and scripts, of every chance to laugh at goodness advantage is taken.

Now, passing to the end of the psalm, let us see what this singer had to say about that way of life. He says : ‘ The wicked are like the chaff which the wind driveth away.’ We only get the full impact of that statement when we observe the singer’s contrast. Speaking of the righteous, he says : *He shall be like a tree planted by the streams of water, that bringeth forth its fruit in its season.* Some day, when the wind blows up a hurricane, look at a tree planted, rooted ; and then at some chaff. If you do so, you will have caught the significance of this declaration concerning the wicked. Thank God, there are winds of God blowing over all human history, winds of God blowing to-day, trying, testing, sweeping winds ; and they carry away the chaff. The wicked are not like the tree : *The wicked are not so, but are like the chaff which the wind driveth away.*

Therefore, he says further, they ' shall not stand in the judgment.' Do not postpone the activity suggested by that word judgment. There is to be a great assize, a great white Throne, a great day of judgment ; but judgment is already operating. We live every day in the presence of judgment. Judgment is discrimination, that which makes the difference between right and wrong. The wicked cannot stand in the judgment. There is a discrimination at work in the world and in human history. It is operating to-day, right here and now and everywhere ; the discrimination which wickedness cannot bribe, and cannot deceive. They ' shall not stand in the judgment.'

And once again, ' Nor sinners in the congregation of the righteous.' That is they are excluded from the gathering together of the righteous. Wickedness can get by a great many operations of so-called law. But wickedness cannot get by the eternal principle of discrimination, which is dividing sharply forevermore between right and wrong ; and the winds of God that sweep across history and human life are forevermore driving the chaff away. John the Baptist said of your Lord and mine, our blessed and adorable

Redeemer, God's holy Son, the Son of man, He shall come, and His fan shall be in His hand, and He shall gather the wheat into His garner, and the chaff destroy in the unquenchable fire. That is the Biblical outlook upon wickedness.

Now let us look at the other side. Here is another way : *Blessed is the man that walketh not in the counsel of the wicked, nor standeth in the way of sinners, nor sitteth in the seat of scoffers.*

This is a negative description of another man, and another way of life. 'Walketh not,' that is, he refuses the philosophy ; 'standeth not,' that is, he declines the activity ; 'sitteth not,' that is, he denies the unanimity. The counsel of wickedness ; this man refuses, denies the philosophy. The way, resulting from the philosophy of sinners, this man does not go near it. He declines all the activity that comes out of the philosophy. There is a session of the scoffers, and the ribald laughter of the intellectuals who have dismissed God and goodness altogether ; and there is a great unanimousness about it. No, there is not. There is a man in the minority, and he won't sit in the seat of the scoffers. The righteous man is the man who declines to vote with the majority, when the majority is laughing at the philosophy of goodness.

Now we come to the positive. 'His delight is in the law of Jehovah.' This man is a man who delights in the law of Jehovah, in the fact of it, and in every expression of it. This is the man who believes that the universe is under the mastery of law, that lawlessness in any form is contrary to the highest in the universe. This is the man who says there is delight, and he finds it in the law of Jehovah. He delights in the fact that God is governing; and that there is a judgment that discriminates between good and evil. He not only delights in the fact of it; he delights in every expression of it. He knows that every command of God is love-inspired. He knows that every denial of God is love-inspired. He knows the truth of what Browning sang, ' I report, as a man may of God's work—all's love, yet all's law.' Law is the outcome of love. This man is a man who sings of law, rejoices in law, delights in law.

And then follows another statement about him. He not only delights in it, but ' in His law doth he meditate day and night.' I should not like to take away any value there is in the word ' meditate,' but I would like to tell you what it really means. It means he talks to himself! He talks to himself about the law of God. He talks to himself day and night; he soliloquizes. Just as a boy when he is learning his lessons, he learns the law, he repeats the law, he ponders the law. He thinks out loud about it, day and night. There are people who really delight in the law of God as a great principle for the safeguarding of humanity, but who spend little time talking to themselves about it, repeating it to themselves, going over and over it, like a lad conning his lesson until he has got it, and it has got him to the end of time. This man may make a gesture to the law of God on Sunday morning, once a day on Sunday, and then mostly late ! Lots of people are doing that ; making their gesture to God Almighty, and then forgetting Him and His law for the rest of the week. This man is the man who delights in it, and keeps himself in touch with it. He talks to himself about it, he ponders it ; it is the secret of his life ; he meditates on the law of God day and night.

Then the singer drops into figurative poetry. He tells you what that man is like. He is ' Like a tree planted by the streams of water.' Planted, not growing wild ; ' planted by the streams of water, that bringeth forth its fruit in its season,' its own fruit, according to its nature, in its season. ' Whose leaf also doth not wither.' Then he swings back from the figure of the tree to the man, ' And in whatsoever he doeth he shall prosper.'

That is a daring poetic figure. This Hebrew singer takes a tree, and makes it the poetic figure of the man he is talking about. The figure is found elsewhere in these psalms. Listen to psalm thirty-seven and verse thirty-five : *I have seen the wicked in great power, And spreading himself like a green tree in its native soil.* I purposely went to that psalm, for that describes the wicked, ' spreading himself like a green tree in its native soil.' But notice he was spreading himself like a tree, in his native soil, not by the rivers of water. What happened to him ? The

singer goes on, *But one passed by, and, lo, he was not ;
Yea, I sought him, but he could not be found.* He was
gone. That is the wicked man, like a tree planted
in his own soil.

Then I turn over again, and I find another place
where one of these singers is singing—perhaps the
same singer, who knows ? I am in psalm fifty-two,
and there he says, *But as for me, I am like a green
olive-tree in the house of God. I trust in the loving kindness
of God for ever and ever.* He is not planted in his own
soil.

I am inclined to go on just once more, and again
I find in psalm ninety-two, verses twelve and thirteen
and on : *The righteous shall flourish like the palm-tree ;
he shall grow like a cedar in Lebanon. They are planted
in the house of Jehovah ; they shall flourish in the courts
of our God. They shall still bring forth fruit in old age ;
they shall be full of sap and green ; to show that Jehovah
is upright.*

Trees, trees, trees ! I, too, have seen the wicked
spreading himself like a tree in his own soil ; but
I looked again, and he had vanished ! But this man,
whose delight is in the law of the Lord, who meditates
in it day and night, is planted by the streams of
water. His life is rooted in the true sources of life.
The man who delights in the law of the Lord is the
man whose roots run down and find the streams that
water and feed him. This man shall bring forth
fruit, ' bringeth forth its fruit in its season.' Joseph
Bryant Rotherham has this interesting and arresting

little comment on that. A man who brings forth
fruit in his season is the man who, in all the processes
of life, brings forth fruit according to purpose ;
' that is, learning and liveliness in youth, steady
work and sturdy endurance in middle life, patience
and serene hope in old age.' That is the fruit of
true humanity, rooted in God. A tree planted by
the rivers of water ; that is the righteous.

Once more. ' Whatsoever he doeth shall prosper.'
Here the marginal reading is undoubtedly correct,
' He shall prosper in whatsoever he doeth.' That is
a much profounder word. It is not always so that
what a righteous man does prospers. He fails in it
sometimes, but he prospers. What he does may fail,
or seem to fail. His plans may be defeated. His
possessions go, but he prospers. Joseph was as
prosperous in Pharaoh's prison, as when he was
associated with the throne. Job was prosperous in
the darkness, as surely as when he passed back into
the light. For Joseph, the adversity of circumstances
passed, and the prosperity came ; and for Job the
outward prosperity came again ; but they were both
prosperous all the way through. Quietly now, and
reverently, Jesus, in whatever He did, prospered.
Yet did you ever see any story of any life that,
measured by the philosophy of godlessness, was a
more ghastly failure ? He went from the world, with
hands and feet pierced with nails, transfixed to a
Roman gibbet ! Do you call that prosperity ? Yes,
He was prosperous even there, and the pleasure of

the Lord prospered in His hands,—crucified hands ! That is the ultimate word in interpretation of the psalm.

Bring all this to the test of experience. How much there is that seems to contradict it as we look out upon the world to-day. Is not that so ? Does it not seem all through as though wickedness was successful ? Oh yes, and there are psalms that deal with that. Glance at the seventy-third. In the course of it the singer says, *Behold, these are the wicked ; and, being always at ease, they increase in riches, surely in vain have I cleansed my heart, and washed my hands in innocency ; for all the day long have I been plagued, and chastened every morning.* Don't we often feel like that ? Well, hear him further : *If I had said, I will speak thus ; behold, I had dealt treacherously with the generation of thy children.* That is how things looked, but he says, *When I thought how I might know this, it was too painful for me ; until I went into the sanctuary of God, and considered their latter end.*

It does look as though the wicked were having a good time. There are no pangs in their death ; they have an easy time. The righteous are again and again seen battered and bruised with life ; *until* . . . Until when ? Until they go to the sanctuary of God, the true view-point for life. When we go to the sanctuary of God, life is seen in its long issues, and never measured by its immediate appearances.

It is an old-fashioned view that righteousness pays, but it does. It is an old - fashioned view that wickedness does not, but it never does. The winds of God are blowing, the discriminations of God are active ; and like chaff that the wind drives, the wicked are driven away ; all the way of wickedness runs out ; there is no goal, no arrival, no destination. But the man who delights in the law of the Lord, and meditates in it, his life is like a tree planted by the streams, taking hold of the true sources of life ; and he brings forth his fruit, and his leaf does not wither, and in whatsoever he does, he prospers, for he marches through the passing phases of time to the lasting destiny and glory of eternity.

The Christian in Danger

C. S. LEWIS

✝

A Syrian ready to perish was my father.—DEUT. xxvi. 5.

THE CHRISTIAN IN DANGER

C. S. LEWIS

A UNIVERSITY, as you all know, is a society for the pursuit of learning. You will be expected, while you are here, to make yourselves, or to start making yourselves, into what the Middle Ages called clerks : into philosophers, scientists, scholars, critics, or historians. And at first sight this seems to be an odd thing to do during a great war. What is the use of beginning a task which we have so little chance of finishing ? Or, even if we ourselves should happen not to be interrupted by death or military service, why should we—indeed how can we—continue to take an interest in these placid occupations when the lives of our friends and the liberties of Europe are in the balance ? Is it not like fiddling while Rome burns ?

Now it seems to me that we shall not be able to answer these questions until we have put them by the side of certain other questions which every Christian ought to have asked himself in peacetime. I spoke just now of fiddling while Rome burns. But to a Christian the true tragedy of Nero must be not that he fiddled while the city was on fire but that he fiddled on the brink of hell. You must forgive me for this crude monosyllable. I know that many wiser and better Christians than I in these days do not like to mention heaven and hell even in a pulpit. I know too, that nearly all the references to this subject in the New Testament come from a single source. But then that source is our Lord Himself. People will tell you it is St. Paul, but that is because they are ignorant. These overwhelming doctrines are dominical. They are not really removable from the teaching of Christ or of His Church. If we do not believe them, our presence here in Church is great tomfoolery. If we do, we must sometime overcome our spiritual prudery and mention them.

The moment we do so we can see that every Christian who comes to a university must at all times face a question compared with which the questions raised by the war are relatively unimportant. He must ask himself how it is right, or even psychologically possible, for creatures who are every moment advancing either to heaven or to hell, to spend any fraction of the little time allowed them in this world on such comparative trivialities as literature or art, mathematics or biology. If human culture can stand up to that, it can stand up to anything. To admit that we can retain our interest in learning under the shadow of these eternal issues, but not under the shadow of a European war, would be to admit that our ears are closed to the voice of reason and very wide open to the voice of our nerves and our mass emotions.

This is indeed the case with most of us ; certainly with me. For that reason I think it important to try to see the present calamity in a true perspective. The war creates no absolutely new situation ; it simply aggravates the permanent human situation so that we can no longer ignore it. Human life has always been lived on the edge of a precipice. Human culture has always had to exist under the shadow of something infinitely more important than itself. If men had postponed the search for knowledge and beauty until they were secure, the search would never have begun. We are mistaken when we compare the war with 'normal life.' Life has never been normal. Even those periods which we think most tranquil, like the nineteenth century, turn out, on closer inspection, to be full of crises, alarms, difficulties, emergencies. Plausible reasons have never been lacking for putting off all merely cultural activities until some imminent danger has been averted or some crying injustice put right. But humanity long ago chose to neglect those plausible reasons. They wanted knowledge and beauty now, and would not wait for the suitable moment that never comes. Periclean Athens leaves us not only the Parthenon but, significantly, the Funeral Oration. The insects have chosen a different line ; they have sought first the material welfare and security of the hive, and presumably they have their reward. Men are different. They propound mathematical theorems in beleaguered cities, conduct metaphysical arguments in condemned cells, make jokes on scaffolds, discuss the last new poem while advancing to the walls of Quebec, and comb their hair at Thermopylæ. This is not *panache*; it is our nature.

But since we are fallen creatures the fact that this is now our nature would not, by itself, prove that it is rational or right. We have to inquire whether there is really any legitimate place for the activities of the scholar in a world such as this. That is, we have always to answer the question, ' How can you be so frivolous and selfish as to think about anything but the salvation of human souls ? '; and we have, at the moment, to answer the question, ' How can you be so frivolous and selfish as to think of anything but the war ? ' Now there is one part of our answer which will be the same for both questions. The one implies that our whole life can, and ought, to become exclusively and explicitly religious ; the other, that it can and ought to become exclusively national. I believe that our whole life can, and indeed must, become religious in a sense to be explained later. But if it is meant that all our activities are to be of the kind that can be recognized as ' sacred ' and opposed to ' secular,' then I would give a single reply to both my imaginary assailants. I would say ' Whether it ought to happen or not, the thing you are recommending is not going to happen.' Before I became a Christian I do not think

I fully realized that one's life, after conversion, would inevitably consist in doing most of the same things one had been doing before ; one hopes, in a new spirit, but still the same things. Before I went to the last war I certainly expected that my life in the trenches would, in some mysterious sense, be all war. In fact, I found that the nearer you got to the front line the less every one spoke and thought of the allied cause and the progress of the campaign ; and I am pleased to find that Tolstoi, in the greatest war book ever written, records the same thing—and so, in its own way, does the *Iliad*. Neither conversion, nor enlistment in the army, is really going to obliterate our human life. Christians and soldiers are still men ; the infidel's idea of a religious life, and the civilian's idea of active service, are fantastic. If you attempted, in either case, to suspend your whole intellectual and æsthetic activity, you would only succeed in substituting a worse cultural life for a better. You are not, in fact, going to read nothing, either in the Church or in the line ; if you don't read good books, you will read bad ones. If you don't go on thinking rationally, you will think irrationally. If you reject æsthetic satisfactions you will fall into sensual satisfactions.

There is therefore this analogy between the claims of our religion and the claims of the war ; neither of them, for most of us, will simply cancel or remove from the slate the merely human life which we were leading before we entered them. But they will

operate in this way for different reasons. The war
will fail to absorb our whole attention because it is
a finite object, and therefore intrinsically unfitted to
support the whole attention of a human soul. In
order to avoid misunderstanding I must here make
a few distinctions. I believe our cause to be, as
human causes go, very righteous, and I therefore
believe it to be a duty to participate in this war.
And every duty is a religious duty, and our obligation
to perform every duty is therefore absolute. Thus
we may have a duty to rescue a drowning man, and
perhaps, if we live on a dangerous coast, to learn life-
saving so as to be ready for any drowning man when
he turns up. It may be our duty to lose our own
lives in saving him. But if any one devoted himself
to life-saving in the sense of giving it his total
attention—so that he thought and spoke of nothing
else and demanded the cessation of all other human
activities until every one had learned to swim—he
would be a monomaniac. The rescue of drowning
men is, then, a duty worth dying for, but not worth
living for. It seems to me that all political duties
(among which I include military duties) are of this
kind. A man may have to die for our country ; but
no man must, in any exclusive sense, live for his
country. He who surrenders himself without reserva-
tion to the temporal claims of a nation, or a party,
or a class—is rendering to Cæsar that which, of all
things, most emphatically belongs to God—himself.

It is for a very different reason that religion cannot

occupy the whole life in the sense of excluding all
our natural activities. For, of course, in some sense,
it must occupy the whole of life. There is no
question of a compromise between the claims of God
and the claims of culture, or politics, or anything
else. God's claim is infinite and inexorable. You
can refuse it ; or you can begin to try to grant it.
There is no middle way. Yet in spite of this it is
clear that Christianity does not exclude any of the
ordinary human activities. St. Paul tells people to
get on with their jobs. He even assumes that
Christians may go to dinner parties, and, what is
more, dinner parties given by Pagans. Our Lord
attends a wedding and provides miraculous wine.
Under the ægis of His Church, and in the most
Christian ages, learning and the arts flourish. The
solution of this paradox is, of course, well known to
you. 'Whether ye eat or drink or whatsoever ye
do, do all to the glory of God.' All our merely
natural activities will be accepted, if they are offered
to God, even the humblest ; and all of them, even
the noblest, will be sinful if they are not. Christianity
does not simply replace our natural life and substitute
a new one ; it is rather a new organization which
exploits, to its own supernatural ends, these natural
materials. No doubt, in a given situation, it demands
the surrender of some, or of all, our merely human
pursuits. It is better to be saved with one eye, than,
having two, to be cast into Gehenna. But it does
this, in a sense, *per accidens*—because, in those special

circumstances, it has ceased to be possible to practise this or that activity to the glory of God. There is no essential quarrel between the spiritual life and the human activities, as such. Thus the omnipresence of obedience to God in a Christian's life is, in a way, analogous to the omnipresence of God in space. God does not fill space as a body fills it, in the sense that parts of Him are in different parts of space, excluding other objects from them. Yet He is everywhere— totally present at every point of space—according to good theologians.

We are now in a position to answer the view that human culture is an inexcusable frivolity on the part of creatures loaded with such awful responsibilities as we are. I reject at once an idea which lurks in the minds of some modern people that cultural activities are in their own right spiritual and meritorious—as though scholars and poets were intrinsically more pleasing to God than scavengers and bootblacks. Writers like Matthew Arnold, who have popularized the English word *spiritual* in the sense of the German *geistlich*, have encouraged a most dangerous and most anti-Christian error. Let us clear it forever from our minds. The work of a Beethoven, and the work of a charwoman, become spiritual on precisely the same condition, that of being offered to God, of being done humbly ' as to the Lord.' This does not, of course, mean that it is for any one a mere toss-up whether he should sweep rooms or compose symphonies. A mole must dig to the glory of God and a cock must crow. We are members of one body, but differentiated members, each with his own vocation. A man's upbringing, his talents, his circumstances, are usually a tolerable index of his vocation. If our parents have sent us to Oxford, if our country allows us to remain there, this is *prima facie* evidence that the life which we, at any rate, can best lead to the glory of God at present is the learned life. By leading that life to the glory of God, I do not, of course, mean any attempt to make our intellectual enquiries work out to edifying conclusions. That would be, as Bacon says, to offer to the author of truth the unclean sacrifice of a lie. I mean the pursuit of knowledge and beauty, in a sense, for their own sake, but in a sense which does not exclude their being for God's sake. An appetite for these things exists in the human mind, and God makes no appetite in vain. We can therefore pursue knowledge as such, and beauty, as such, in the sure confidence that by so doing we are either advancing to the vision of God ourselves or indirectly helping others to do so. Humility, no less than the appetite, encourages us to concentrate simply on the knowledge or the beauty, not too much concerning ourselves with their ultimate relevance to the vision of God. That relevance may not be intended for us but for our betters—for men who come after and find the spiritual significance of what we dug out in blind and humble obedience to our vocation. This is the teleological argument, that the existence of the impulse and the faculty prove that they must have a proper function in God's scheme—the argument by which Thomas Aquinas proves that sexuality would have existed even without the Fall. The soundness of the argument, as regards culture, is proved by experience. The intellectual life is not the only road to God, nor the safest, but we find it to be a road, and it may be the appointed road for us. Of course, it will be so only so long as we keep the impulse pure and disinterested. That is the great difficulty. As the author of the *Theologia Germanica* says, we may come to love knowledge—*our* knowing— more than the thing known ; to delight not in the exercise of our talents but in the fact that they are ours, or even in the reputation they bring us. Every success in the scholar's life increases this danger. If it becomes irresistible, he must give up his scholarly work. The time for plucking out the right eye has arrived.

That is the essential nature of the learned life as I see it. But it has indirect values which are specially important to-day. If all the world were Christians, it might not matter if all the world were uneducated. But, as it is, a cultural life will exist outside the Church whether it exists inside or not. To be ignorant and simple now—not to be able to meet the enemies on their own ground—would be to throw down our weapons, and to betray our un- educated brethren who have, under God, no defence but us against the intellectual attacks of the heathen.

Good philosophy must exist, if for no other reason, because bad philosophy needs to be answered. The cool intellect must work not only against cool intellect on the other side, but against the muddy heathen mysticisms which deny intellect altogether. Most of all, perhaps, we need intimate knowledge of the past. Not that the past has any magic about it, but because we cannot study the future, and yet need something to set against the present, to remind us that the basic assumptions have been quite different in different periods and that much which seems certain to the uneducated is merely temporary fashion. A man who has lived in many places is not likely to be deceived by the local errors of his native village ; the scholar has lived in many times and is, therefore, in some degree immune from the great cataract of nonsense that pours from the press and the microphone of his own age.

The learned life then is, for some, a duty. At the moment it looks as if it were your duty. I am well aware that there may seem to be an almost comic discrepancy between the high issues we have been considering and the immediate task you may be set down to, such as Anglo-Saxon sound laws or chemical formulæ. But there is a similar shock awaiting us in every vocation—a young priest finds himself involved in choir treats and a young subaltern in accounting for pots of jam. It is well that it should be so. It weeds out the vain, windy people and keeps in those who are both humble and tough. On that kind of difficulty we need waste no sympathy. But the peculiar difficulty imposed on you by the war is another matter ; and of it I would again repeat, what I have been saying in one form or another ever since I stood up—do not let your nerves and emotions lead you into thinking your predicament more abnormal than it really is. Perhaps it may be useful to mention the three mental exercises which may serve as defences against the three enemies which war raises up against the scholar.

The first enemy is excitement—the tendency to think and feel about the war when we had intended to think about our work. The best defence is a recognition that in this, as in everything else, the war has not really raised up a new enemy but only aggravated an old one. There are always plenty of rivals to our work. We are always falling in love or quarrelling, looking for jobs or fearing to lose them, getting ill and recovering, following public affairs. If we let ourselves, we shall always be waiting for some distraction or other to end before we can really get down to it. The only people who achieve much are those who want knowledge so badly that they seek it while the conditions are still unfavourable. Favourable conditions never come. There are, of course, moments when the pressure of the excitement is so great that only superhuman self-control could resist it. They come both in war and peace. We must do the best we can.

The second enemy is frustration—the feeling that

we shall not have time to finish. If I say to you that no one has time to finish, that the longest human life leaves a man, in any branch of learning, a beginner, I shall seem to you to be saying something quite academic and theoretical. You would be surprised if you knew how soon one begins to feel the shortness of the tether ; of how many things, even in middle life, we have to say ' No time for that,' ' Too late now,' and ' Not for me.' But nature herself forbids you to share that experience. A more Christian attitude, which can be attained at any age, is that of leaving futurity in God's hands. We may as well, for God will certainly retain it whether we leave it to Him or not. Never, in peace or war, commit your virtue or your happiness to the future. Happy work is best done by the man who takes his long-term plans somewhat lightly and works from moment to moment ' as to the Lord.' It is only our *daily* bread that we are encouraged to ask for. The present is the only time in which any duty can be done or any grace received.

The third enemy is Fear. War threatens us with death and pain. No man—and specially no Christian who remembers Gethsemane—need try to attain a stoic indifference about these things : but we can guard against the illusions of the imagination. We think of the streets of Warsaw and contrast the deaths there suffered with an abstraction called Life. But there is no question of death or life for any of us ; only a question of this death or of that—of a machine-gun bullet now or a cancer forty years later. What does war do to death? It certainly does not make it more frequent: 100 per cent. of us die, and the percentage cannot be increased. It puts several deaths earlier: but I hardly suppose that that is what we fear. Certainly when the moment comes, it will make little difference how many years we have behind us. Does it increase our chances of a painful death? I doubt it. As far as I can find out, what we call natural death is usually preceded by suffering: and a battlefield is one of the very few places where one has a reasonable prospect of dying with no pain at all. Does it decrease our chances of dying at peace with God? I cannot believe it. If active service does not persuade a man to prepare for death, what conceivable concatenation of circumstances would? Yet war does do something to death. It forces us to remember it. The only reason why the cancer at 60 or the paralysis at 75 do not bother us is that we forget them. War makes death real to us: and that would have been regarded as one of its blessings by most of the great Christians of the past. They thought it good for us to be always aware of our mortality. I am inclined to think they were right. All the animal life in us, all schemes of happiness that centred in this world, were always doomed to a final frustration. In ordinary times only a wise man can realize it. Now the stupidest of us knows. We see unmistakably the sort of universe in which we have all along been living, and must come to terms with it. If we had foolish un-Christian hopes about human culture, they are now shattered. If we thought we were building up a heaven on earth, if we looked for something that would turn the present world from a place of pilgrimage into a permanent city that could satisfy the soul of man, we are disillusioned, and not a moment too soon. But if we thought that for some souls, and at some times, the life of culture, humbly offered to God, was, in its own small way, one of the appointed approaches to the Divine reality and the Divine beauty which we hope to enjoy hereafter, we can think so still.

THE END

ACKNOWLEDGMENTS

THE Editor and the Publishers are indebted to the following for special permissions to reproduce sermons included in this book :

To the Society for Promoting Christian Knowledge for the SERMON FROM THE LATIN, taken from *The Venerable Bede*, by G. F. Browne ; to the executors of the late Dr. Henry Scott Holland for CRITICISM AND THE RESURRECTION, taken from *On Behalf of Belief*; to the author for THE PSALM OF THE TWO WAYS, by Dr. G. Campbell Morgan ; to the author and the Student Christian Movement Press for THE CHRISTIAN IN DANGER, by C. S. Lewis.

PRINTED IN GREAT BRITAIN BY
THOMAS NELSON AND SONS, LTD.